Perfect D

DRESDEN

CW00665835

Contents

 TOP 10   4

That Dresden Feeling   6

For chapters: See inside front cover

TOP 10

Not to be missed!
Our TOP 10 hits – from the absolute No. 1 to No. 10 –
help you plan your tour of the most important sights.

⭐ FRAUENKIRCHE ► 58

This church is Dresden's historic landmark. It disappeared from the cityscape for many years after being destroyed in World War II. Since 2005, the massive dome has once again dominated the silhouette of the city's Altstadt (left).

⭐ ZWINGER & GEMÄLDE-GALERIE ALTE MEISTER ► 62

A masterwork of Saxon Baroque: three of the most important museums in Dresden are housed in the pavilions and adjacent Semperbau.

⭐ RESIDENZSCHLOSS ► 70

Prince electors and kings resided here for over four centuries. Today, their treasures can be admired in the Grünes Gewölbe and in the Armoury. The panoramic view from the Hausmannsturm is a must.

⭐ SEMPEROPER & THEATERPLATZ ► 77

This square's unique architectural ensemble creates the ceremonious setting for one of the world's most famous opera houses.

⭐ BRÜHLSCHE TERRASSE ► 80

Locals and tourists alike admire the view from the "Balcony of Europe" down to the steamers on the Elbe and Dresden's Neustadt quarter.

⭐ SCHLOSS & PARK PILLNITZ ► 142

The summer residence of the Dresden royal court is one of the most unusual castle complexes in Saxony and a perfect symbiosis of architecture and nature.

⭐ ELBE CASTLES ► 146

Three 19th-century castles on the banks of the Elbe – between vineyards and parks – seem to be straight out of a fairy tale when seen in the morning mist.

⭐ KÖRNERPLATZ ► 148

Relax and unwind with a stroll around the square. There are half-timbered houses, handicraft shops, two funicular railways, cosy cafés and a view of the so-called "Blue Wonder" bridge.

⭐ GROSSER GARTEN ► 122

The most beautiful of the city's parks has avenues of trees, ponds, open-air stages, a botanical garden, a park railway – and a car factory.

⭐ ÄUSSERE NEUSTADT ► 96

There are countless pubs, bars, galleries and hip shops in the liveliest quarter in Dresden – and this is also where you will find the Kunsthofpassage, a series of quirky, artistic courtyards.

THAT
DRESDEN

Experience the city's unique flair and find out what makes it tick – just like the Dresdeners themselves.

FULL STEAM AHEAD

With some ear-splitting toots the venerable old **paddle-wheel steamer** (▶ 84) sets out from the Terrassenufer quayside. Its journey goes past Dresden's Altstadt, the "Blue Wonder" bridge, Schloss Pillnitz castle and on to Saxon Switzerland. While on board, passengers can admire the polished brass instruments, listen to the swish of the paddle wheels or indulge in a *Schifferbemme* in the restaurant.

PICNIC IN THE MEADOWS

The place to have a picnic in Dresden is on the Elbwiesen. As soon as the first rays of the sun appear, people of all ages head for the meadows on the Elbe banks – many choose the area directly opposite Altstadt or upstream below the Neustadt **Rosengarten** (▶ 109). Those who don't feel like packing their own hamper can sit down in the **Fährgarten Johannstadt** (✚ 191 E2) and watch the *Johanna* ferry cease-lessly crossing the river.

JOURNEY THROUGH TIME

Somewhere a cock is crowing, the sun rises – and you look down from

The Augustusbrücke and meadows on the banks of the Elbe in Neustadt

FEELING

the tower of the Dresden Hofkirche (cathedral) onto the Baroque city's bustling streets. The artist Yadegar Asisi created the **Panometer (➤ 23)** a 360-degree panoramic painting of what a day in the life of the city may have been like in 1695–1760. The exhibit is housed in an old gasometer.

(Gasanstaltstraße 8b, Tue–Fri 10am–5pm, Sat and Sun to 6pm).

CHOCOLATE DELIGHTS

Dresden used to be the chocolate capital of Germany and, if the latest findings are to be believed, milk chocolate was even invented here. Today you will find high-quality chocolate from all around the world in the three branches of **Camondas** (✚ 196 B2, Schlossstraße 22, An der Frauenkirche 20) chocolate shop in Altstadt. The real hit is a

That Dresden Feeling

 Insider Tip

chocolate ice-cream on a stick
(spring to autumn), produced by
Dresden's Neumann ice-cream
manufacturer. Delicious!

LA DOLCE VITA

The **Elbhangfest** is probably the
most authentic of the city's festivals.
It takes place every year on the last
weekend in June and is held on the
7km (4mi) stretch between the
"Blue Wonder" bridge (⊞ 195 D4)
and Pillnitz. People dressed in their
summery-best stroll through the
old village centres along the way,
music can be heard everywhere,
street artists entertain the crowds
and vendors offer culinary delights
and other wares for sale. A lovely
way to spend the day.

WINE WITH A VIEW

Just 3km (2mi) upstream from
the centre of Dresden, the vintner
Lutz Müller has his vineyards below
the Elbe castles. On weekends in
spring – if the weather is fine –
he opens his **Straußwirtschaft**
(⊞ 194 C5, Bautzner Str. 130)
near the Kavaliershaus of **Schloss
Albrechtsberg**. In addition to his
prize-winning wines, he also
serves tartes flambées from a
wood-burning stove. And, of
course, there is also an unbeat-
able view of the Elbe Valley.

PUB CRAWL

In the warm months, **Neustadt's
nightlife** takes place mainly outside:
on the terraces and in the courtyard
gardens of the countless pubs, cafés
and bars. Dresdeners and visitors
from all around the world stroll
through the streets or settle down
on the benches and enjoy the
feeling of being young.

THE JOY OF ANTICIPATION

The large Christmas markets in
the city centre attract hundreds
of thousands of visitors every year.
The **Christmas market** near the
"Blue Wonder" bridge is smaller
and more intimate and has stands
run by artists and craftsmen from
the region. The half-timbered houses on Friedrich-Wieck-Straße
(⊞ 195 E3) form the market's
romantic backdrop.

**Dresden's Christmas market has the
tallest Christmas pyramid**

The Magazine

The ELBE VALLEY

Dresden's greatest treasure is not to be found in a museum. It is the River Elbe with a landscape created both by the river itself and human hands.

Canal Grande

The Elbe flows in a wide arch for 30km (19mi) through Dresden and its banks are lined with meadows up to 400m (1300ft) wide and framed by a cultural landscape that has developed over the centuries. Inspired by a trip to Venice, King August the Strong made the river his "Canal Grande" and had castles and palaces erected along its banks with moorings for the court's ceremonial gondolas. The fact that the city became known as "Florence on the Elbe" and not "Venice on the Elbe" is due to Johann Gottfried Herder who described it as the "German Florence" due to its artistic treasures. Even today, after destruction and reconstruction, the unique combination of architecture, culture and nature is the reason for Dresden's very special charm.

Lifeline Elbe

Generations of farsighted city planners are to be thanked for the unique synthesis of the urban environment and, largely unspoiled, river landscape that makes Dresden unique among modern European cities. For years, Dresden has been one of the top ten city destinations in Germany – and an increasing number of tourists from all around the world have come to

PRAISED

"Dresden has a great, solemn location in the centre of the garland of the Elbe heights ...The river suddenly leaves its right bank and turns quickly towards Dresden, to kiss its beloved."

Heinrich von Kleist, 1801

The Elbe banks in Neustadt – a stroll in a breathtaking setting

LOST HERITAGE TITLE

In 2004, UNESCO added the cultural landscape of the Dresden Elbe Valley to the World Heritage List. Shortly thereafter, it became clear that a new four-lane Elbe bridge, which was approved by a local referendum in 2005, would endanger this status. A bitter conflict between the supporters and opponents of the Waldschlösschen Bridge flared up. Although the World Heritage Commission placed the Dresden Elbe Valley on its Red List of threatened World Heritage Sites, the city went ahead and the controversial bridge was officially opened in 2013. The deletion from the World Heritage List – painful and hardly flattering – had already taken place four years previously after various mediation attempts failed.

appreciate the city's monuments, art, culture and it's river. It goes without saying that the locals do!

More than anything else, the Elbe determines their attitude towards life. As soon as the first warm rays of the sun can be felt, the Dresdeners flock to the Elbwiesen – the meadows on the river banks – complete with their prams, dogs and picnic baskets or set off on their bikes along the Elbe Cycle Route. They take pride in showing visitors the panoramic view of Altstadt from the Neustadt side of the Elbe. And, in summer, the banks become the setting for festivals and open-air cinema.

Improved water quality has brought back Elbe beavers, otters and the Elbe salmon and local swimmers can now enjoy a dip in the river. It appears that the relationship between the Dresdeners and their river has become even closer since the flooding in August 2002. At least it has to the Elbwiesen – as natural floodplains they protected the city from even worse damage.

An Ill-fated
AFFAIR

They are the most colourful couple in the history of Saxony: Anna Constantia Countess von Cosel (1680–1765, née von Brockdorff and divorced von Hoym), and Friedrich August I (1670–1733), Prince Elector of Saxony and King of Poland, better known as "August the Strong". Their liaison would fill the gossip columns today…

August the Strong …

As the second son of the Saxon Prince Elector Johann Georg III, Friedrich August was not born to rule but to take up a military career. However, his brother Johann Georg IV died in 1694 after a reign lasting only three years and the 24-year-old Friedrich August had to take over the affairs of government. The only child from his marriage to Christiane Eberhardine von Brandenburg-Bayreuth, Friedrich August II, was born in 1696. The Prince Elector, who converted to the Catholic faith, was elected King of Poland in 1697 and again in 1709.

Friedrich August I, who was known as "the Strong" due to his legendary physical strength and virility, was to become Saxony's most magnificent ruler; he got his inspiration for his lavish lifestyle from France's Sun King Louis XIV. During his reign, the Saxon court developed into a European city of art and culture.

Above: The bust of August by Paul Heermann in the Sculpture Collection

Below: Copperplate engraving of Countess von Cosel

The Countess' flight in porcelain

...and the Countess Cosel

Anna Constantia von Brockdorff, who grew up in Depenau in Holstein and was elevated to Countess von Cosel in 1706, was not the only – but definitely the most famous – of August the Strong's mistresses. After the birth of an illegitimate child and two years of unhappy marriage to the Saxon Tax Director Adolf Magnus von Hoym, the beautiful, well-educated young woman became August's "left-hand consort" with a promise to marry her after his rightful wife's death. The Prince Elector ended the seven-year liaison in 1713 and demanded that the marriage promise be returned to him. Anna Constantia lost power, property and security. She fled to Berlin but was extradited by the Prussians. Countess Cosel was taken to Stolpen Castle on 24 December 1716 where she lived for 49 years until her death on 31 March 1765. She had survived her paramour by 32 years.

FRIEDRICH AUGUST

August the Strong bore the title of Friedrich August I (1670–1733) Prince Elector of Saxony and, from 1697, King of Poland as August II. He passed on his name twice: to his only legitimate son and successor Friedrich August II (1696–1763), also Prince Elector of Saxony and King of Poland as August III. And, to the son he fathered with Countess Cosel: Friedrich August von Cosel (1712–70).

The Wettin family tree also lists Friedrich August III (1750–1827), known as "the Just", Prince Elector of Saxony and – by the grace of Napoleon – King Friedrich August I of Saxony after 1806, King Friedrich August II (1797–1854) and finally Friedrich August III (1865–1932) the last Saxon king.

The 13th of February

This date represents the greatest catastrophe in the history of Dresden: 13 February 1945. In just a few hours, British and American bombers reduced the city, which had been considered one of the most beautiful in Europe, to ash and rubble.

Destruction

The end of World War II, which had claimed lives of millions of victims, was rapidly approaching at the beginning of 1945. Many Dresdeners already believed that they had once again had a narrow escape: the artistic city on the Elbe was even considered the "safest air-raid shelter in the Reich". That was until the 13th of February. During the night from Mardi Gras to Ash Wednesday the sirens started to howl at 9:39pm. The first bombs fell at 10:13pm. In two waves of attack, three hours apart, more than 750 British Lancaster bombers dropped their deadly cargo over Dresden's city centre. A third attack – this time carried out by American squadrons – took place at midday on the following day.

The firestorm created by the explosive and incendiary bombs left a 15km² (6mi²) field of rubble in its wake. The Historical Commission set up in 2005 estimated that at least 25,000 people lost their lives. The dome of the burned-out Frauenkirche remained standing above the smouldering ruins until the morning of 15 February, when the burned columns gave way and Dresden's landmark collapsed.

Reconstruction and Reconciliation

A new Dresden emerged from the rubble of the city in the decades following the war – a great feat that still continues. In the seven decades since the night of the bombs, many of the unique monuments that were hit have been faithfully reconstructed. Zwinger, Hofkirche and the Semperoper opera house are back to their former splendour while construction work on the Residenzschloss is slowly but steadily approaching completion.

The rebirth of the Frauenkirche and its consecration in autumn 2015 marked the crowning achievement of the reconstruction activities. In the

"TO THE BITTER END"

Victor Klemperer, who described the events in his diary, gave one of the most moving eyewitness accounts of the bombing. In an incredible turn of fate, the attack saved him and many other of the approximately 100 Jews still living in Dresden as the deportation orders, delivered on 13 February, could no longer be carried out.

Dresden city centre after the destruction

days of the GDR, the ruin was regarded as an anti-war symbol. From the early 1980s, the citizens of Dresden made a pilgrimage to the ruined church every year on 13 February. During its reconstruction, the Frauenkirche became a symbol of reconciliation. People from all over the world – including many American and British citizens, not only from Dresden's partner city Coventry – supported the work through donations. Alan Smith, the son of one of the bomber pilots who had taken part in the attack on Dresden, created the tower cross that was financed by the British Dresden Trust.

ART **TREASURE**

Dresden's art and cultural history is full of many great names.
The city has a unique heritage that is proudly cultivated by
its inhabitants, and one that always inspires new generations
of artists.

Music

The city's oldest music ensemble, the **Dresden Kreuz Choir**, is one of the
most famous boys' choirs in the world and has around 150 young singers –
known as the Kruzianers. The choir's history goes back for more than
700 years.

The city of Dresden has two world-class orchestras – the time-honoured
Saxon Staatskapelle Dresden, founded in 1548 as the court orchestra,
now sits in the pit of the Semperoper and the **Dresden Philharmonic**,
which was formed in 1870 having developed from the traditional town
band over the centuries. **Heinrich Schütz** (1585–1672) composed
the first German opera *Die Tragicomoedia von der Dafne* in the Saxon
Residenz in 1627; **Carl Maria von Weber** (1786–1826) – after whom the
Dresden conservatory is named today – wrote the German national opera,
Der Freischütz, on the Elbe. Like Schütz and Weber, **Richard Wagner**
(1813–83) was also court conductor in Dresden. Three of his operas –
Rienzi, The Flying Dutchman and *Tannhäuser* – premiered here. He
had also started working on his *Lohengrin* before he had to leave the city
because of his participation in the 1849 May Uprising. **Richard Strauss**
(1864–1949), who was a frequent guest conductor at the Dresden Opera,
called the Saxon Staatskapelle "the world's best opera orchestra". Nine

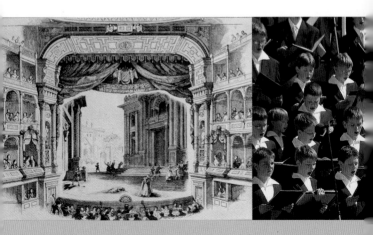

of his operas, including *Der Rosenkavalier,* had their premiere in Dresden and are still in the repertoire of the Semperoper.

SHAPED BY THE CITY

"If it happens to be true that I know not only what is bad and ugly, but also what is beautiful, then I have the fortune of growing up in Dresden to thank for this."

Erich Kästner

Dance

The history of modern dance began in Hellerau in Dresden in 1910 when the Swiss music teacher **Émile Jacques-Dalcroze** (1865–1950) founded the Educational Institute for Rhythmic Gymnastics. The dancer and choreographer **Mary Wigman** (1886–1973), who studied here until 1913, founded her own school in Dresden in 1920 that then developed into a centre for expressive dance. Wigman's most famous pupil, **Gret Palucca** (1902–93) soon caused a sensation with her solo performances and also opened her own School for New Artistic Dance in 1925. The Palucca University of Dance is the only independent university of dance in Germany.

Literature

Theodor Körner (1791–1813) was only destined to have a short career as a poet and dramatist. The author of *Lützows wilde, verwegene Jagd (Lutzow's Wild Hunt),* who was Lützow's aide-de-camp, died at 21 in a battle against Napoleon. The writer of adventure yarns, **Karl May** (1842–1912), lived for a time in Dresden and later moved to Radebeul. Dresden's most famous author, **Erich Kästner** (1899–1974), created a monument to his birthplace with *Als ich ein kleiner Junge war (When I was a Little Boy).* The Romance scholar **Victor Klemperer** analysed the language of the Third Reich in *LTI – Lingua Tertii Imperii* and bore witness to the Nazi persecution of the Jews in Dresden in his diaries (➤ 14).

Left to right: Premiere of Wagner's *Rienzi* in Dresden in 1842; The Kreuz Choir; A lesson at the Palucca University of Dance in Dresden

Fine Arts

Balthasar Permoser (1651–1732), one of the most famous sculptors of the Baroque age, was active in Dresden for more than 40 years. **Ernst Rietschel** (1804–61) and his master pupil **Johannes Schilling** (1828–1910) were the dominant figures in the area of sculpture in the 19th century.

The Venetian **Bernardo Bellotto**, known as **Canaletto** (1721–80) left his mark on Baroque Dresden with his scenes of the city, and they are still famous today. In 1764, the painter began teaching at the recently founded Kunstakademie, today's Academy of Fine Arts.

Many other famous artists lived and taught in Dresden: **Caspar David Friedrich** (1774–1840) and **Adrian Ludwig Richter** (1803–84), **Robert Sterl** (1867–1932) and **Oskar Kokoschka** (1886–1980), **Otto Dix** (1891–1969) and **Hans Grundig** (1901–58).

Prominent contemporary artists such as **Gerhard Richter** (born 1932) and **A.R. Penck** (born 1939) were born in Dresden.

And finally, **"Die Brücke" (The Bridge)**, a group of Expressionist artists (▶ 24; with Karl Schmidt-Rottluff, Ernst Ludwig Kirchner and others) founded in 1905, which provided some of the most significant influences for the history of European art in the 20th century.

Top to bottom: Pulpit by Permoser in the Hofkirche; Caspar David Friedrich, portrayed by Georg Friedrich Kersting; A Kokoschka painting in the Galerie Neue Meister; Bernardo Bellotto, known as Canaletto, painted several versions of Dresden from the right bank of the Elbe

THE CHANGING CITY

Today, the silhouette of Dresden's Altstadt is almost the same as it was before its destruction during World War II. Locals and visitors alike admire historic Dresden most of all, so it is no surprise that modern architecture is often not well received here.

The 18th Century

Great architects have left their mark on Dresden; the city is characterised by building styles from three centuries. The favourite architect of August the Strong, Matthäus Daniel Pöppelmann (1662–1736), drew up the plans for the Zwinger, Taschenbergpalais and the Japanische Palais, as well as Pillnitz and Moritzburg castles and the Matthäuskirche church. George Bähr (1666–1738) made his way up from being a carpenter's apprentice to become the city's master carpenter. He had already built several village churches before the City of Dresden commissioned him to draw up the plans for the Frauenkirche. Bähr did not live to see the completion of his masterpiece, which was finished in 1743.

Wallpavillon in the Zwinger

The 19th Century

During his days in Dresden, Gottfried Semper (1803–79) designed a theatre (burned down in 1869), an opera house, the Picture Gallery in the Zwinger and the synagogue that was destroyed in the Night of Broken Glass in 1938. He created the plans for today's Semperoper while in exile after being forced to flee after his participation in the Dresden May Uprising of 1849.

The myth of Baroque Dresden, preserved in Canaletto's paintings (► left), has managed to survive wars and upheaval. However, the farewell to the Baroque city started long before the bombardment night in 1945. Quite a number of buildings, which were considered old fashioned, were sacrificed in the construction boom after the end of the 19th century. For example, the 150-year-old palace on the Brühlsche Terrasse had to make way for

The Magazine

the Kunstakademie (Academy of Fine Arts, designed by Constantin Lipsius) and other historical-style buildings. The buildings erected in the years around 1900 were then considered to be too large, too elaborate and not sufficiently typical of Dresden. In 1955, Fritz Löffler, author of the standard work on architectural history *Das alte Dresden*, wrote: "The glass dome of the Academy, which the locals call the lemon squeezer, formed a permanent offence to the eye seen against the Frauenkirche".

The 20th and 21st Centuries

Hans Erlwein (1872–1914) was the last outstanding personality to leave an indelible mark on the face of the city. As head of the city's planning department, around 50 buildings including the Italienisches Dörfchen (Italian Village), the abbatoir in Ostragehege and the Erlweinspeicher – now a hotel – were created before his death in an accident in 1914. The City of Dresden has awarded the Erlwein Prize since 1997.

In addition to the reconstruction of the most important architectural monuments – Zwinger, Hofkirche, and Semperoper – the creation of living space became a priority after World War II. New housing settlements sprung up, in the 1950s as a ring around the centre, and in the 1970s outer districts of Prohlis and Gorbitz. Ensembles such as the Altmarkt development with the Kulturpalast and Prager Straße, which are considered exemplary testimonies to the urban construction of their time, were also created.

The citizens of Dresden are to be thanked for the Frauenkirche being reconstructed after the change in the political system in 1989. The public controversies that go hand in hand with any new construction plans show just how difficult it is to fill the Dresdeners with enthusiasm for modern archi-

tecture. The reconstruction of the Neumarkt around the Frauenkirche in particular has been a point of contention between traditionalists and modernists for years. The most severe critics even feel that the collection of copies of town houses is a kind of "Baroque Disneyland".

The most outstanding examples of contemporary architecture created since 1990 include the Sächsischer Landtag (Saxon State Parliament, by Peter Kulka), the Ufa Kristallpalast (coop Himmelb(l)au), the Neue Synagoge (Wandel, Lorch and Hirsch) and the extension to the Museum of Military History (Daniel Libeskind).

Top to bottom: The original Prager Straße; Peter Kulka's Saxon State Parliament

"We are leaving our
ROLLES behind us"

In the autumn of 1989, Dresden was the starting point of the peaceful revolution that resulted in the collapse of an entire political system. The civil courage of the citizens of Dresden forced the state authorities to enter into a dialogue with the people for the first time.

The atmosphere was troubled in the summer of 1989. The GDR leaders refused to recognise *glasnost* and *perestroika* and, instead, brazenly falsified the results of local elections. Thousands of young people from the GDR then left the country, via the border between Hungary and Austria, which had been opened, or sought refuge in one of the Federal Republic of Germany's embassies.

"We want to get out"

The situation escalated when the SED (Socialist Unity Party) leaders closed the border to Czechoslovakia and it became known that the refugees from the embassy of the FRG in Prague would be passing Dresden on their way into the west. The first confrontations between those wanting to leave the country and the security forces – paving stones against water cannons – took place at the Hauptbahnhof, the main station, on 3 October.

Hundreds of people were arrested at the peaceful demonstrations held on that evening and in the following days. In the meantime, the cries had changed from "We want to get out" to "We're staying here; we want reforms".

'We're staying here"

On 6 October, the eve of the 40th anniversary of the GDR, members of the State Theatre came on stage after a performance and read a remarkable resolution. It began with the words "We are leaving our roles behind us" and demanded fundamental democratic rights. Two evenings later, the "Group of 20" was formed from those taking part in the demonstration march on Prager Straße; with their resoluteness, these men and women forced the Lord Mayor to sit down at the negotiating table.

POST-INDUSTRIAL

There are a whole series of remarkable historic industrial buildings, away from Dresden's Altstadt, in districts that were hardly – or not at all – affected by the bombardments on 13 February 1945.

The imposing buildings from the 19th, and first half of the 20th century, were mostly used for their original purposes in GDR times. After the operations were closed following the fall of Communism, several of the buildings were elaborately renovated and converted for new use.

The most outstanding – in the real sense of the word – example of this is the **Yenidze**. The entrepreneur Hugo Zietz had his Oriental Tobacco and Cigarette Factory, which was named after a tobacco-growing region, erected on the western periphery of Altstadt in the years after 1907. He got around the ban on building high smokestacks by hiding his 62m (203ft) high chimney beneath the shell of a minaret. The building was constructed in the style of a mosque complete with colourfully glazed dome. The spectacular design, by architect Martin Hammitzsch, was met with fierce disapproval and hostility. During the GDR period, it was used as a storage and administration building for the Dresden tobacco-buying association and today houses offices, a restaurant with a terrace and a theatre in the dome where readings take place.

From a Museum to a Fair

Dresden was an important camera-producing city for many decades. The **Ernemannwerke**, which was later known as **VEB Pentacon**, was built on Sachaundauer Straße in Dresden from 1898–1938. Dresden's most famous architectural historian, Fritz Löffler, described the high-rise building, crowned with its five-storey **Ernemannturm** tower that dominates the complex, as a "factory building in the New Objectivity style". The silhouette of the tower served as the Pentacon logo and was the symbol of the GDR's photo industry for decades.

The dome of the Yenidze by night

Gasometer on the outside; panoramic view of Baroque Dresden on the inside

Technische Sammlungen Dresden has housed their collection of exhibitions on the history of technology and industry here since 1993.

The first two **gas storage** facilities were built for the Dresden-Reick Gas Institution between 1878 and 1881. A third, larger one designed by the city planner Hans Erlwein, was added in 1909. When gas production stopped in 1974, one of the two older gasometers was taken down. In 2006, the artist Yadegar Asisi installed a 360-degree panorama – 27m (89ft) high and 105m (344ft) wide – in the remaining circular brick building. The panorama and gasometer were united under the name of **Panometer**. Standing on a platform, the viewer is presented with a panoramic view – historical events but interpreted with some artistic liberty – from the tower of the Dresden Hofkirche over the Baroque city; a revised version was installed in 2012. The panoramic presentation of the destroyed city, shown in the first quarter of 2015 on the occasion of the 70th anniversary of the bombardment of Dresden, is really spectacular.

When the abattoir on Leipziger Straße (today, a venue for events) became too small, a new abattoir complex consisting of 68 individual buildings, designed by Hans Erlwein in the revivalist *Heimatstil* style, was erected in Ostragehege in 1906. The ensemble, in the form of a settlement, combined cattle halls and abattoir, administration and residential buildings. After the abattoir closed in 1995, sections of the **Neuer Schlachthof** were converted into the **Dresden Trade Fair** grounds.

Cultural Powerhouse

At the end of the 19th century, "an electrical light works" went online to the west of the city centre; in keeping with the taste of the time, it was built in the Historicist revivalist style. When the power plant was renovated in 1927/1928, the architect Paul Wolf, Dresden's city planner at the time, extended the ensemble with steel-skeleton buildings in the New Objectivity style, which were matched to the existing buildings through the use of red clinker bricks. The four smokestacks led to the **Kraftwerk Mitte** being popularly called the "Battleship Aurora". After the complex was shutdown in 1994 it was partially demolished in 2006, before the Dresden City Council decided to use it to house the Dresden Staatsoperette and the Theater Junge Generation.

The Magazine

"THE BRIDGE"

At the beginning of the 20th century, four architecture students in Dresden formed a group of artist known as "Die Brücke" (The Bridge). The group had a decisive influence on the development of modern art and made Dresden the cradle, and one of the main scenes, of German Expressionism.

Karl Schmidt (1884–1976) and Erich Heckel (1883–1970), who had been friends since their high-school days in Chemnitz, became acquainted with Ernst Ludwig Kirchner (1880–1938) and Fritz Bleyl (1880–1966) while they were studying architecture at the Technical University in Dresden. The four students, who were between 20 and 25 years of age at the time, were united in their love of art and their search for new forms of expression. On 7 June 1905, they founded their group. Karl Schmidt extended his name with that of his birthplace and called himself Karl Schmidt-Rottluff from that time on. In the following years, members of Die Brücke included Max Pechstein, Otto Mueller and – for a brief period – Emil Nolde.

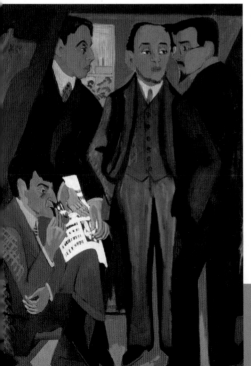

In a New Way

The young guns broke with the traditional academic style of art and, instead of simply depicting reality, they placed their own subjective perception of objects, landscapes and people in the centre of their work. They reduced forms to their essential parts, rejected the dictates of perspective and proportion and used colour to express emotions. In this way, they created drawings that appeared to have been dashed off on the spur of the moment,

Ernst Ludwig Kirchner:
A Group of Artists (1925)

Karl Schmidt-Rottluff: *Woman's Head and Mask*, Galerie Neue Meister

powerful woodcuts and dazzlingly-coloured oil paintings. The favourite motifs of the group included views of the city of Dresden, such as Friedrichstadt, where the artists lived and worked, as well as depictions of female nudes for which their girlfriends – and later wives – often modelled. The Expressionists painted landscapes and bathing scenes in the outdoors at the ponds and lakes around, Moritzburg north of Dresden, and on the North and Baltic Seas.

Beginning and No End

The first Brücke exhibition in Dresden took place in the Karl-Max-Seifert Lamp Factory in Dresden-Löbtau in 1906; however, what was most probably the most important one was held in the Galerie Arnold in September 1910. There were numerous travelling exhibitions, and seven portfolios of prints were published in the years up to 1912. The group moved to Berlin in 1911 and, after quarrels, dissolved in 1913.

The works of the Brücke artists were deemed as "degenerate art" in Nazi Germany and many were lost in the turmoil of World War II. The pioneers of Expressionism did not find their rightful place in the history of art until recent times.

IN THE ARTIST'S FOOTSTEPS

The Dresden State Art Collections have some works by Brücke artists in their collections; these include Ernst Ludwig Kirchner's *Railway Bridge on Löbtauer Straße in Dresden* and the scene can still be seen today at the junction of Löbtauer and Roßthaler Straße.

A venue for artistic and other events was rebuilt at the Dippelsdorf Pond in Moritzburg in 2005; it was modelled on the "Red House" that was used by the artists and well-known from various drawings and paintings. Guided tours of the "Brücke-Weges" (Bridge Path) takes you to the places that inspired the artists while they were staying in Moritzburg.

FESTIVE EVENTS

Dresdeners like to celebrate and they really let their hair down. The city and district festivals held every year in summer attract hundreds of thousands of visitors.

Festive parade at the Stadtfest city festival

Jubilee

The city celebrated its 800th anniversary in 2006. The **Stadtfest** city festival, organised as a run-up to the great event, has been held every year since the end of the 1990s on a weekend in August. Dresden's entire city centre is turned into the festival site for the party that draws the most visitors on the city's calendar of events.

Birthday of a Republic

On the weekend before the monetary union came into effect in June 1990, the **Bunte Republik Neustadt** (Colourful Republic of Neustadt) or "BRN" was proclaimed. It was intended to be a cheerfully defiant act of self-determination, with a provisional government, demarcation lines and its own currency. Over time, the "BRN" became an annual event, a district festival that is probably unique in regulation-crazy Germany. Attempts to put the organization "back on the right track" and make a single body responsible were only moderately successful. Dozens of independent operators have replaced a central organiser. However, there is one set date and the basic rules are respected. For one weekend in the middle of June, Neustadt is turned into a huge party zone. There are concerts, theatre performances on squares and in courtyards, open-air pubs, portable players on windowsills and community-run, kerbside bratwurst stands.

Festival on the Banks

The last weekend in June is reserved for the **Elbhangfest**. This is when the people of Dresden celebrate their lifestyle. The festival takes place on the Elbe stretch between Loschwitz and Pillnitz. Old village centres, the meadow-lined banks of the Elbe and the Elbhang with its villas, gardens and vineyards form the setting for what is probably the most charming of all of Dresden's festivities. Around 200 events take place in the 7km (4mi) stretch. There are musical and theatre performances, lectures, readings and exhibitions as well as an arts and crafts market and – last but not least – all kinds of culinary treats. The festival, which was initiated in 1991 as a benefit event for the Pillnitz Vineyard Church and the George-Bähr church in Loschwitz, has a different motto every year and is traditionally opened with a huge festive parade.

A Shot at the Bird

The oldest festival in Dresden can be traced back to a crossbow bird shooting contest and has been held at Whitsun since the 15th century. Around 1800 the **Vogelwiese** developed into a popular festival with fairground rides and sideshows – and has stayed that way to this very day. The showmen present their attractions at the Volksfestgelände near the Marienbrücke for around three weeks in summer. After the fall of Communism, the tradition of crossbow shooting was also reintroduced. The spring and autumn festivals are usually held at the same location in April and October.

celebrating at the Elbhangfest street festival

New Departures

There are more than 40 museums in the Saxon capital. The incomparable treasures of the world-famous Dresden State Art Collections receive the most attention. And it is not always easy for the other museums to assert themselves.

However, in recent years, some exhibitions have blossomed from being insiders' tips to being real highlights in the Dresden museum landscape with their fascinating subjects and exciting new forms of presentation.

Human Adventure

The Deutsches Hygiene-Museum (German Hygiene Museum, ► 132) is such a place. It portrays itself as a forum for science, culture and society – with the main focus on man. The imaginative permanent exhibition deals with all things human and has no taboos: from sexuality and birth to death. Using unique exhibits, impressive models and media installations, information is conveyed in an interesting and stimulating fashion. An experience-

The Hygiene Museum has many interactive displays featuring aspects of human life

oriented 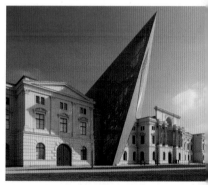 Children's Museum devotes itself, with great fantasy, to our five senses. The museum regularly creates a stir with its elaborately staged – and, not infrequently, provocative – special exhibitions. These have included subjects such as religion, wealth, abortion, beauty and migration.

Technology of Yesterday and Tomorrow

The Technische Sammlungen Dresden (Dresden Technical Collections, Junghansstr. 1–3, tel: 0351 4 88 72 01, www.tsd.de, Tue–Fri 9am–5pm, Sat and Sun 10am–6pm, entrance €5) is located quite a way off the beaten track in the former Ernemann camera factory building (later, Zeiss Ikon and Pentacon). This is where the story of the city's industrial history is told. Dresden was a camera city, pioneer in the field of office and computing technology, as well as micro technology. A section of the exhibition is devoted to the 1992 Dresden DEFA studio for animated films; the more than 100 fascinating experiments in the 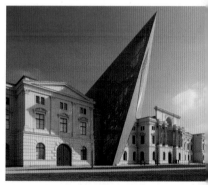 "mathematics adventureland" will impress both adults and children alike. In 2014, the "Cool X. Energy in a Digital World" exhibit brought the future into the museum. Micro- and nanotechnology are the main focus of this presentation that was conceived in cooperation with the top-level Saxon "Cool Silicon" cluster. Visitors can immerse themselves in the world of high technology and gain astonishing insights through interactive experiments.

A Cultural History of Military Power

The building that houses the **Militärhistorische Museum der Bundeswehr** (▶ 108) is suggestive of the city's new ideas on museums. This Military History Museum has an impressive wedge-shaped extension, designed by the star architect Daniel Libeskind, which slices into what was once the Saxon army arsenal. The chronological exhibition of German military history in the old historic section throws a completely new light on the subject. However, it is the section in the Libeskind wedge that is the real sensation;

The Military History Museum's new landmark: the Libeskind Wedge

here, the connections (frequently surprising) between politics and war, and military and civilian everyday life, are demonstrated. A multi-layered – in the true meaning of the world – staging extends over several floors and brings together a World War II V-2 rocket, dishes from the Mittelbau Dora Concentration Camp – where the rocket was built by prisoners living under horrific conditions – as well a dollhouse from 1944 that belonged to a girl living in London. The dollhouse was set up for the war with blackened windows. And, hovering high above all of this – as a witness to the civil use of rocket technology – the landing capsule of a Soyuz spaceship.

MADE in DRESDEN

Numerous inventions – ranging from everyday articles to trailblazing technical achievements – began their triumphant progress in the Saxon city.

Necessity is the mother of invention. And it was a woman – a woman from Dresden – who liberated her fellow sufferers from their corsets when she registered a "woman's undershirt as a breast supporter" with the Imperial Patent Office in September 1899. The **brassiere** created by the brilliant Christine Hardt was also special because the undershirt "can be separated from its adaptable straps for washing" as can be read in patent specification number 110888.

Practical

We have another Dresden housewife to thank for an idea that was as simple as it was brilliant, and makes it possible for us to enjoy our drip-brewed coffee today. In 1908, 35-year-old Melittta Bentz was fed up with having annoying grounds in her coffee so she developed the **coffee filter** by drilling holes into the bottom of a brass pot, and lining it with a sheet of blotting paper from one of her son's exercise books. She had her invention patented and founded the company, which still bears her name today, with a start-up capital of 73 *Reichspfennig* in the same year.

Delicious and Healthy

In 1821, the Dresden doctor and pharmacist, Friedrich Adolph August Struve, developed artificial **mineral water,** a scientifically exact copy of natural mineral water. He went on to establish an entire chain of institutions for drinking cures.

In 1823, Gottfried Heinrich Christoph Jordan and Friedrich Timaeus founded the first German chocolate factory and, sixteen years later, produced the world's first **milk chocolate** – for the price of one *Thaler* a pound.

The chemist Ottomar Heinsius von Mayenburg mixed natural limestone, essential oils, oxygen-rich salts and peppermint together in his Altstadt laboratory in the attic of the Löwenapotheke pharmacy in 1907 – and revolutionised dental hygiene. His Chlorodont brand of **toothpaste** replaced the tooth powder that had previously been in use. The entrepreneur and founder of the Hygiene Museum, Karl August Lingner, had launched his antiseptic **Odol mouth wash** 15 years before in Dresden and became the world's most important mouthwash manufacturer.

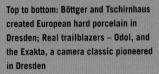

Top to bottom: Böttger and Tschirnhaus created European hard porcelain in Dresden; Real trailblazers – Odol, and the Exakta, a camera classic pioneered in Dresden

Trailblazers

Johann Andreas Schubert, engineer and professor at the Dresden Technical School, came up with a really revolutionary invention. After having blessed the Elbe with the first passenger steamer, he constructed the first German **locomotive**, the *Saxonia*. He took his place in the driver's seat on 8 April 1839 and, from there, took part in the inaugural journey of the first long-distance railway in Germany – between Dresden and Leipzig. The year 1839 also saw the birth of the photo industry in Dresden; not quite one hundred years later in 1936, the Ihagee Camera Works launched the Kine Exakta, the first **35mm reflex camera** to be mass-produced. Although **cinema** was not initiated in Dresden, the Ernemann Kino cine camera was produced here in 1903.

In 1962 Nikolaus Joachim Lehmann – professor of mathematics at Dresden's Technical College, now the Technical University – was the first computer researcher in the world to build a **"calculating machine on the table".** The D4a worked with transistors and is considered the forerunner of today's personal computers.

Even one of the most famous Saxon products, **Meissen porcelain**, was not invented in Meißen but in Dresden. In 1708 Johann Friedrich Böttger and Ehrenfried Walther von Tschirnhaus successfully produced the Europe's first hard porcelain.

FINE **WINE**

Saxony is the most northeasterly of the thirteen German wine-producing regions and stretches from Pirna over Dresden to Diesbar-Seußlitz.

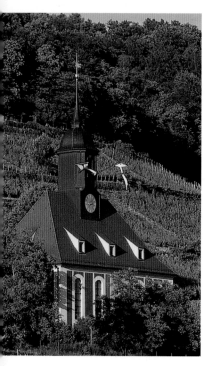

Left: Matthäus Daniel Pöppelmann's Vineyard Church below the Pillnitz vineyards

Prime Location

The vineyards in the Elbe Valley go back many centuries; the first documented mention dates back to 1161. Terraced vineyards, historic wine cellars and picturesque churches dot the landscape.

The mild climate provides perfect growing conditions and, with an average of 1570 hours of sunshine a year, Saxony surpasses many other areas of cultivation in Germany while the great variety of vineyard soil types gives the wines their typical character.

Grape Varieties

The Müller-Thurgau, Riesling and Pinot Blanc varieties are grown on about half of the areas of cultivation in Saxony. Although the amount of red wine produced has increased to around 15 per cent in recent years, mainly dry white wine varieties, which are renowned for their strong and fruity acidity, are still the most cultivated. The Meißner Schieler is not a separate variety but wine pressed from red and white grapes. Another

FESTIVALS

The wine festival period along the Saxon Wine Route begins at the end of August. The largest and most famous are the Autumn and Wine Festival in Radebeul (with an international touring theatre festival) on the village green in Altkötzschenbroda, the Meißen Wine Festival and the Federweißerfest in Diesbar-Seußlitz.

special feature of the area is the *Sachsenkeule*, a traditional wine bottle with a bulbous shape. It fell out of favour for many years but has recently started becoming increasingly popular.

Vintners

Today, more than two dozen wine-growing enterprises and around 2,500 smaller independent farmers cultivate an area of around 460ha (1140 acre). The most famous include the Saxon State Estate Schloss Sackerbarth, the Schloss Proschwitz's Prinz zur Lippe Winery, Vincenz Richter in Meißen, Hoflößnitz in Radebeul and Jan Ulrich (no, not the cyclist) in Diesbar-Seußlitz, as well as Schuh in Sörnewitz. The Saxon Winegrowers' Cooperative Meißen has approximately 1,500 members. And, wine is not only consumed in Dresden: the Königliche Weinberg in Pillnitz run by Klaus Zimmerling's winery produces a first-rate tipple and the vintner Lutz Müller took over the vineyards below the castles on the Elbe in the 1990s.

Wine Tourism

The 55km (34mi) long Saxon Wine Route, from Pirna to Diesbar-Seußlitz, was established in 1992. Many estates now offer wine tastings and guided tours and you can find out all you need to know about the region's history of wine in the Viticulture Museum in Hoflößnitz.

The 90km (56mi) Saxon Wine Trail was established in 2004. The trail leads to the most beautiful vineyards and lookout points, as well as the best vintners' taverns, cellars and restaurants. Holidaying on vineyard estates has also become popular.

Top to bottom: Grape harvest in Pillnitz; Viticulture Museum Hoflößnitz in Radebeul; View from Spitzhaus Restaurant terrace above Radebeul

DYNAMIC
DRESDEN

Scientific curiosity and a pioneering spirit have a long tradition in Dresden. So it comes as no surprise that the Saxon metropolis has outpaced other large cities in the eastern part of Germany.

City of Science and Research

The unparalleled development of its scientific infrastructure has resulted in Dresden having the highest concentration of technical and scientific research and development capacities in the new German states. Eleven universities, colleges and specialist educational establishments – with a total of 45,000 students – have their home in the city on the Elbe; they include the Dresden Technical University, founded in 1828, the only University of Excellence in the east of Germany, and that, since 2012.

THIRST FOR KNOWLEDGE

Since 2003, Dresden's education and research facilities have organised the "Long Night of Science" (www.wissenschaftsnacht-dresden.de). Universities, research institutes and laboratories open their doors for guided tours, lectures and demonstrations, exhibitions, films and music. The permanently rising numbers of people attending shows just how much the Dresdeners are interested in science. The 🎓 **Children's University** (www.ku-dresden.de) and the Junior Doctor project are devoted to promoting young talent. Dresden was the City of Science in 2006.

And that's not all. Dresden is now considered the German city with the highest concentration of research institutions – including the eleven facilities of the Fraunhofer Society, five Leibnitz and three Max Planck Institutes, the Helmholtz Centre Dresden Rossdorf, as well as a research centre of the German Research Council Dresden. Dresden is the leading electronic location in Europe; every second European chip is produced here. Pioneering work is also being done in areas such as nanotechnology, new materials and photovoltaics, as well as biotechnology and sciences. Research networks, competence centres and facilities such as DRESDEN-concept, Silicon Saxony and Dresden Exists act as catalysts that promote synergies and boost development.

The Eastern Upswing

The enormous scientific potential, as well as the creative atmosphere of a city of art and culture, has made the Saxon capital an attractive and dynamic business location – with great prospects for the future. The number of employed people, who have graduated from a specialist college or university, is higher than average in Dresden. Innovative enterprises in particular appreciate this reservoir of motivated and highly qualified workers.

Thousands of new workplaces have been created in recent years; the unemployment rate is always well below the average for eastern Germany. Numerous companies in the technology-oriented field settled in Dresden after the fall of Communism; they include giants in the semiconductor area such as Infineon Technologies and Globalfoundries. The former Sächsischen Serumwerk became GlaxoSmithKline Biologicals, the time-honoured Elbe Airplane Works are now a sister company of EADS and Volkswagen's Gläserne Manufaktur (transparent factory) is a production facility and tourist attraction at the same time – not only for Volkswagen fans.

Tourist attraction and an economic factor: VW's Gläserne Manufaktur, a transparent factory

Jingle Bells...

The Striezelmarkt in Dresden is one of oldest and most famous Christmas markets in Germany. The name refers to a traditional pastry that has been sold at the market since the Middle Ages.

The history of the Striezelmarkt began in 1434 when the sovereign gave permission for a market on the day before Christmas Eve. Today, the time-honoured Christmas market, in Dresden's Altmarkt, attracts hundreds of thousands of locals and visitors every year with its bright lights, aromas of Christmas and colourful market stalls. The most recent redesign with winding lanes and festive illumination on the surrounding buildings has made the market even more charming. The stately Christmas tree, the Erzgebirge Christmas pyramid – the highest at almost 15m (50ft) – and a *Schwibbogen* (a decorative arched candle holder), complete with observation platform, high enough to walk under, are just a few of the attractions. In addition to the 🎁 Advent calendar – Father Christmas opens one of the small doors every day – there is now also a children's carousel and a small Ferris wheel. Around 250 vendors offer traditional crafts – Christmas decorations from Lauscha in Thuringia, Moravian stars and, first and foremost, wooden products from the Erzgebirge: Christmas pyramids, nutcrackers and *Räuchermänner*, wooden figures of men smoking – as well as culinary delights.

Dresdner Stollen

The *Striezel*, which is known as stollen today, that gave the Dresden Christmas market its name was a pre-Christmas cake made of flour, yeast and water. That changed in 1450 when the Pope gave permission, in a "butter letter", for more substantial ingredients to be added. Today, almonds and sultanas, candied orange peel, lemon zest, rum and a

DRESDNER PFLAUMENTOFFEL

These little figures, made out of dried prunes with a ladder, ruff and top hat, were modelled on the chimney sweep lads (often no older than ten) from about 200 years ago and were made by poor families and sold by their children. Today the *Pflaumentoffel* are said to bring luck and are a symbol of the Striezelmarkt.

Every year in December Altmarkt dazzles with festive lights

number of secret spices make the stollen a unique delicacy. By the way, only those with the golden quality seal of the Stollen Protection Association are allowed to be called Original Dresdener Stollen®.

The Stollen Festival has been held on the second Saturday in Advent since 1994, something that can also be traced back to August the Strong. After being paraded through Altstadt, a stollen weighing 3–4 tons is sliced with a gigantic special knife at the Striezelmarkt and then sold under the patronage of a Stollen Maiden.

Christmas Cheer Everywhere

For a the past few years the Striezelmarkt has been joined by other markets such as those on Pragerstraße and Hauptstraße (rather modest), the Mediaeval Christmas in the Stallhof, the small Elbhang Christmas Market in Loschwitz and, above all, the Advent on Neumarkt next to the Frauenkirche. The atmospheric Advent market is just as it was in the 1900s, with traditionally decorated market stalls.

Insider Tip

DID YOU KNOW...

- ...that the first Dresdeners were actually Sorbs and that the name Dresden comes from the Sorb word *Drezdany* meaning "swamp dwellers"?
- ...that Dresden takes twelfth place in terms of population when compared with other large cities in Germany but covers the fourth largest surface area (after Berlin, Hamburg and Cologne)? 62 per cent is covered with forests and green areas, making it one of the greenest cities in Europe.
- ...that around 15 per cent of the people living in Dresden are Evangelical Lutherans and barely 5 per cent are Roman Catholic; the overwhelming majority does not belong to any religious denomination?
- ...that Dresden is particularly popular with visitors from the USA, Switzerland, Austria, Great Britain and Japan?
- ...Dresden Saxon sounds different from the way the language is spoken in Leipzig or Chemnitz? And that, through Luther's translation of the Bible into *Meißner Kanzleideutsch* (chancery or pulpit German), the Saxon language had a major influence on the development of today's standard German?
- ...that more than 500,000 people live in Saxony's capital city and that – in contrast to the trend in eastern Germany – the population is on the increase and the city is now Germany's childbirth capital?
- ...that the components for the cars that are manufactured in the Gläserne Manufaktur are transported by a goods tram – the CarGoTram – especially constructed for the purpose?
- ...that the two most famous Dresdeners loiter in the Gemäldegalerie Alte Meister – and that they are the two cherubs in Raphael's *Sistine Madonna*?

Dresden is a young up-and-coming city that is popular with tourists

Finding Your Feet

First Two Hours

Dresden Airport

Dresden's airport is located in Klotzsche on the northern edge of the city around 9km (6mi) from the centre. Airport information: tel: 0351 88133 60, www.dresden-airport.de.

Airport Transfers

- The airport is liked to the Dresden **S-Bahn** (suburban train) network. The S2 line runs every half hour; the trip to the Dresden-Neustadt station takes around 15 minutes and 25 minutes to the main station.
- A **taxi** ride to the city centre is around €20 and takes 15–30 minutes, depending on the time of day and the traffic.
- The trip to the centre by **bus and tram** takes approximately 35 minutes. Take bus 77 to the Infineon Nord stop and then transfer to tramline 7 in the direction of Gorbitz.
- By **car,** you reach the centre of Dresden via Karl-Marx-Straße, Königsbrücker Landstraße and then Königsbrücker Straße. The trip takes 15–30 minutes depending on the time of day and traffic.

Railway Stations

Long distance trains stop at the **Hauptbahnhof** main station (reconstructed using a design by Sir Norman Foster) south of the city centre; those coming from the north and east usually stop at the **Bahnhof Neustadt** station on the right side of the Elbe.

Railway Information

Service Hotline: tel: 0180 6 99 66 33, www.bahn.de; **main station DB-Service-Point** in the main hall in front of the tracks on the ground floor: daily 6am–10:30pm; **Lost and Found Hotline:** tel: 0900 1 99 05 99, www. fundservice.bahn.de, lost articles can be collected at the counter in the waiting room in the south hall (Tue, Fri noon–6pm).

Arriving by Car

We recommend the Dresden-Hellerau exit if you are arriving from the north (A13 from Berlin) or the east (A4 from Görlitz) and the Dresden-Altstadt exit if you are coming from the west (A4 from Eisenach). The Dresden-Südvorstadt exit is the quickest way to reach the centre for those drivers arriving from Prague via the A17.

Arriving by Boat

Various organisations (such as www.flusskreuzfahrten-elbe.de and www. flusskreuzfahrten.de) offer boat trips that stop in Dresden.

Visitor Information

- **Dresden Information** offers tourist info, an accommodation service, city tours, excursions, and also sells Dresden and Regio Cards.
- **Telephone Service Centre:** tel: 0351 50 15 01, www.dresden.de, email: info@dresdeninformation.de, Mon–Sat 9am–6pm.
- There are two **tourist information offices** in the city: Dresden Information at Frauenkirche (Neumarkt 2, in the basement of the QF-Passage, Mon–Fr 10am–7pm, Sat 10am–6pm, Sun 10am–3pm) and Dresden Information in the main station (Wiener Platz 4, Hauptbahnhof, Mon–Sun 8am–8pm)

Getting Around

Dresden has a well-developed network of tram; bus, suburban and regional trains that connect the city to the countryside. The city is also developing an extended network of cycle paths – but at a slow pace – and it is easy to cover lengthy east-west distances on the Elbe Cycle Route. Visitors can take tours of the city by bus, rickshaw, Trabi (an old East German car), carriage, horse-drawn bus or steamer.

Public Transport

- **Trams** are the most important means of transport in the city centre and there are 12 regular lines. The main junctions are Pirnaische Platz and Postplatz. The trams run every 10 to 20 minutes during the day and every half-hour or hour from midnight to 5am.
- The 28 **city bus lines** operate mainly in the outer districts. Some buses run 24 hours a day (hourly during the night) and others only during the day. Lines 75 and 62 cross the city centre.
- Alita – **call-up taxis** – are used to replace trams and buses on certain routes at times when demand is low. You need to order an Alita 20 minutes in advance (tel: 0351 8 1 11 11); they then come to the named ÖPNV stop and cost the same as a normal ticket.
- Three **S-Bahn** lines run from the city centre to the airport, the outlying districts and the surrounding countryside. The **S1** runs from the main station to Saxon Switzerland as far as Schöna; Neustadt station lines go to Meißen; the **S2** goes from Pirna via the main station, Mitte and Neustadt stations to the airport; the **S3** goes to Freital and Tharandt and, on workdays, to Freiberg as the S30.
- The numerous **regional railways and buses** make **excursions** into Dresden's beautiful surroundings an easy matter. A steam-powered **narrow-gauge railway,** the Lößnitzgrundbahn (known as the "Lößnitzdackel" or Lößnitz Dachshund), runs regularly between Radebeul East and Moritzburg/Radeburg, special trips are also available (www.loessnitzgrundbahn.de, www.traditionsbahn-radebeul.de).

Information

- **Dresdner Verkehrsbetriebe (DVB)**: tel: 0351 8 57 10 11 (service telephone), www.dvb.de. The DVB transport customer centre is at Postplatz 1 (Wilsdruffer Kubus, Mon–Fri 9am–7pm, Sat 9am–6pm, Sun 10am–6pm). The DVB also operates **service points** in the city centre at Hauptbahnhof/Wiener Platz, Albert- and Pirnaischer Platz and on Prager Straße (Mon–Fri 8/9am–6/7pm, Sat 8/9am and 5/6/7pm, main station also Sun 9am–6pm).
  The **Verkehrsverbund Oberelbe** (VVO) transport association also has an information hotline tel: 0351 8 52 65 55 or www.vvo-online.de. Smartphone users can use free Dresdner Verkehrsbetrieben (DVB) apps.

Tickets

- The city centre of Dresden is one of the 21 tariff zones of the Verkehrsverbund Oberelbe. If you want to travel beyond the city limits, ask for information at one of the DVB service points. Tickets are valid for buses, trams and other rail services. Special tickets are required for ferries and funicular railways. You can find tourist ticket information on the www.dvb.de website.

Finding Your Feet

- **Tickets** are available from service centres and ticket counters of the participating organisations. Only certain tickets are available from vending machines or from public transport drivers. There are reduced fares for children aged 6 to 14 years.
- Note that all tickets purchased in advance (except tickets that are valid for a year or other set lengths of time) **must be stamped** at a validating machine before starting your trip!
- **Single tickets** for one zone are valid for one hour after validation. Registration for mobile-phone tickets at www.handyticket.de.
- One strip on the more economical **4-trip tickets** must be cancelled for each zone and hour.
- The **4-trip tickets** are the only **short distance tickets** available and they are sold at the normal price. A cancelled strip permits the holder to travel as far as the fourth stop after the starting point. Changes are not allowed.
- **Day tickets** are worthwhile if you make at least three trips in a single day. They are valid until 4am on the day after being cancelled; the same applies to **day tickets for families** (for a maximum of two adults and four children from 6 to 14 years of age).
- For a longer stay in Dresden, buy a **weekly** or **monthly ticket**; they are more economical if you make more than 10 or 26 trips respectively.
- A bicycle day ticket has to be bought for the respective tariff zone (zone 1 for Dresden) if you want to take your **bike** or **dog** with you.
- If you are caught **without a ticket**, you will have to pay €40.
- The **Dresden City Card for one day** (€9.90; families €13.90) makes it possible for you to use all of the means of transport operated by the ÖPNV (except funicular railways) until 4am on the following day and also entitles you to discounts from numerous tourist partners. In addition, the **Dresden City Card for two days** (€29.90; families €54.90) includes entrance to the twelve museums of the State Art Collections Dresden (except the Grünes Gewölbe). The **Dresden Regio Card** (€79.90; families €119) is also valid on the scheduled services of the Verkehrsverbund Oberelbe in the Dresden surrounds and includes discounts from 120 partners. You can get the tourist passes at the Tourist Information Offices, the DVB service points and at other locations.

Funicular Railway

There is a **funicular railway** from Körnerplatz to Weißer Hirsch (Mon–Fri 7am–9pm, Sat/Sun 9am–9pm; shorter Nov–Mar); a **suspension railway** from Pillnitzer Landstraße near Körtnerplatz to Oberloschwitz (daily 10am–8pm shorter Nov–Mar). They both run every 10–15 minutes.

By Car

If you decide to drive in Dresden you should be prepared for roadworks and detours, as well as traffic jams on the bridges over the Elbe at rush hours. There are sufficient city centre **parking spaces** (with a fee) – on the street, in multi-storey car parks and underground parking – and the prices are moderate (usually €1–1.50/hour with economic daily rates in the Centrum Galerie and elsewhere). The electronic signboards of the **parking information system** show where there are empty spaces (see also www.dresden.de/freie-parkplaetze).

Taxi

Taxis from the **Funk-Taxi Dresden** service can be found at more than 100 taxi ranks throughout the city and can be also be called by telephone (tel: 3522

12 11) or you can use the free Taxi Dresden app. The **Chauffeurservice 8×8** (tel: 0351 88 88 88 88) charges a few cents more for driving to the location but nothing extra for waiting time.

Velotaxi and Rickshaw

Hi-tech three-wheelers and rickshaws operate in the city centre. Half an hour costs from €15 (1 person) or €20 (2 persons): **Rikscha-Service** (tel: 0351 8 03 07 70), **8×8 Rikscha** (tel: 0351 41 89 99 55), **City Rikscha** (tel: 0152 04 31 60 10), **Rikscha Taxi** (tel: 0160 92 70 86 03).

Carriage and Horse-drawn Bus

Ride through the city in a horse and carriage or horse-drawn bus, they depart from Neumarkt or Schlossplatz.

Bicycle and Scooter

- The **Elbe Cycle Route** (www.elberadweg.de) is one of the most popular long distance routes for cycling in Germany. The most beautiful section starts in Dresden's Altstadt and runs upstream along the Elbe past the "Blue Wonder" and Schloss Pillnitz castle to Saxon Switzerland (➤ 158).
- Some hotels, hostels and guest houses provide **hire bikes**. In addition, the **nextbike** hire system and their partner **sz-bike** operate a number of locations where bikes can be hired. Registration (with credit card) and rental by app or hotline (tel: 030 69 20 50 46, www.nextbike.de, www.sz-bike.de, €9/24 hours). **Scooters** (with helmet about €25/day) and bicycles can be hired from **Roll On Dresden** (Königsbrücker Str. 4a/ Albertplatz, tel: 0351 2 14 25 01, www.rollondresden.de). You can even get a seven-seater bike from **ConferenceBikes Dresden** (tel: 0351 65 31 88 88, www.cbikes.de).

Elbe Ferries, Paddle Steamers and Boats

- Ferries link the two sides of the Elbe in Dresden: **Johannstadt–Neustadt** (Mon–Fri 6:30am–11pm, Sat/Sun 9:30am–11pm, in winter up to 6:30pm), **Niederpoyritz–Laubegast** (Mon–Fri 6am–10pm, Sat/Sun 9am–10pm), **Kleinzschachwitz–Schloss Pillnitz** (car ferry, 5:30am–midnight, cars Mon–Fri 5:30am–9pm, Sat/Sun 8am–9pm). Single trip €1.50, return €2, with car €3.50/6.
- The **Sächsische Dampfschifffahrt** steamers set out downstream to Diesbar-Seußlitz and upstream to Bad Schandau (tickets/departure on Terrassen-ufer, information: tel: 0351 86 60 90, www.saechsische-dampfschiffahrt.de).
- **Elbe Taxi** (tel: 0351 4 17 24 24 40, 0177 1 98 88 08, www.elbe-taxi.de) speedboats offer everything from **sightseeing tours** to their 20-minute **Cruise & Fun** trip through the city.
- Canoes are available from **Kanu Dresden** (May–Oct daily, Apr upon request, tel: 0351 1 60 52 23, www.kanudresden.de).
- **Floßexpeditionen** offers a variety of different **rafting trips** on the Elbe. The motorised rafts are covered but it is still a good idea to be properly equipped with sun protection or a raincoat – depending on the weather (tel: 0351 2 73 10 37, www.flossexpedition.de).

Plane and Balloon

- **Sightseeing flights** in small planes depart from the airport in Dresden or the Riesa Airfield (45km /28mi away) and are a good way to get a bird's eye view of the city, Meißner and Moritzburg, as well as Saxon Switzerland. The **August der Starke** flight service (tel: 0351 8 81 55 55, www.rundflug

dresden.de) and **Dresdner Luftfahrtgesellschaft mbH** (tel: 0351 65 87 75 85, www.sachsenrundflug.de) are two companies that offer flights.

■ In good weather **hot-air balloons** can regularly be seen in the skies over Dresden. Companies such as **Ballon-Sport und Luftwerbung Dresden GmbH** (tel: 0351 47 96 52 50, www.ballon-sport-dresden.de), **Ballonfahrten Dresden** (tel: 0351 4 16 17 00, www.ballon-dresden.de) and **Sky-Lift Ballonfahrten** (tel: 0351 4 11 71 14, www.sky-lift.de) depart from the Elbwiesen. You will have to pay around €180 per person for a trip.

City Tours

■ Some of the **starting points** for city tours are at Augustusbrücke/Schloss- and Theaterplatz, Wilsdruffer Straße/corner of Schlossstraße or Stadtmuseum.

■ The **Dresden Information** tourism service offers a great variety of themed walking or driving tours.

■ The **Dresdner Verkehrsbetriebe** transport service also offers a variety of guided walking and bus tours of the city (tel: 0351 8 57 10 11, www.dvb.de).

■ **Igeltour Dresden** (tel: 0351 8 04 45 57, www.igeltour-dresden.de) organises imaginative tours on various subjects, exploring individual districts and other excursions in Dresden and surrounds – walking, by bus or bike.

■ **Programmgestaltung Matthes** (tel: 0351 4 11 67 56, www.programm gestaltung-matthes.de) and **Barokkoko** (tel: 0351 8 33 60 00, www. erlebnisrundgang.de) offer city tours lead by "August the Strong", "Countess Cosel" or "Count Brühl". **Jana Malschewski-Böhm** guides visitors through the history of Dresden with walking or bus tours (www. discoverdresden.com) while the **Nachtwächter** will help you discover Neustadt's Baroque district (tel: 0162 2 65 91 55, www.nachtwaechter-dresden.de/english-offers).

■ **Stadtrundfahrt Dresden's** double-decker buses have 22 stops (you can hop on and off as often as you like). If you start after 4pm, the city tour ticket is also valid on the following day (www.stadtrundfahrt.com). The red **Rote Doppeldecker** also cover various routes in Dresden (www. stadtrundfahrt-dresden.de).

■ **Videobustour** (information on dates from: tel: 030 44 02 44 50, www.video bustour.de) offer tours with a multimedia experience using historical film, images and sounds.

■ **Trabi Safari** offer you the chance to drive through the city in an old car from the GDR – complete with four-speed manual gearbox – commentary is provided via the radio (tel: 0351 82 12 01 43, www.trabi-safari.de).

■ Trend conscious tourists can opt to spend time on a futuristic two-wheeler with a **Segway Tour**. Companies include **Segway Store Dresden** (tel: 0351 7 95 76 99, www.dresden-roller.de), **Segway Tour Dresden** (tel: 0351 4 86 71 01, www.seg-tour-dresden.de) and **SegCity** (tel: 0173 2 19 02 40, www.seg-stadtfuehrung-dresden.de).

Accommodation

There is somewhere in Dresden to stay to suit every taste and budget: the city has more than 21,000 beds in around 180 hotels and guest houses, in addition to 1,000 beds in backpacker hostels and camping sites. Those who plan to stay for a longer period can book a holiday apartment.

Information and Reservations

The **Dresden Information** (➤ 40) arranges stays in hotels, guest houses, private rooms and holiday apartments, as well as various attractive packages.

Backpackers and Hostels

■ The offers range from a double room to a dormitory for 10 people with shared bathroom. A bed can be had for as little as €15.

■ The **Jugendgästehaus Dresden**, the largest youth hostel in Saxony, is only a five-minute walk away from the Zwinger (Maternistr. 22, tel: 0351 49 26 20, www.jugendherberge-sachsen.de, overnight stays with youth hostel ID). Comparable accommodations are offered by **City Herberge** (Hotel & Hostel, Lingnerallee 3, tel: 0351 4 85 99 00, www.city-herberge. de) opposite the town hall and the low-priced **A&O Dresden** hotel and youth hostel directly behind the Dresden's main station (Strehlener Str. 10, tel: 0351 46 92 71-59 00, www.aohostels.com/de/dresden).

■ The **hostels** in Äußere Neustadt are extremely popular and it is therefore wise to book in advance. They have a laid-back, international atmosphere, individually decorated rooms, free WiFi and hire bikes and are sometimes open around the clock. Options include: **Guesthouse Mezcalero** (Königsbrücker Str. 64, tel: 0351 81 07 70, www.mezcalero. de), **Hostel Mondpalast** (Louisenstr. 77, tel: 0351 5 63 40 50, www.mond palast.de), **Lollis Homestay** (Görlitzer Str. 34, tel: 0351 8 10 84 58, www.lollishome.de), **LaLeLu Mini-Hostel** (Königsbrücker Straße 70, tel: 0173 3 51 52 17, www.lalelu-hostel.de). The **Hostel kangaroo-stop** (Erna-Berger-Str. 8–10, tel: 0351 31 43 455, www.kangaroo-stop.de) and the **Family Hostel Dresden** (Hechtstraße 27, tel: 0351 20 58 68 57, www.familyhostel-dresden.de) are particularly suitable for families.

Camping and Caravans

The **Campingplatz Dresden-Mockritz** in the south of the city (Boderitzer Straße 30, tel: 0351 4 71 52 50, www.camping-dresden.de) is open most of the year. The **Campingplatz Wostra** is located in the southeast of Dresden near the Elbe and the Wostra nudist beach (An der Wostra, tel: 0351 2 10 32 54). The year-round caravan park, **Wohnmobilstellplatz am Blüherpark,** is only stone's throw away from the historic Altstadt (administered by the Cityherberge, Zinzendorfstraße, tel: 0351 4 85 99 00, www.wohnmobil-dresden.de). The second caravan park in Neustadt, **Große Meißner Straße/ Wiesentorstraße** (tel: 0170 7 18 76 43) is not even 50m (160ft) from the Elbwiesen and the panoramic view over Altstadt. Also close to the Elbe is the **Wohnmobilstellplatz Sachsenplatz** (tel: 0162 9 84 36 62, wohnmobil stellplatz-dresden.de).

Accomodation Prices

For a double room per night (incl. breakfast):

€ less than €100   €€ €100–€150   €€€ €150–€200   €€€€ over €200

Aparthotel am Zwinger €€

This hotel has 45 apartment-style rooms in several Gründerzeit houses. It is close to the Zwinger and not even a ten-minute walk from the Frauenkirche. All have their own kitchens or a more basic unit and many have a separate living room in addition to one or more bedrooms. Breakfast and lunch (Mon–Fri) in the hotel's Maximus Restaurant.

Finding Your Feet

⊞ 190 A2 ✉ Maxstraße 3–7
☎ 0351 89 90 01 00; www.pension-zwinger.de
🚋 Tram 6, 11 Kongresszentrum

art'otel Dresden €€

The ultramodern hotel is only 300m (1000ft) away from the Zwinger and Semperoper. The rooms and public areas are by the Italian designer Denis Santachiara; the approximately 750 works of art – including the 6.50m (21ft) high statue of a naked man on the roof – throughout the hotel are original creations by A.R. Penck who was born in Dresden.

⊞ 190 A2 ✉ Ostra-Allee 33
☎ 0351 4 92 20; www.artotels.com
🚋 Tram 6, 11 Kongresszentrum

Insider Tip

Backstage €

An old dairy factory building at the east end of Äußere Neustadt was converted into a unique hotel. The twelve rooms were designed by artists and craftsmen and are a real feast for the eyes. Unusual materials such as wood, bamboo and natural stone were used. Restaurant, garden and special package deals.

⊞ 191 D3 ✉ Prießnitzstraße 12
☎ 0351 8 88 77 77; www.backstage-hotel.de
🚋 Tram 11 Diakonissenkrankenhaus

Hotel Bülow Palais & Residenz Dresden €€€–€€€€

In Innere Neustadt, the Baroque (built in 1730) Bülow Residenz is one of the most exclusive addresses in Dresden. It was expanded with the addition of the nearby Bülow Palais, which was built in a historical style in 2010. Both establishments are noted for their elegance and first-class service. The award-winning Caroussel Restaurant also moved from the Residenz into the Palais. Benjamin Biedlingmaier has been the chef de cuisine since 2013.

⊞ 196 B4 ✉ Königstraße 14/Rähnitzgasse 19
☎ 0351 8 00 32 91; www.buelow-residenzen.de
🚋 Tram 4, 9 Palaisplatz; 3, 6–8, 11 Albertplatz

Hilton Dresden €€€

Built in the last years of the GDR, the Hilton is right opposite the Frauenkirche and some of the rooms and suites have a view of Dresden's famous landmark. The hotel also has a modern business centre, an excellent gym and spa, as well as twelve restaurants, cafés and bars.

⊞ 196 B2 ✉ An der Frauenkirche 5
☎ 0351 8 64 20; www.hilton.de/dresden
🚋 Tram 1, 2, 4; Altmarkt

Hotel Martha Dresden €€

This hotel, which is very peaceful in spite of its location on the edge of Innere Neustadt, is over 100 years old. Cheerful rooms, a sunny conservatory and the pleasant staff ensure that guests feel comfortable.

⊞ 196 B4 ✉ Nieritzstraße 11
☎ 0351 8 17 60; www.hotel-martha-dresden.de
🚋 Tram 4, 9 Palaisplatz; 3, 6, 11 Bahnhof Neustadt

Ibis Hotels Bastei/Lilienstein/Königstein €

The three almost identical hotels on "Prager", Dresden's popular shopping street, have a total of 918 rooms between them. This is the right choice for anyone who wants to stay in a peaceful, reasonably priced location without any traffic noise.

⊞ 192 B3 ✉ Prager Straße 5, 9, 13
☎ 0351 48 56 20 00; www.ibis-dresden.de
🚋 Tram 3, 7, 8, 10; bus 66 Hauptbahnhof; tram 3, 7–9, 11 Hbf-Nord

Hotel Taschenbergpalais Kempinski €€€€

The top hotel in Dresden is located in the heart of Altstadt. The Taschenbergpalais, which August the Strong gave to his mistress Countess Cosel as a present, was reconstructed in the mid-1990s. Behind the Baroque façade, one discovers all of the luxury and comfort of a grand hotel: spacious rooms and suites with exquisite furnishings (there is a view of the Zwinger and Theaterplatz from the 360m²/4000ft² Crown Prince's Suite), top-class gastronomy, first-class service and exquisite gym and spa facilities.

🖽 196 A2 ✉ Taschenberg 3 ☎ 0351 4 91 20; www.kempinski.com/de/dresden

🚋 Tram 1, 2, 4, 8, 9, 11, 12; bus 75, 94 Postplatz

Maritim Hotel Dresden €€€

The former Erlwein warehouse has housed an elegant luxury hotel since 2006. Built more than 90 years ago – by Dresden's then head of city planning Hans Erlwein – the hotel is next to the International Congress Center. It has 328 spacious rooms and suites, a spa and a conservatory with a restaurant and terrace along the Elbe as well as a 38m (125ft) high glass atrium.

🖽 190 B2 ✉ Ostra-Ufer 2/Devrientstr. 10–12
☎ 0351 21 60; www.maritim.de
🚋 Tram 6, 11 Kongresszentrum

Motel One – Dresden am Zwinger €

This budget hotel was opened in 2013, it has a modern exterior and a functional contemporary interior. Pleasant rooms and bathrooms and excellent value for money for the location. There is a second Motel One on Palaisplatz in Neustadt.

🖽 192 B4 ✉ Postplatz 5
☎ 0351 43 83 80; www.motel-one.com
🚋 Tram 1, 2, 4, 8, 9, 11, 12; bus 94 Postplatz

Pullman Dresden Newa €€

The hotel is part of an ensemble that was built on Prager Straße in the 1960s. A complete modernisation transformed the somewhat out-dated prefabricated building into a real gem: modern, clean, elegant, and urban. The rooms are small but chic, air-conditioned and have panorama windows.

🖽 192 B3 ✉ Prager Straße 2c
☎ 0351 4 81 40;
www.pullmanhotels.com/Dresden
🚋 Tram 3, 7, 8, 10; bus 66 Hauptbahnhof; tram 3, 7–9, 11 Hbf-Nord

Hotel Schloss Eckberg €€–€€€

The romantic castle, which was built in Tudor style the middle of the 19th century, occupies a prominent position high above the Elbe. The 17 princely – in the real sense of the word – rooms and suites are furnished with antiques and decorated with exquisite fabrics. Marble baths complete the picture. The restaurant impresses with excellent international cuisine and a terrace with a breathtaking view over the Elbe Valley. The Kavaliershaus in the park offers much more reasonably priced accommodation.

🖽 195 D5 ✉ Bautzner Straße 134
☎ 0351 8 09 90; www.schloss-eckberg.de
🚋 Tram 11 Elbschlösser

Schloss Hotel Dresden-Pillnitz €€

The hotel is located in a renovated annex of Schloss Pillnitz (➤ 142). The rooms and suites are comfortable and there is a varied selection of restaurants. An early-morning stroll through the deserted castle park is an unforgettable experience.

Insider Tip

🖽 195 off F1 ✉ August-Böckstiegel-Str. 10
☎ 0351 2 61 40; www.schlosshotel-pillnitz.de
🚋 Bus 63 Pillnitzer Platz

Swissôtel Dresden Am Schloss €€€

The new building has a reconstructed historical façade and opened its doors in 2012. It houses 235 elegant rooms and suites, equipped with state-of-the-art technology and creative bathrooms. There is also a small but excellent spa in the 15th-century sandstone cellar and two restaurants.

🖽 196 B2 ✉ Schlossstr. 16 ☎ 0351 50 12 00; www.swissotel.de/hotels/dresden
🚋 Tram 1, 2, 4 Altmarkt

Therese-Malten-Villa €€

This pretty neo-Renaissance villa, opposite Schloss Pillnitz, belonged to a singer at the Dresden Court

Finding Your Feet

Opera at the beginning of the 20th century. Today, it is a cosy guest house, with simple but tastefully-decorated rooms, a kitchen for the guests with terrace and a garden. Self-catering or with breakfast if desired.

✉ Wilhelm-Weitling-Straße 3
☎ 0351 2 05 35 21; www.dresden-pension.net
🚊 Tram 2 Kleinzschachwitz Freystraße

The Westin Bellevue Dresden €€€

The hotel close to the banks of the Elbe in Neustadt is surrounded by a wonderful garden. If a tree does not get in the way, guests can enjoy the famous "Canaletto view" from some of the rooms. The ensemble includes a Baroque town house, complete with interior courtyard, which lends it a special charm.

➕ 196 B3 ✉ Große Meißner Straße 15
☎ 0351 80 50; www.westinbellevuedresden.com
🚊 Tram 4, 8, 9 Neustädter Markt

Zur Königlichen Ausspanne € *Insider Tip*

Idyllic guest house set in the former carriage house of a stately manor on the banks of the Elbe. The building was converted in 1999. Guests sleep in rooms with country-style furnishing and wake up to the sound of birds chirping. Private concerts are held under the vaulted ceiling of the fireplace hall. Minimum stay of two nights.

➕ 195 off F2 ✉ Eugen-Dieterich-Straße 5
☎ 0351 2 68 95 02; http://koenigliche-ausspanne.de 🚌 Bus 63 Staffelsteinstraße

Food and Drink

Dresdeners are no longer enjoying just local fare. At one time menus were limited to Saxon specialities – from the Erzgebirge, Vogtland and the Oberlausitz – and reflected Czech, Russian or Hungarian influences but after the fall of Communism, the entire culinary universe found its way to Dresden.

Typical

- **Sweet:** About 150 years ago the poet and dramatist Robert Prutz said that Dresdeners were *Kuchenfresser* or "cake eaters". This is still true today, most of Dresden's specialities are sweet: the **Dresdner Eierschecke** (a substantial layered sponge cake) and, of course, the **Dresdner Stollen**. There is also the ***Schälchen Heeßen*** (hot, sweet coffee); don't forget, the coffee filter was invented in Dresden – and, although they drink less coffee than in many other parts of Germany, the Saxons are still sometimes referred to as "coffee Saxons". However, that the Dresdeners only drink *Bliemchengaffee* (little flower coffee), which is so weak that you can see the little flowers at the bottom of the cup, is just a rumour. The **Russisch Brot** (Russian bread) and ***Schmätzchen*** (sweet biscuits) produced by the Dr Quendt bakery, as well as the Vadossi company's Nudossi spread – the East German equivalent of Nutella – and ***Pulsnitzer Pfefferkuchen*** (gingerbread) can all be recommended as **sweet souvenirs**.
- **Hearty:** Saxon cuisine is characterised by succulent roasts with tasty sauces, all kinds of potato dishes, and hearty stews. **Dresdner Sauerbraten** and ***Sächsische Kartoffelsuppe*** (potato soup), the latter often with marjoram and frankfurters, are almost always on the menu. Other popular dishes are jacket potatoes served with *Quark*

(curd cheese) and linseed oil from Lausitz, *Erzgebirgische Glitscher* (potato fritters) and Sorbian *Hochzeitssuppe* (wedding soup).

■ **Nostalgic:** Sometimes, it is still possible to find those dishes that were de rigueur on most menus in the GDR: the ***Würzfleisch*** (ragout fin), solo, or as ***Schweinesteak au four*** – pork topped with Würzfleisch – and still with "Exzellent" a Dresden-style Worcestershire sauce. But, the real GDR classic actually comes from Russia or the Ukraine: ***Soljanka*** is a spicy soup, usually served with pieces of meat or sausage, onions and sour gherkins, as well as a blob of sour cream.

■ **A good tipple:** Saxon wine has a well-established reputation outside of the borders of Saxony. And the most famous (and best!) beer in the east of the country, Radeberger Pilsener, is not actually brewed in Dresden but 15km (9mi) away in Radeberg.

■ **By the way:** In Dresden a roll is called a ***Semmel***, a slice of bread a ***Bemme***, the *Gugelhupf* is a ***Bäbe*** and a doughnut a *Pfannkuchen*.

Restaurants, Cafés, Pubs

Hundreds of new places to eat and drink opened in Dresden after the fall of Communism.

■ **Altstadt and Innere Neustadt:** There are several cafés and restaurants in the vicinity of the major sights that serve both traditional Saxon and international food. There are also eateries serving food from Japan, Australia, the Czech Republic and many other countries. And, you should not forget the gourmet restaurants in several of the luxury hotels: the **Caroussel** (▶ 112), **Intermezzo** (▶ 87), **Canaletto** (▶ 111).

■ **Äußere Neustadt:** This district has the highest number of pubs and restaurants – especially on Görlitzer Straße, Alaunstraße and Louisenstraße. There are trendy restaurants, fashionable pubs, snack bars, cafés and bars, and places serving fusion cuisine.

■ **Eating outside:** Almost all of the restaurants have outside dining places in summer. There is a particularly romantic feeling about eating in one of the many **restaurants with a view of the Elbe**. And, of course, there are countless **beer gardens** in the green city of Dresden.

■ **Vegetarian:** It is not always easy to find vegetarian dishes in the restaurants in Altstadt: exceptions include the **Laden Café aha** (▶ 134) and the **BrennNessel** (▶ 87). In contrast, vegetarian dishes are becoming very popular in Neustadt – even at snack bars. Pure vegetarian/vegan: **Flax** (Schönfelder Str. 2), **Lotus Bio-Imbiss** (Louisenstr. 58), **Falscher Hase** (Rudolf-Leonhard-Straße 3).

Insider Tip

Snacks

There are **food courts** in the city centre (Markthalle Café Prag, Centrum- and Altmarktgalerie) and all kinds of novel fast-food eateries in Äußere Neustadt. Burgers and chips are on offer at: **Burgermeister** (Louisenstr. 54), **Kantine No 2** and **Kochbox** (Görlitzer Str. 2/3), **Devils Kitchen** (Alaunstr. 39). Additional tips: **Crêperie La Galette** (Rothenburger Str. 9), **Suppenbar** (Rothenburger Straße 37), **Curry & Co** (Louisenstraße 62).

Restaurant Prices

Expect to pay per person for a main course without drinks.

€ less than €12   €€ €12–20   €€€ more than €20

Shopping

Chic new department stores and shopping centres, arts and crafts shops, quirky boutiques and numerous galleries make a shopping spree in Dresden a real pleasure. Even the exclusive brands have finally made a home for themselves on the Elbe.

Where can you find it?

- **Prager Straße, Seestraße, Centrum Galerie, Altmarkt-Galerie:** The "Prager" is Dresden's classic shopping mile. The large department stores and fashion chains have opened their doors here and in the adjacent streets. There are also two malls with the usual range of shops and restaurants: the **Centrum Galerie** on Prager Straße and the **Altmarkt-Galerie** between Altmarkt and Wallstraße.
- **Neumarkt:** The shops around Neumarkt, the QF-Passage and the surrounding streets, are mainly popular with tourists.
- **Innere Neustadt:** Discerning customers usually find what they are looking for in the boutiques, galleries and antique shops on Königstraße and its adjoining alleyways. Craftsmen offer their wares for sale in the arcades on Hauptstraße.
- **Äußere Neustadt:** New shops seem to open here all the time – and others close just as quickly. The area is popular with hip young people in particular, and they are sure to find just about everything their heart desires: trendy clothes, skater gear, jewellery and vinyl records.
- **Körnerplatz:** This is where the main galleries and arts and craft shops are located.

Markets

- Special **spring and autumn markets** are held on Altmarkt. In the period before Christmas, the **Striezelmarkt** (►36) attracts millions of visitors to Dresden's city centre.
- The **Elbeflohmarkt** flea market near the Albert Bridge is held all year round from 8am to 2pm every Saturday and on some Sundays.
- Mainly regional products are offered at the **Sachsenmarkt** on Lingnerallee every Friday from 8am to 5pm.

Galleries

The large number of galleries in the city shows quite clearly that Dresden is a real city of art. Most of them are in Neustadt near Körnerplatz. The city's calendar of events for all of the galleries is available from the cultural establishments and online at www.dresden.de/en/Culture.php

Souvenirs

- You come across the image of the **angels in Raphael's *Sistine Madonna*** all over the world but their home is right here in Dresden. You can take them back with you on mouse pads, coffee mugs, t-shirts, umbrellas…
- There are various **Frauenkirche** devotional objects in the souvenir shops on Neumarkt such as the wristwatches made with genuine sandstone chips from the ruins of the Frauenkirche.
- **Arts and crafts:** There is a large selection on offer that includes authentic Erzgebirge Christmas decorations, Sorbian Easter eggs, blue-dyed fabric and ceramics from Lausitz.

- **Meissen Porcelain:** In Dresden, you will find the famous porcelain at three authorised dealers; at Karstadt, in the **Hotel Hilton** (➤46) and the Meissen Outlet in the QF-Passage.
- **Saxon wine and Dresdner stollen:** There are about two dozen wine estates in and around Dresden and many of them produce high-quality wines. Only genuine Dresden Christstollen® bears the Stollen Association seal of quality.
- **Museum shops:** Stylish Dresden souvenirs are for sale in the shops of the State Art Collections Dresden (in the Residenzschloss, the Albertinum and elsewhere), as well as in the city's Stadtmuseum.

Entertainment

Dresden is usually considered a city of high culture – with the Semperoper as the flagship. However, the Saxon capital also has a very lively jazz and rock scene, as well numerous bars, clubs and cinemas. And, Dresdeners have fun until the small hours of the morning.

Information

- The **tourist information offices** in the QF-Passage on Neumarkt and at the Hauptbahnhof station (➤40) are the best places to go for information on what is happening in Dresden.
- The monthly **SAX** city magazine (€1.80, www.cybersax.de) has the most comprehensive calendar of events.
- The regional daily newspapers **Sächsische Zeitung** (with the Augusto calendar of events on Thursday, www.sz-online.de) and **Dresdner Neueste Nachrichten** (www.dnn-online.de) provide the latest information on Dresden and the vicinity.
- The free cinema calendar gives details of the films being shown (www.kinokalender.com) and theatre box offices and ticket agencies will tell you all about upcoming events.

Opera, Theatre, Concerts

- Many visitors come to Dresden just to go to one of the – usually sold out – **Semperoper** (➤77, 90) performances. But the city has many other first-rate cultural events to offer. There are innovative productions in the **Schauspielhaus** (➤90) and the **Kleine Haus** (➤115), concerts with the Kreuz Choir in the **Kreuzkirche** (➤127), master concerts at **Schloss Albrechtsberg** (➤146) and events in the **Zwingerhof** (➤90). The **Staatsoperette** (Pirnaer Landstr. 131, tel: 0351 2 07 99 99, www.staatsoperette-dresden.de), which was founded in 1947, is one of the few venues for light-hearted music still operating in Europe.
  The youth are catered for in the **🔢 Theater Junge Generation** (Meißner Landstr. 4, tel: 0351 4 96 53 70, www. tjg-dresden.de), which also has a **puppet theatre**. It is on the western edge of the city and is one of the largest children's theatres in Germany.
- The home of the **Landesbühnen Sachsen** (Meißner Str. 152, tel: 0351 8 95 42 14, www.landesbuehnen-sachsen.de) is located in nearby Radebeul. In summer, the multi-genre theatre also performs on the **Felsenbühne Rathen** (➤160) in Saxon Switzerland.

Finding Your Feet

- The **Kulturpalast**, the home of the **Dresdner Philharmonie**, is being reno-vated at the moment and the orchestra now performs in the Albertinum, the Schauspielhaus and the German Hygiene Museum (www.dresdner philharmonie.de).
- Famous pop and rock stars perform in the **Alter Schlachthof** (Gothaer Str. 11, www.alter-schlachthof.de) while the **Dresdner Messe** (Messering 6, www.messe-dresden.de) has plenty of space for mega-events.
- The European Centre of the Arts in the **Festspielhaus Hellerau** (Karl-Liebknecht-Str. 56, tel: 0351 8 89 38 84, www.hellerau.org) organises avant-garde music, dance and theatre performances.

Clubs
The best locations for all kinds of alternative music are: **beatpol** (Altbriesnitz 2a, tel: 0351 4 21 03 97, www.beatpol.de), the **Scheune** (➤ 116) and the **Groovestation** (Katharinenstr. 11–13, tel: 0351 35 18 02 95 94, www. groovestation.de). There are also many clubs for dance fans such as **Katy's Garage** (➤ 116), **m5 Nightlife** (➤ 90) and the **Musikpark Dresden** (Wiener Platz 9, tel: 0351 48 52 51 30, www.mp-dd.de). It is also worth taking a look at what is happening in the **Saloppe** (➤ 156) from May to September. The **Strasse E** (➤ 116) is the home of a whole slew of clubs. The **Blue Note** (Görlitzer Straße 2b, tel: 0351 8 01 42 75) is a legendary bar with live music most nights and a cult spot for all night owls.

Insider
Tip

Cinema
Dresden is the cinema capital of eastern Germany. There are four Multiplexes – two of them are in the centre of town, the traditional **Rundkino** (➤ 131) dates back to GDR days and has six cinemas and right next door is the futuristic **Kristallpalast** which has eight cinemas. Both cinemas usually show blockbusters but also have live transmissions of operas and sporting events. Arthouse cinemas such as the **Schauburg** (➤ 116), the **Programmkino Ost** (Schandauer Str. 73, Tel: 0351 3 10 37 82, www.programmkino-ost.de), the **Thalia** (➤ 116) and the **KIF** (Kino in der Fabrik, Tharandter Str. 33, tel: 0351 4 24 48 60, www.kif-dresden.de) provide more variety. Most of the cinemas also have sneak previews, premieres with guests, original-language films and special film weeks.

Gays and Lesbians
The **Boys Bar** is the longest-surviving gay bar in Dresden; it organises regular karaoke parties and film evenings and is open until 3am during the week and until 5am on weekends (Alaunstraße 80, tel: 0351 56 33 630, www.boys-dresden.de). The **Queens & Kings** is a popular small bar for gays, lesbians and their friends (Görlitzer Str. 2) while the newer **Valentino** café-bar is another popular meeting place to have coffee, cake and ice-cream; most of the guests are in the 30-plus age group (Jordanstr. 2, tel: 2109595, www.valentino-dresden.de). **Christopher Street Day** is celebrated in Dresden with a parade and a variety of events in June/July.

Tickets
Tickets for concerts, theatre performance, parties and sport events are avail-able from the Tourist Information Office (➤ 40), **saxTicket** (Schauburg side entrance, Königsbrücker Str. 55, tel: 0351 8 03 87 44, www.saxticket.de), at the concert ticket office in **Florentinum** (Ferdinandstr. 12, tel: 0351 8 66 60 11, www.konzertkasse-dresden.de) and various SZ ticket offices (sz-ticketservice.de).

The Historic Altstadt

 **Little Treats**

Trabi Safari
Climb behind the steering wheel of a
legendary Trabant and set out in convoy
on a rather unique **city tour** (➤ 44).

Oasis of Tranquillity
Need a break from sightseeing? There
are two peaceful benches in the **Brühlscher
Garten** at the eastern end of Brühlsche
Terrasse (➤ 80).

City Tour with Nobility
Have a costumed August the Strong or
Countess Cosel show you around the
Zwinger – even more fun in a group (➤ 62).

Getting Your Bearings

Zwinger, Semperoper, Frauenkirche – it is the old Dresden, the "Florence on the Elbe", that was born again out of the ruins of war that once again fascinates visitors from around the world with its wealth of art and culture. The legend lives on.

Dresdeners refer to the Innere Altstadt – the correct name for the area between Theaterplatz and Neumarkt – simply as Altstadt. However, calling the area on the left side of the Elbe "Neuendresden" (new Dresden) was only introduced after the area on the right bank was destroyed by fire in 1685 and rebuilt as "Neue Stadt bey Dresden" (New Town near Dresden).

Today, this historic old town – that covers an area of only half a square kilometre – contains a world-famous opera house, a palace steeped in history, two unique Baroque churches and a dozen top-class museums. All of these united in a picturesque panorama that will not only gladden the hearts of romantics.

Weisseritzstr.

S
Dresden-Mitte

Kabarett Breschke & Schuch

Wettiner-platz

**The *Procession of Princes* (Fürstenzug)
depicts members of the House of Wettin**

Getting Your Bearings

View from the Frauenkirche dome over
the Art Academy and the Elbe Valley

Internationales Congress Center

Sächsischer Landtag

Elbe

Theater-kahn

🔢12 Augustus-brücke

🔢13 Sächsische Dampfschiffahrt

Schlossplatz

Hofkirche

⭐ Brühlsche Terrasse

⭐4 Semper-oper & Theater-platz

Zwingerteich

⭐2 Zwinger & Gemäldegalerie Alte Meister

Schau-spielhaus

⭐3 Residenz-schloss

Johanneum · Verkehrsmuseum Dresden

🔢14

Neue Synagoge

🔢18

🔢16 Cosel-palais

Rathenau-platz

🔢11 Cholera-brunnen

Neumarkt 🔢15

⭐ Frauen-kirche

0   300 m
0   300 yd

Wilsdruffer Str.

Landhaus · Stadtmuseum & Städtische Galerie

🔢17

Pirnaischer Platz

At Your Leisure

TOP 10

The Historic Altstadt

Two Perfect Days

The splendour of the Wettin dynasty is on display in Dresden's Altstadt – allow at least two days to discover all of the area's treasures. This itinerary will help you not to miss a single highlight. More info about the individual sights can be found in the pages (➤ 58–86).

Day One

Morning
The museums do not open until 10am but you can enter the ☆**Zwinger** (right; ➤ 62) and Zwinger courtyard at 6am. That will give you plenty of time to explore the Baroque jewel in peace. Try to spend at least two – three, would be even better – hours in a highlight like the ☆**Gemäldegalerie Alte Meister** (Old Masters Gallery, ➤ 62).

Afternoon
There are many different kinds of restaurants – ranging from elegant to down-to-earth, rustic – in the Hotel Taschenbergpalais Kempinski (➤ 46) to the east of the Zwinger. Take a look at the **11 Cholera-brunnen** (➤ 84) fountain when you are on your way to lunch.

Evening
Once you have regained your strength, you can visit another museum in the Zwinger. Or maybe take a stroll over ☆**Theaterplatz** (➤ 77). Finally, you should try to take part in a guided tour of the ☆**Semperoper** (➤ 77) or the **Hofkirche** (left; ➤ 78) church. Let the day come to a close with the panoramic view of Altstadt and the steamers of the **13 Sächsische Dampfschifffahrt** (➤ 84) from the **12 Augustusbrücke** (➤ 84) bridge and then treat yourself to dinner in the Italienisches Dörfchen (➤ 88) to make the day complete.

Day Two

Morning
Set out to climb up into the dome of the ⭐**Frauenkirche** (above; ➤ 58), from where you have a wonderful view of Alstadt. Then head to Augustus-straße with the **Fürstenzug** (➤ 72) mural and left through the Georgentor on to Schlossstraße with the Löwentor entrance to the ⭐**Residenzschloss** (➤ 70). Here, you should visit the **Grünes Gewölbe** (➤ 73) or **Türckische Cammer** (➤ 73). After you have finished your tour, go over the Stallhof back to ⏴⏵**Neumarkt** (➤ 85).

Afternoon
Take a break from all this walking to have lunch on Münzgasse or in one of the restaurants around Neumarkt – the Grand Café & Restaurant of the ⏴⏵**Coselpalais** (➤ 85) is a good option.

Evening
This is the time to visit a museum that particularly interests you: the ⏴⏵**Verkehrsmuseum** in the Johanneum (➤ 84) is all about transport, the ⏴⏵**Stadtmuseum** (➤ 86), **Dresden Fortress** (➤ 83) with witnesses from the pre-Baroque era, or maybe the **Albertinum** (➤ 81) with the **Galerie Neue Meister** gallery and **Sculpture Collection**. Then take a stroll over the ⭐**Brühlsche Terrasse** (➤ 80) with the ⏴⏵**Neue Synagogue** (➤ 86) at its eastern end. You might like to end the day with an evening steamer cruise or a glass of wine on the terrace of one of the restaurants on Neumarkt.

Yenidze
Internationales Congress Center
Könneritzstr.
Dresden-Mitte
Ostrallee
Sächsischer Landtag
Elbe
Augustus-brücke
Semperoper & Theater-platz
Sächsische Dampfschiffahrt
...iner-atz
Zwinger & Gemäldegalerie Alte Meister
Johanneum · Verkehrsmuseum Dresden
Brühlsche Terrasse
Schweriner Str.
Residenz-schloss
Frauen-kirche
Cosel-palais
Neue Synagoge
Cholera-brunnen
Neu-markt
Landhaus · Stadtmuseum & Städtische Galerie

0   300 m
0   300 yd

⭐Frauenkirche

This impressive church is Dresden's landmark. The Frauenkirche rises proudly over Altstadt and it is hard to believe that its mighty dome, the "Stone Bell", disappeared from the cityscape for more than half a century before being carefully restored.

Inspired by the domes of Italian churches, the Dresden master carpenter, George Bähr, drew up the plans for one of the most impressive Protestant houses of worship in Europe and the foundation stone was laid in 1726. Both the architect and August the Strong, who supported its construction in spite of his conversion to Catholicism, were no longer alive when construction was completed in 1743.

Baroque gem: the Frauenkirche flooded with light

Destruction and Resurrection

The dome of the Frauenkirche managed to withstand both the Prussian shelling of the Seven Years' War and the firestorm of 13 February 1945 but the burned-out building collapsed two days later in the early hours of 15 February. As an anti-war memorial, the ruin became the symbol of the peace movement in the 1980s and, for that reason, not all Dresdeners were in favour of its reconstruction after the fall of Communism. Recovery of stones that could be used again began in 1993 and,

SIGN OF RECONCILIATION

The donations of people from many countries contributed to the reconstruction of the Frauenkirche. The **tower cross** – donated by the British Dresden Trust – was created by a London goldsmith, the son of a bomber pilot who had taken part in the raid on Dresden.

Frauenkirche

The "Stone Bell"

with it, the reconstruction of the most important domed religious building north of the Alps. The entire world looked on as the Frauenkirche developed into a symbol for civic pride and an impressive manifestation of reconciliation.

After its consecration on 30 October 2005, Dresdeners and their guests were once again able to marvel at the magnificence of this Baroque masterpiece. The interior of the church – a central nave with five galleries – has space for 1,800 people. The restoration is true to the original Baroque design. Both the **altar** and **organ façade** were reconstructed by Johann Christian Feige; the organ itself was built in the spirit of Silbermann by the Kern Company from Strasbourg. The tower cross, which was rediscovered when the rubble was cleared away, can be seen inside the church and George Bähr's **tomb** is in the crypt – now a place of contemplation.

SECOND-HAND LUTHER

Next to the Frauenkirche is a monument to the reformer that was created by Adolf Donndorf in 1885. The head was one that his teacher, Ernst Rietschel, had planned for a Luther memorial in Worms and never used.

TAKING A BREAK

Look for a place on the terrace of one of the restaurants on Neumarkt with a view of the Frauenkirche.

➕ 196 B2 ✉ Neumarkt
☎ 0351 65 60 61 00
(visitor info); www.frauenkirche-dresden.de
🕐 Daily 10am–noon, 1pm–6pm
(except when services or other events are being held)
🚋 Tram 1, 2, 4 Altmarkt 💵 Free

INSIDER INFO

- You can listen to **music in the Frauenkirche** at organ prayers and vespers followed by tours of the church (Mon–Sat noon, Mon–Wed, Fri 6pm), scared music on Sunday (every two weeks, 3pm) and at the Dresdner Organ Cycle (Wed 8pm; alternating with the Kreuzkirche and the cathedral). Tickets for all events can be purchased from the ticket service of the **Frauenkirche** (Georg-Treu-Platz 3, 1. Upper floor, Mon–Fri 9am–6pm, Sat 9am–noon, tel: 0351 65 60 67 01, ticket@frauenkirche-dresden.de) and from other ticket offices in the city.
- The ascent to the 🔟 **Frauenkirche observation platform** at a height of 67m (220ft) (lift and then a steep winding staircase inside the dome; Mon–Sat 10am–6pm, Sun 12:30pm–6pm, Nov–Feb to 4pm; tickets and admission at entrance G; €8), this is also an exciting adventure for youngsters.
- The 25-minute film *Fascination Frauenkirche* is screened in the crypt (€3) and there is also a small exhibition about the destruction and reconstruction of the church.
- The Frauenkirche treats music lovers to atmospheric evenings with **organ music by candlelight** at 9pm on the Sundays in Advent.

Insider Tip

Symbol of Reconciliation

The Frauenkirche, whose dome can be seen from afar looming proudly in the city's silhouette, has risen again – this time as a symbol of reconciliation. Around 8,400 sandstone blocks from the exterior shell and interior walls were recovered and reused in the façade, where their dark patina makes them immediately recognisable.

❶ **Church crypt:** The crypt takes the form of a Greek cross and replaced the cemetery of the previous church. Today, it serves as a place of silence.

❷ **Altar:** The altar area towered over the pile of rubble for decades. Two thousand pieces – around 80 per cent – from the altar were rescued and carefully reused in the reconstruction. The statue of Christ is original; the Annunciation is a replica. The *cross of nails* on the altar table symbolises reconciliation.

❸ **Organ:** The magnificent organ façade was carefully reconstructed following historical models. After an organ dispute, which played out in public, the decision was taken against the reconstruction of the original Silbermann organ and in favour of a technically modern instrument made by Daniel Kern, an organ maker from Strasbourg.

❹ **Interior:** The Baroque central building of the church was erected on a square layout. The circular interior is surrounded by eight supporting pillars for the dome and five galleries. The church has seating for 1,800. The high sermon area takes the form of a Protestant box theatre encircling the centre pulpit.

❺ **Stair towers:** Only one of the original four stair towers survived the collapse – and only partially – and was a prominent feature of the ruins for many decades.

❻ **Dome:** The interior of the dome soars almost 37m (121ft) above the body of the church and is vaulted over by George Bahr's "Stone Bell". A ramp, on which donkeys used to transport the stones needed to build the dome, winds its way up to the top. Today, this provides access to the observation platform at a height of 67m (220ft) from where visitors can enjoy the same view admired by Goethe.

❼ **Tower cross:** The lantern on the tower cross has shined again as a symbol of reconciliation since 2004. It is a gift from Great Britain and was crafted in the London workshop of the goldsmith Alan Smith, the son of a Royal Air Force Pilot who took part in the raid on Dresden in 1945. The original cross was recovered from the rubble in 1993 and now stands in the southern section of the church.

The ruined Frauenkirche in Dresden became an anti-war memorial in GDR days

Frauenkirche

The ceiling painting on the inner dome, which was originally created by the Venetian artist Giovanni Battista Grone, shows the Four Evangelists and allegories of Christian virtues

⭐2 Zwinger & Gemäldegalerie Alte Meister

It is a masterpiece of Saxon Baroque and one of the finest examples in the history of European architecture. The Zwinger, together with the museums in its pavilions and in Gottfried Semper's adjacent gallery building, are a must on any visit to Dresden.

This unique ensemble of courtly architecture was commissioned by August the Strong and built from 1709–32. It is to the west of the Residenzschloss and is named after a section of the city's fortifications. The architect Daniel Pöppelmann and the sculptor Balthasar Permoser drew up the plans for the pavilions and galleries, arranged around a courtyard to mirror each other.

The **Kronentor** gate, with its onion-shaped dome and the royal crown borne by Polish eagles, is the main portal to the Zwinger and one of Dresden's major landmarks. It rises up, forcefully but elegantly, above the Long Gallery. The **Wallpavillon** is at the apex of the western gallery of arches; the figure of *Hercules Saxonicus* on the gable pays tribute to August the Strong. A staircase leads through the Wallpavillon to the roofs of the galleries. The **Nymphenbad**, a courtyard with fountains, cascades and 16 statues of nymphs, is located behind the French Pavilion.

The pavilion on the eastern side was given a glockenspiel made of Meissen porcelain in the 1930s and is known as the **Glockenspiel Pavilion**. The design of the Zwinger courtyards and fountains was also carried out in the first third of the 20th century.

The Gemäldegalerie, designed by Gottfried Semper in which the old masters are displayed, closed off the Zwinger, which previously opened up towards the Elbe. The Zwinger is bordered on two sides by a moat and pond, as well as a small park. The memorial to Carl Maria von Weber by Ernst Rietschel is between the gallery and the Semperoper.

Following the severe damage caused by the Allied bombers on 13 February 1945, reconstruction of the Zwinger began in the same year – and continued until the mid-1990s.

Wallpavillon and Zwinger courtyard

Upper left: Herms on the Wallpavillon in the Zwinger

Porcelain Collection

The most refined – and, with more than 20,000 individual pieces, largest – collection of ceramics in the world is the result of one of August the Strong's passions, one that he himself described as a "maladie des porcellaines". The precious items, which were evacuated during World War II and then taken as spoils of war to the Soviet Union, were returned to the GDR in 1958. The organisation of the exhibition in the Glockenspiel Pavilion and adjacent galleries is according to the Prince Elector's designs. The main focus

Above: The Kronentor with the royal crown borne by eagles

is on **Chinese porcelain** from the Tang to Ming dynasties and Kangxi era, as well as early **Japanese Imari and Kakiemon porcelain** from Arita. In addition, exceptional objects illustrate the history of the **Porzellan Manufaktur Meissen** (➤ 165) from the infancy of European hard porcelain in 1708 to the late 18th century. New York architect Peter Marino recently revamped parts of the gallery with designs that included an opulent interior decorated with leather wall-coverings, baldachins and gilded wall brackets.

CLASSICAL MUSIC ON MEISSEN PORCELAIN

The glockenspiel in the Glockenspiel Pavilion plays every 15 minutes and there are melodies by Vivaldi, Mozart, Bach and other composers at 10:15am, 2:15pm and 6:15pm from Easter to December.

🔁 Mathematisch-Physikalischer Salon

Established under August the Strong in 1728, the museum has one of the world's oldest and most important collections of historic scientific instruments and timepieces. The majority of the most precious pieces displayed in the exhibition halls, which were reopened in 2013 after six years of renovation, date from the 16th to 19th century and portray the impressive knowledge and artistic and technical skill of scholars and craftsmen in times gone by. An Arab celestial globe from around 1300, a 350-year-old mechanical calculator by Blaise Pascal and a 16th-century astronomical clock by Eberhard Baldwein are just three of the most important exhibits. The almost 1m (3ft) high "Drumming Bear" automaton clock from 1625 is something that children and adults alike can appreciate. Animations provide fascinating insights into the mechanisms and operation of selected items. As part of the guided guided tour, visitors can replicate experiments made in the 18th century.

Insider Tip

In the 18th century, an observatory for observing the heavens was added to pavilion in the centre of the museum and it provided the official time for Dresden and all of Saxony until well into the 20th century. Today, the ceremonial hall on the upper floor houses gigantic reflectors and telescopes.

Gemäldegalerie Alte Meister

Countless reproductions have made them all well-known: Giorgione's ***Sleeping Venus***, Liotard's ***Chocolate***

Sundial from the Mathematisch-Physikalischer Salon

Giorgione's Sleeping Venus

Girl, Vermeer's ***Girl Reading a Letter by an Open Window***, Albrecht Dürer's ***Bernhard von Reesen*** and Titian's ***Tribute Money***. The originals are all here in the Old Masters Picture Gallery, the most outstanding collection of European painting from the 15th–18th centuries. The majority were collected, in a mere 50 years, by August the Strong and his son and successor Friedrich August II.

One hundred years after the construction of the Baroque Zwinger, Gottfried Semper provided the artworks with a worthy setting with his Italian Renaissance-style Gemäldegalerie (1847–1855). The Semper building is not actually part of the Zwinger ensemble but closes it off on the Elbe side.

STAATLICHE KUNSTSAMMLUNGEN DRESDEN (STATE ART COLLECTIONS)

The twelve individual museums under the auspices of the State Art Collections provide an almost unparalleled variety and quality. Nine of the museums are in the historic Altstadt: **Old Masters Picture Gallery, Porcelain Collection** and **Mathematisch-Physikalischer Salon** in the Zwinger and adjacent Semper Gallery, **Historic and New Grünes Gewölbe, Collection of Prints, Drawings and Photographs, Coin Cabinet** and **Armoury with Riesensaal** and **Türckische Cammer** in the Residenzschloss, **New Masters Picture Gallery** and **Sculpture Collection** in the Albertinum. The **Museum of Saxon Folk Art** and **Puppet Theatre Collection** exhibits its treasures in the Jägerhof and the **Museum of Decorative Arts** resides in Schloss Pillnitz. The Ethnographical Museum Dresden – together with the Grassi Ethnographical Museum in Leipzig – and the Ethnographical Museum Herrnhut have been administered by the State Art Collections Dresden since 2010; their exhibits can also be seen in the multimedia content on the individual websites. Museums, special exhibitions and the Hausmannsturm in the Residenzschloss are closed on Tuesday; the other museums, on Monday. **Art & Info Visitors Centre:** Residenzschloss, corner Taschenberg/Schlossstraße, daily 10am–6pm.

The Historic Altstadt

THE MADONNA AND HER CHERUBS

Raffaello Santi, who is known simply as Raphael, painted what is probably the most famous picture in the Old Masters Picture Gallery for the high altar in the San Sisto monastery church in Piacenza in 1512/1513. The *Sistine Madonna* came to Dresden in 1754 after being purchased by Prince Elector Friedrich August II. The Madonna with the baby Jesus in her arms steps towards the viewer with great self-assuredness, almost challengingly but the two **cherubs** at her feet have long upstaged her. They have gone on to become an independent motif of popular culture and it can safely be said that, today, they are the most famous Dresdeners on earth.

More than 500,000 visitors view the old masters every year – and they are on the increase. In recent years, it was noticed that the building no longer fulfilled requirements for air conditioning, accessibility and fire protection and a project for a gradual renovation, which will take several years to complete, was started in 2013. The renovations – in line with heritage requirements – of the eastern wing of the gallery that housed the armoury for centuries will be followed in a second stage by the renovation of the west wing. During the entire construction period, almost 400 of the most important works in the collection will be shown in a temporary exhibition in the wing that is not being worked on. The newly-conceived arrangement intends to make European artistic history understood as "a homogenous historical narrative" and make it possible to compare contents and styles beyond territorial borders – with themes such as "Devotional Pictures from van Eyck to Botticelli", "European Baroque from El Greco to Poussin" and "Sensitivity and Enlightenment". While building is taking place, visitors will still be able to view the most popular paintings such as Correggio's *Nativity*, Rembrandt's *Rembrandt and Saskia in the Scene of the Prodigal Son*, Canaletto's veduta of Dresden and, of course, the *Sistine Madonna* – in the magnificent new frame she received for her 500th birthday.

TAKING A BREAK

The stylish **Alte Meister** café and restaurant, at the western end of the Sempergalerie, serves fresh cuisine.

МИН НЕТ — *Insider Tip*

If you look closely, you will still be able to make out the 1945 Cyrillic inscription at the Theaterplatz entrance to the Gemäldegalerie. The German translation next to it says, "The Museum was inspected. No mines. Checked by Chanutin"

Zwinger & Gemäldegalerie Alte Meister

✚ 196 A2 🕐 6am–10pm (Zwingerhof)
🚊 Tram 1, 2, 4, 8, 9, 11, 12; bus 94 Postplatz; tram 4, 8, 9 Theaterplatz

View over
the Zwinger
courtyard with
the Semper
Gallery in
the shade
on the right

State Art Collections Dresden
Porcelain Collection (Glockenspiel Pavilion), Mathematisch-Physikalischer
Salon, Gemäldegalerie Alte Meister (Sempergalerie) ☎ 0351 49 14 20 00;
www.skd.museum 🕐 Tue–Sun 10am–6pm 💶 All museums and special
exhibitions in the Zwinger: €10; only Porcelain Collection or only Mathematisch-
Physikalischer Salon: each €6; day ticket for admission to all of the museums
(except the Historisches Grünes Gewölbe): €19

INSIDER INFO

- The staircase in the Zwinger Wallpavillon leads to both the Nymphenbad as well as to the rooftops of the Long Gallery (entrance to the roofs also from stairs at the Glockenspiel Pavilion). There is a wonderful **view** over the entire complex from the top.
- Various **events** are held in the Marble Hall and – in summer – in the Zwinger courtyard. Information and tickets from the individual organisers or Schlösserland Sachsen (www.schloesserland-sachsen.de).
- There are various museum guides for children in the 👬 *Zwei Engel im Museum* series.
- The State Art Collections **programme,** with information on guided tours and lectures, is available from the museums.
- If you plan to spend several days in the city, you might consider buying the **Dresden City Card** or **Dresden Regio Card** (► 186). Admission is free for those under 17 years of age.
- You will be (almost) alone in the Zwinger if you get there at 6am in the **morning**!

Baroque Masterpiece

August the Strong's symbol of splendour and power was created as an Orangery and setting for courtly festivities in the years after 1709. When construction was completed, the celebrations for the marriage of the Prince Elector and the daughter of the Austrian Emperor took place here. After 1728, the Zwinger was the Palais Royal du Sciences, today it is home to some world-famous museums.

❶ Wallpavillon: The staircase to the fortress wall was built over with the pavilion designed by Daniel Pöppelmann from 1715–19. The *Hercules Saxonicus* on the gable – an allusion to August the Strong – is an original work by Balthasar Perlmoser whose workshop provided the sculptural decorations for the Zwinger.

❷ Kronentor: The delicate construction with its partially-gilded onion-shaped dome rises up out of the Long Gallery by the Zwinger moat and forms the main entrance to the Zwinger courtyard. Four Polish eagles bear the royal crown at the top.

❸ Sempergalerie: Since 1855, the gallery, which was built in the High Renaissance style, has closed off the Zwinger, which was previously open to the Elbe. Today, it houses the Old Masters Painting Gallery.

❹ Mathematisch-Physikalischer Salon: The oldest of the four corner pavilions has housed a collection of scientific instruments since 1728. The museum, which stretches over the two adjacent galleries, was reopened in 2013 after years of renovation work.

❺ Zwingerhof: The almost square central section of the courtyard measures 106m × 116m (448ft × 380ft); the entire longitudinal axis 204m (670ft). The arrangement as we see it today mainly dates from the first third of the 20th century.

❻ Nymphenbad: The fountains between the Wallpavillon and Sempergalerie, unites Baroque architecture, sculpture and aquatic art in the narrowest of spaces. Two of the sweeping staircases lead from the parterre to the wall plateau.

From the southwestern corner of the Zwinger you have a view of the moat, the Long Gallery and Kronentor

⭐❸ Residenzschloss

The former residence of the Witten dynasty is a monument of Saxon history and culture. It saw rulers come and go, was rebuilt and survived wars. After the last one, it appeared that its fate had been sealed. But a magnificent palace rose again out of the ashes of the ruins.

The first documented mention of a *castrum* dates back to 1289. Around 200 years later, Moritz von Sachsen developed the mediaeval castle into a stately Renaissance palace. At the beginning of the 18th century, August the Strong had the halls and apartments refashioned in the

Baroque style and the **Taschenbergpalais** (now a luxury hotel; ➤ 46), which was later expanded, built for his mistress Countess Cosel. The last major reconstruction work took place between 1889 and 1901 on the occasion of celebrations for the 800th anniversary of the House of Witten. The **bridges** to the **Taschenbergpalais** and Kreuzkirche church were also constructed at that time to replace those from the middle of the 18th century. The Residenzschloss was razed by fire during the bombardments on the 13 February 1945. Although the decision was made to reconstruct the palace immediately after the war – and later in 1985 – the lack of financial means, and also

The Renaissance façade of the Residenz seen from Schlossstraße

NAPOLEON'S STONE

There is a paving stone marked with an "N" near the two lanterns on the west side of Schlossplatz (seen from Georgentor). It is said that from this spot, on 26 August 1813, Napoleon, the Emperor of France, sent out his troops to fight the Battle of Dresden – it was to be his last successful campaign.

political will, prevented the comprehensive reconstruction of the historical edifice for half a century. The **Georgenbau** – a stately gabled building with façade decorations – between Schlossstraße and Schlossplatz, and the adjacent Stallhof, were both restored between 1964 and 1979, before work began on other sections of the palace.

Risen from the Ruins

A new beginning was rung in when the cupola was placed on the remains of the **Hausmannsturm** tower on 2 October 1991. Since then, the south and west wings have been reconstructed and the almost completely destroyed east wing rebuilt. A more-or-less original copy of the Prince Elector's chancellery, today House of the Cathedral, was built from 1997–99. After the millennium, the **Grünes Gewölbe, Kupferstich-kabinett** (Museum of Prints, Drawing and Photographs) and **Art Library** moved into their new rooms in the palace; the **Armoury** found its final home with the **Riesensaal** (Hall of the Giants) and **Türckische Cammer** (Turkish Chamber). The small palace courtyard was transformed into a central foyer with a transparent roof, the east wing can once again be accessed via the Englische Treppe (English Staircase), the Prince's gallery connects it with the west wing. The court chapel, with its reconstructed twined-rib vault and Renaissance portal – the "Beautiful Gate" – can be visited during events and on guided tours (only with time slot tickets, €5). And, the main palace courtyard with its stair towers and Sgraffito façades has once been restored to its former glory.

Stallhof and Fürstenzug *(Procession of Princes)*

The **Langer Gang** (Long Gallery), which was built from 1586–91, connects the Georgenbau and Stallhof stables – the later Joanneum and today's Transport Museum (Verkehrsmuseum, ►84). With its open arched hall supported by 22 Tuscan columns and rich Sgraffito decoration, it is one of the few remaining – and one of the most beautiful – examples of Renaissance architecture in Dresden. The adjacent **Stallhof** was once used for tournaments and hunts.

Bridge between the Residenz-schloss and Hofkirche in front of the Hausmanns-turm

Row of columns in the Stallhof

The Historic Altstadt

The exterior façade of the Long Gallery on Augustus-straße is decorated with a very special series of family portraits – the *Fürstenzug (Procession of Princes)*. The 35 rulers from the House of Wettin from 1127 to 1904 are united – larger-than life and on horseback – on this mural created in Sgraffito technique in 1876. The last Saxon king is missing: Friedrich August III was only eleven years old when the mural was completed. The regents are followed by the nobility, soldiers, artists, scholars and – last but not least – Wilhelm Walther, the creator of the Fürstenzug, together with his assistants. From 1904–07 environmental issues made it necessary to transfer the 102m (335ft) depiction to 25,000 Meissen porcelain tiles, making it the world largest porcelain mural.

Sgraffito decorations in the main palace courtyard

Grünes Gewölbe

The Green Vault is the oldest – and richest – treasury museum in Europe and is located in the western wing of the palace. The name is derived from the green walls of the secret repository where the Saxon rulers stored their royal treasures from the 16th century. August the Strong had the treasury converted into a magnificent public collection after 1721.

The treasures survived World War II in the casemates of the Königstein Fortress. They were seized by the Red Army at the end of the war and taken to the Soviet Union but found their way back to Dresden in 1958 at the behest of the government in

SGRAFFITO

In this artistic technique, which was very popular in the Renaissance period, ornaments and figures are depicted by scratching into the top layer of paint to reveal the contrasting colour of the layer underneath.

Procession of Princes on Augustusstraß

Moscow. The collection was transferred from the Albertinum into rooms in the western wing of the Residenzschloss between 2004 and 2006. As in the days of August the Strong, more than 3,000 precious exhibits are once again on display in the original rooms on the ground floor – most of them free standing, on ornate tables and consoles and in front of elaborately decorated walls. The Pretiosensaal (Valuables Hall) with its almost completely mirrored walls is the highlight of the ensemble; the Juwelenzimmer (Jewels Room) houses seven glittering sets of jewellery in its showcases. The **Neues Grünes Gewölbe** (New Green Vault), one floor higher up, has more than 1,000 exhibits including masterpieces by the court goldsmith Melchior Dinglinger, such as the golden table service that belonged to August the Strong and the *Royal Household in Delhi on the Birthday of the Grand Mogul Aurung Zeb* – a group of figures made of gold and precious stones.

Right: *Royal Household in Delhi on the Birthday of the Grand Mogul Aurung Zeb* in the Grünes Gewölbe

Rüstkammer

The history of this exquisite Armoury collection of ceremonial weapons and costumes dates back to Albrecht the Brave-Hearted who founded the ducal armoury in the 15th century. Extravagant clothes, weapons of all kinds, as well as magnificent suits of armour and armaments provide insights into the culture, ceremonies and festivities at the Saxon court, as well as hunting and the art of warfare, between the Renaissance and Baroque periods. Since 2013 there have been 350 items on display – elaborately staged in the **Riesensaal** (Hall of the Giants), which was reconstructed in its original dimensions of 57 × 13m (187 × 43ft). The **Türckische Cammer** (Turkish Chamber), which was opened three years prior, is the home of one of the largest and most impressive collections of Ottoman art outside of Turkey. The rulers of Saxony collected its exotic treasures during the 16th–19th centuries. The highlights include a 20 × 8 × 6m (66 × 26 × 20ft) richly decorated Ottoman tent, as well as a group of eight carved Arab steeds.

Stronghold of the Arts and Science

The magnificent reconstructed Residenzschloss palace is characterised by Renaissance and neo-Renaissance elements. Now housing the Grünes Gewölbe, Kupferstichkabinett and the Armoury, it attracts both the curious and art connoisseurs alike.

❶ **Georgenbau:** The stately gate building was given the neo-Renaissance appearance we see today when the palace was reconstructed between 1899 and 1901. The 4m (13ft) high equestrian statue on the gable on the Elbe side is of the building's namesake, Count Georg the Bearded.

❷ **Hausmannsturm:** Be sure not to miss out on the fantastic view from the 39m (128ft) tower which overlooks the palace complex and Altstadt. The tower's Baroque cupola, which was designed by Wolf Caspar Klengel and destroyed in World War II, was rebuilt in 1991.

❸ **Grünes Gewölbe:** In the Historical Green Vault, August the Strong's treasury has risen again as an all-embracing Baroque work of art. Tickets for the vault are all allocated a specific time slot. The New Green Vault, one floor higher up, has more modern displays of over 1,000 items of jewellery and goldsmith treasures.

❹ **Kupferstichkabinett:** The museum exhibits drawings, prints and photographs from its own holdings as well as temporary exhibitions with loan items.

❺ **Türckische Cammer:** From the 16th–19th centuries Saxony's regents collected Ottoman ceremonial weapons, armour, saddles and costumes. All of them are on display in the Turkish Chamber.

❻ **Riesensaal:** Visitors can admire more than 350 precious weapons and suits of armour from the armoury in the restored Hall of Giants.

A daringly curved transparent roof has transformed the palace's smaller courtyard into a foyer

Residenzschloss

The glittering treasures of the
jewel room in the Historical
Green Vault

The Historic Altstadt

Kupferstichkabinett

The museum's impressive collection of 500,000 prints, drawings and photographs, which was started 450 years ago, makes it one of the world's oldest and most important institutions of this kind. The **Studiensaal** (Study Hall) is where interested visitors can have a close-up look at originals and there are also **special exhibitions**.

Münzkabinett

The Coin Cabinet collection of one of the oldest museums in the city and has around 300,000 items: coins and medals, decorations, banknotes and historical documents. The new presentation in the Georgenbau consists of a permanent exhibition and temporary exhibitions, as well as the special library with 32,000 titles.

TAKING A BREAK

Try a latte macchiato in the small **cafeteria**.

✚ 196 A2 🚇 Tram 1, 2, 4, 8, 9, 11, 12; bus 94 Postplatz; tram 4, 8, 9 Theaterplatz; tram 1, 2, 4 Altmarkt

Museums of the State Art Collections Dresden

✉ Central Foyer: Kleiner Schlosshof, entrances from Sophienstraße, Taschenberg 2 or Schlossstraße (Löwentor)
☎ 0351 49 14 20 ; www.skd.museum
🕐 All museums, special exhibitions, Hausmannsturm (only Apr–Oct) Wed–Mon 10am–6pm 🎟 Neues Grünes Gewölbe, Türckische Cammer, Rüstkammer im Riesensaal, Fürstengalerie, Hausmannsturm (day ticket): €12; Historisches Grünes Gewölbe (time slot ticket): €12 (online booking plus advance booking fee €2); Court Chapel (time slot ticket with guided tours): €5; day ticket for single admission to all the museums of the State Art Collections except the Historisches Grüne Gewölbe: €19

Art & Info Visitor Centre

✉ Entrance at the corner Schlossstraße/Taschenberg 🕐 Daily 10am–6pm

Kupferstichkabinett Study Hall

🕐 Mon, Wed, Thu, Fri, 1st Sat in the month 10am–1pm, Mon, Wed also 2pm–4pm, Thu also 2pm–6pm ☎ 0351 49 14 32 21 (registration) 🎟 Free

Münzkabinett Library

✉ Georgenbau, Schlossstraße 25
🕐 Mon 10am–5:30pm, or by appointment ☎ 0351 49 14 32 31 🎟 Free

---

INSIDER INFO

- You will have the **best view** over the entire palace complex from the Hausmannsturm's observation platform.
- Take Albrecht the Degenerate and Friedrich the Bitten home with you. You will find all kinds of **concertina folders** of the *Procession of Princes* in the souvenir and museum shops near the palace.

⭐4 Semperoper & Theaterplatz

Dresden's opera house sets the tone on Theaterplatz, forming a part of an ensemble of buildings – designed by important architects and reflecting various epochs and styles – that is unrivalled throughout the world.

King Johann stands guard over the Semperoper square

Gottfried Semper's first royal court theatre was destroyed by fire in 1869. The architect drew up the plans for the second theatre – today's **Semperoper** – while he was in political exile. He was sought for being a barricade builder in the uprising in May 1849 and had been forced to leave Dresden. His son Manfred took over building operations from 1871–78.

"IT'S HIGH TIME TO CELEBRATE A BEER..."
In the mid-1990s an advertising campaign for beer, of all things, made the Semperoper phenomenally famous. Some people even think that the opera house is the most beautiful brewery in Germany...

After being destroyed in World War II, a replica Semperoper was rebuilt from 1977 and reopened on 13 February 1985 with a performance of Carl Maria von Weber's *Der Freischütz*. With its arcaded façade and panther quadriga over the protruding, richly decorated, main entrance, it is one of the most impressive theatre buildings in Europe. Ernst Rietschel created the sculptures of Goethe and Schiller that are next to the portal, for the first court theatre. Pay special attention to the elaborate

From left
to right:
Semperoper
auditorium;
Performance
of *Don Carlos*

ceilings paintings in the auditorium, the ornate imitation marble in the vestibule and foyer, the splendid curtain and the famous two-window, five-minute clock above the stage.

Great musicians such as Carl Maria von Weber, Richard Wagner and Richard Strauss all left their mark on Dresden's operatic tradition. The ensemble of the **Saxon State Opera** has an excellent reputation and one of the world's oldest orchestras, the **Saxon Staatskapelle**, founded in 1548, has its home in the Semperoper.

Theaterplatz

There can be no doubt that this is one of the most beautiful squares in Europe – if not the world – where tourists swirl around in enchantment and the locals proudly act as tour guides for their relatives. The square is lined with Semper's opera house, the **Gemäldegalerie** (► 62), the **Residenzschloss** (► 70) and the **Hofkirche**.

The **Italianisches Dörfchen** (Italian Village) was built by the city planner, Hans Erlwein, on the site where the Italian builders who worked on the **Hofkirche** once lived. Although it is "only" a restaurant, its colourful wall and ceiling paintings have made it a tourist attraction. The plans for the **Altstädter Wache** guardhouse, which was erected from 1830–32, were drawn up by Friedrich Schinkel which explains why this late example of Berlin Classicism is also known as the "Schinkelwache". It now houses the Semperoper visitors' service centre and a café.. The centre of the square is dominated by Johannes Schilling's equestrian statue of King Johann who ruled Saxony from 1854–73 and managed to translate Dante's *Divine Comedy* on the side.

Hofkirche (St Trinitatis Cathedral)

The Catholic counterpart to the Frauenkirche, the Hofkirche, stands right next to the Residenzschloss at an angle to the Elbe. The Italian architect Gaetano Chiaveri created this filigreed masterwork in the late Roman Baroque style. The 78 figures that decorate the façade and balustrades come from the workshop of the sculptor Lorenzo Mattielli. In order to spare Protestant Dresden the spectacle of Catholic processions, a gallery was

HOMESICK
August the Strong was also King of Poland and as such, his body is buried in Wawel Castle in Cracow. But his heart found its way back to the homeland and now rests in the Hofkirche's crypt.

The Dresden boy's choir in front of the Silbermann organ

included in the nave just for this purpose. The fanciful pulpit by Permoser forms a delightful contrast to the otherwise sober interior of the church. The House of Wettin tomb is in the crypt. In the memorial chapel, which was originally dedicated to St John of Nepomuk, a Pietà made of Meissen porcelain, by the Dresden sculptor Friedrich Press, is dedicated to the "victims of 13 February and all unjust violence". The Silbermann organ in the Hofkirche was evacuated in World War II and was the only one of the three instruments of this kind to survive.

In 1980, the church was made the Cathedral of the Holy Trinity of the Dresden-Meißen Diocese.

TAKING A BREAK

Have a small *Heeßen* in the **Café Schinkelwache** or in the **Italienisches Dörfchen** café.

➕ 196 A2 🚊 Tram 4, 8, 9 Theaterplatz

INSIDER INFO

- Ten themed **Semperoper tours** are held when there are no rehearsals or performances taking place (tel: 0351 3 1 73 60, www.semperoper-erleben.de, from €10). **Special tours** for children tell them all about life in the theatre; in "Semper and the Detectives", the youngsters attempt to find an opera singer's lucky charm.
- The **Hofkirche is open to the public** when no services are being held; there are also regular guided tours (up-to-date times in the showcase at entrance A, information tel: 0351 4 1 47 12, www.kathedrale-dresden.de).
- You can hear the **Silbermann organ** in the cathedral at the organ prelude (Wed, Sat 11:30am–noon) and within the framework of the Dresden Organ Cycle (Wed 8pm, alternating with the Kreuz- and Frauenkirche).
- If you manage to get one of the sought-after tickets for a Semperoper performance, have a glass of sparkling wine on the **terrace** overlooking the Elbe on the first floor in the interval – the view is breathtaking (information on opera tickets ➤ 90).

Insider Tip

⭐5 Brühlsche Terrasse

Known as the "Balcony of Europe", the terrace is named after Count Brühl, the man who once owned it. Today, tourists and locals alike promenade here and enjoy the Altstadt backdrop and sweeping views of the Elbe and Neustadt.

Count Heinrich von Brühl – Royal Polish and Electoral Saxon Prime Minister – was a favourite of Friedrich August II, the son of August the Strong. At the beginning of the 18th century, the Brühlsche Terrasse was still part of the town's fortress, which had gradually lost its military importance. Friedrich August II handed over large sections of the fortress complex on the Elbe side to Count von Brühl between 1739 and 1748. The Count had old vaults and courtyards filled in then had his favourite architect Johann Christoph Knöffel create a pleasure garden with pavilions, a gallery and belvedere 10m (33ft) above the banks of the Elbe. Count Brühl's palaces have not survived; most of them had to make way for new buildings when the complex was redesigned in the late 19th early 20th century.

Gottfried Semper next to the Academy of Fine Arts

Brühlsche Terrasse

The Brühlsche Terrasse Opens to the Public

In 1814, the Russian Prince Repnin-Wolkonski, who had been appointed General Governor of occupied Saxony after the Battle of Leipzig, ordered that the 500m (1640ft) long Brühlsche Terrasse be made open to the public. He had a **flight of steps** erected to provide access to the garden complex on the fortress walls and, what was once reserved for the aristocracy, was available to all. Today, the ascent from Schlossplatz is flanked by a group of figures by Johannes Schilling showing *The Four Seasons*. At the top, you pass the **Old Parliament** (also House of the Estates), designed by the architect Paul Wallot from 1901–07. The **Sekundogenitor**, erected for the second-born prince from 1897, once served as a painting gallery and now houses the restaurants of the Hilton Hotel. Johannes Schilling's Rietschel Monument is located on the terrace balustrade opposite the neo-Baroque building. A few steps further on, the statue *Earth and Planets* by the Dresden artist Vinzenz Wanitschke recalls the bastions of the old Dresden city fortifications that were named after the Roman gods of the planets. The Frauenkirche is the reason that all eyes and cameras are focused on the city from this position; its dome rises up majestically above the houses on Münzgasse, which you can get to via a double stairway.

Artworks

The monumental neo-Renaissance **Kunstakademie** (today's Academy of Fine Arts) was created by Constantin Lipsius at the end of the 19th century. The ribs of the glass dome have given it its nickname of the "lemon press". It is crowned by a statue of Pheme, the Goddess of Fame. The State Art Collections Dresden has temporary exhibitions in the **Lipsius Bau**, the exhibition building next to the Art Academy on the Brühlsche Terrasse. The Semper Monument, which was also created by Schilling, is on the sweeping flight of steps leading from Georg-Treu-Platz to the **Dresden Fortress**. Reconstruction of the **Albertinum,** with the **New Masters Gallery** and **Sculpture Collection,** which was created when

Ernst Rietschel, by his pupil Johannes Schilling

The Historic Altstadt

the old arsenal was converted in 1884–87 and is named after King Albert, was completed in 2010. It was given a central foyer in the courtyard as well as a "hovering" flood-proof depot above it and now presents itself as a house for "Art from Romanticism to the Present". The Brühlsche Garden is at the eastern end of the **Brühlsche Terrasse**. Pierre Coudray's **Delphinbrunnen**, the two **sphinxes** and the former house of the court gardener (today, a home for senior citizens) at the southeastern corner date from Count Brühl's time. There is also a **monument to Caspar David Friedrich** and a **stele** with the portrait of the "inventor " of porcelain, **Johann Friedrich Böttger**, in the charming little park.

Monument to Caspar David Friedrich at the east end of the Brühlsche Terrasse

Galerie Neue Meister

The New Masters Gallery museum has a collection of modern art works from the early 19th century through to the present day. It includes outstanding works by German Romantic artists (Caspar David Friedrich, Ludwig Richter) and German and French Impressionists, as well as works by the Dresden Expressionist group "Die Brücke". Among the artists representing the second half of the 20th century are Georg Baselitz from the Oberlausitz and Gerhard Richter who was born in Dresden in 1932; the latter in two rooms arranged by the artist himself.

Sculpture Collection

The museum's collection covers five centuries. Objects from the collection of antiques are displayed, side-by-side, in huge glass-fronted display areas by the Georg-Treu-Platz entrance. The works presented in the sculpture hall on the ground floor range from Auguste Rodin to the present day. The Klingersaal shows sculptures from the fin-de-siècle; the Mosaiksaal is devoted to Classicist artists – especially Ernst Rietschel. And many other works from ancient cultures to our day can be admired in the displays on the first

Parau Api (What's New?) by Paul Gauguin

floor, as well as in some exhibition rooms in the New Masters Galley.

Dresden Fortress

The sections of the former fortress complex filled in by Count Brühl were excavated in the 1990s and now provide a fascinating insight into little-known aspects of the Saxon residence. The canon courts and casemates, the old town moat bridge and the brick gate, Dresden's last city gate to be preserved, can all be visited.

TAKING A BREAK

Absolutely traditional: a coffee and slice of Black Forest gateau in **Café Vis-à-Vis** in the Sekundogenitur.

✚ 196 B2 🚋 Tram 4, 8, 9 Theaterplatz; 3, 7; Synagoge

Kunsthalle im Lipsius-Bau
☎ 0351 49 14 20 00; www.skd.museum
🕐 Tue–Sun 10am–6pm 🎟 Varies, depending on the exhibition

**Galerie Neue Meister/Skulpturensammlung
(New Masters Gallery/Sculpture Collection)**
✉ Albertinum ☎ 0351 49 14 20 00; www.skd.museum
🕐 Tue–Sun 10am–6pm
🎟 €10, combined ticket with the Kunsthalle im Lipsiusbau €12.50

Dresden Fortress
✉ Georg-Treu-Platz 1
☎ 0351 4 38 37 03 20; www.schloesserland-sachsen.de
🕐 Only open for guided tours 🎟 €5

INSIDER INFO

- Take a one-hour guided tour down into the subterranean 🏰 **fortress casements** and get to know a different side of Dresden.
- The best time of day on the Brühlsche Terrasse is at **sunset**.

At Your Leisure

⓫ Cholerabrunnen

Baron Eugen von Gutschmid donated the Cholera Fountain after Dresden was spared from a cholera epidemic. The sculptor Moritz Seeling, with a design by Gottfried Semper, created the fountain that consists of an octagonal pool and 18m (59ft) high, neo-Gothic pinnacle tower with 40 gargoyles. It was inaugurated in 1846 and moved from Postplatz to its present location in 1927.

✚ 196 A2 ✉ Sophienstraße (next to Taschenbergpalais)
🚋 Tram 1, 2, 4, 8, 9, 11, 12; bus 94 Postplatz

⓬ Augustusbrücke

The bridge connects Schlossplatz on the left bank of the Elbe with Neustädter Markt on the right side. The first mention of a bridge at this location dates from 1275. Over the centuries, the bridge experienced floods, wars and numerous reconstructions. Today's bridge, with its nine sandstone arches, was built in 1907–10 following plans by the architect Wilhelm Kreis, who later also designed the Hygiene Museum.

✚ 196 B2/3 🚋 Tram 4, 8, 9 Theaterplatz and Neustädter Markt

Detail of the Cholera Fountain

⓭ 🚢 Sächsische Dampfschifffahrt

The world's largest and oldest fleet of **paddle steamers** have their home port on the Terrassenufer in Dresden. Nine historic paddle steamers (as well as two new salon ships named after *August the Strong* and *Countess Cosel*) have been carefully spruced up and now ply their way between Diesbar-Seußlitz and Bad Schandau and from Pirna to Děčín. The oldest one still in service – the *Stadt Wehlen* – was launched in 1879. In addition to the regular service, tours and special cruises are also offered. The fleet review on 1 May and the Steamer Festival with a parade of the boats during the Stadtfest city festival in August are two particularly spectacular events.

✚ 196 B2 ✉ Terrassenufer ☎ 0351 86 60 90; www.saechsische-dampfschiffahrt.de
🕐 Departures May–Sep daily 9am–5pm; Apr, Oct to 3pm, evening cruises and special events
🚋 Tram 4, 8, 9 Theaterplatz; 3, 7 Synagoge
💶 Depending on the route €2.50–€25

⓮ 🚢 Johanneum · Verkehrsmuseum Dresden

This stately building has been rebuilt many times and used for a great variety of purposes during its history: it served as the stables and

garage for the Prince Elector's horses and carriages, housed a porcelain collection, armoury and the Old Masters Gallery. Since 1956 it has housed the **Transport Museum**. The exhibits cover the five realms of travel and include the first German steam locomotive (the *Muldenthal* from 1861), exhibits documenting the East German automobile industry and the GDR aviation industry (that was based in Dresden in the 1950s). The 325m² (3500ft²) 0-gauge model railway guarantees fun for young and old alike. In front of the museum is the **Türkenbrunnen** (Turkish Fountain).

In the Transport Museum

➕ 196 B2 ✉ Augustusstr. 1 ☎ 0351 8 64 40; www.verkehrsmuseum-dresden.de
🕐 Tue–Sun 10am–5pm
🚋 Tram 1, 2, 4 Altmarkt 💶 7 €

🔟 Neumarkt

This area was a gigantic wasteland for more than half a century. After being destroyed in World War II the rubble was cleared away, leaving nothing but an empty space – with the remains of the Frauenkirche in the middle. After the Frauenkirche was rebuilt Neumarkt and its neighbouring streets began to experience a renaissance – with a blend of modern architecture and reconstructed facades. Already completed are: the quarter near the Frauenkirche, with the QF-Passage shopping mall, the former Hotel de Saxe and Salomonis pharmacy, that now both form the Steigenberger Hotel, the Carrée an der Frauenkirche with the Zum Schwan and Zur Glocke houses, and the reconstructed Heinrich Schütz/ Köhlerschen house. The monuments to Martin Luther and King Friedrich August II stand guard over the square (Neumarkt Information Pavilion at Pirnaischer Platz).

➕ 196 B1/2 🚋 Tram 1, 2, 4 Altmarkt

🔟 Coselpalais

The palace, which was designed by Christoph Knöffel, destroyed in the Seven Years' War and rebuilt by Julius Heinrich Schwarze, once belonged to Friedrich August von Cosel, the son of August the Strong and Countess Cosel. With the exception of the wing buildings, the Rococo construction was completely destroyed during the bombing in February 1945. The exterior was

Historic paddle steamers with Altstadt in the background

The Historic Altstadt

reconstructed in the late 1990s and today houses offices and restaurants.

🗺 196 B/C 2 · ✉ An der Frauenkirche 12
🚋 Tram 1, 2, 4 Altmarkt; 3, 7 Synagoge

🔢17 Landhaus · Stadtmuseum & Städtische Galerie

The **Landhaus**, which was the former meeting place of Saxony's provincial diets, is the main work of the architect Friedrich August Krubsacius. The building, which was built in 1770–75, and destroyed by fire in World War II, was rebuilt and has housed the **city museum** since 1965. The permanent exhibition "800 years of Dresden" is complemented by temporary exhibitions. The **Städtische Galerie** presents local art from the region – mainly from the 19th and 20th centuries – as well as contemporary works. Library and museum shop.

🗺 196 C1 · ✉ Wilsdruffer Straße 2 (entrance from Landhausstraße)
☎ 0351 4 88 73 70; www.museen-dresden.de, www.galerie-dresden.de · 🕐 Tue–Sun 10am–6pm, Fri to 7pm · 🚋 Tram 1–4, 7, 12; bus 75, 62 Pirnaischer Platz · 🎫 €5; Fri, free admission from noon (except on public holidays)

The striking Neue Synagoge exterior is a massive sandstone cube

🔢18 Neue Synagoge

Dresden's Jewish community's New Synagogue was consecrated exactly 63 years after the National Socialists destroyed the original synagogue designed by Gottfried Semper. The outline of Semper's building is marked in the courtyard. Only the Star of David from the original building remained intact; a fireman salvaged it and concealed it until after the war.

The star now hangs above the new synagogue's entrance. The new building is a windowless cube turned to the east, the interior is enclosed with by symbolic tent of chain mesh. Today, there is a stele between the Synagogue and Brühlsche Terrasse; it is in remembrance of the pogrom night of 9 November 1938 when the National Socialist mob set this Jewish house of worship ablaze.

🗺 196 C2 · ✉ Hasenberg
ℹ Guided tours (except Fri, Sat and Jewish holidays), times in the Community Centre or under www.hatikva.de, tel: 0351 8 02 04 89
🚋 Tram 3, 7 Synagoge · 🎫 €4–5

Where to...
Eat and Drink

Prices
Expect to pay per person for a main course without drinks.
€ less than €12   **€€** €12–20   **€€€** more than €20

Alte Meister €€ *Insider Tip*
In the evening, the museum café in the Alte Meister is transformed into a stylish restaurant. The evening menu lists fresh seasonal creations and daily specials complete the offer. In summer, you can dine outside on the terrace with a panoramic view of Theaterplatz.
➕ 196 A2 ✉ Theaterplatz 1a
☎ 0351 4 81 04 26 ⏰ Daily 10am–1am
🚋 Tram 4, 8, 9 Theaterplatz

BrennNessel €€
This small restaurant, in a half-timbered house from the mid-17th century, is only a few minutes' walk away from the Zwinger but still off the beaten tourist track, making it a peaceful oasis in the hectic atmosphere of the city. Mainly vegetarian dishes but you will find a farmer's breakfast with ham alongside nettle soup and tofu curry on the menu. In summer, you can enjoy a refreshing beer in the pleasant courtyard. There is also a special vegan menu.
➕ 190 A1 ✉ Schützengasse 18
☎ 0351 4 94 33 19 ⏰ Daily 11am–midnight
🚋 Tram 1, 2, 6, 10; bus 94 Bahnhof Mitte

Coselpalais – Grand Café and Restaurant €€
Its prime location near the Frauenkirche, as well as its opulent menu with international and Saxon specialities, has made the Grand Café in the Coselpalais one of the most frequented restaurants in the city. Excellent gateaux and cakes from the Eisold pastry shop are served on noble Meissen plates in the Porcelain Room.
➕ 196 B2 ✉ An der Frauenkirche 12
☎ 0351 4 96 24 44 ⏰ Daily 10am–midnight
🚋 Tram 1, 2, 4 Altmarkt

Dresden 1900 €€
Dresden's Linie 6 tramcar restaurant enjoyed a cult status for over three decades. This restaurant, which was opened in 2008, follows in the tramcar restaurant tradition. It has – among other things – the oldest preserved tram in Dresden, the *Helene* from 1898, with seating for 14 guests, on the copy of a Postplatz. Saxon dishes and wine, cooking events, regular discussions on art and politics.
➕ 196 B2 ✉ An der Frauenkirche 20
☎ 0351 48 20 58 58 ⏰ Mon–Sat 8am–1am, Sun 9am–midnight, Sunday brunch
🚋 Tram 1, 2, 4 Altmarkt

edelweiss €€
Swiss chalet-style Alpine restaurant perfect for those who like *Rösti* (fried, grated potatoes), *Bündnerfleisch* (air-dried beef), *Kaiserschmarren* (sweet, cut-up pancakes with raisins) and cheese fondue. A hearty "mountain hut breakfast" is served every day until noon. You can watch the hustle and bustle around the Frauenkirche from the terrace on the ground floor or from the balcony upstairs.
➕ 196 B2 ✉ An der Frauenkirche 7
☎ 0351 4 98 98 36 ⏰ Daily 8am–midnight
🚋 Tram 1, 2, 4 Altmarkt

Intermezzo €€€
Jörg Mergner loves the Mediterranean – and that is the reason he serves magical, light

dishes from sunny southern countries. It is no surprise then that Intermezzo is one of the best restaurants in Saxony. The elegant ambience, classical music and perfect service make each visit an unforgettable experience. Be sure to reserve a table in the magnificent interior courtyard in summer.

➕ 196 A2 ✉ Taschenberg 3
☎ 0351 4 91 27 12
🕐 Daily noon–3pm, 6pm–11:30pm
🚋 Tram 1, 2, 4, 9, 11, 12; bus 94 Postplatz

Italienisches Dörfchen €–€€

The restaurant, named in honour of the Italian builders of the Hofkirche, has classic café décor and painted coffered ceilings in the Beer Hall and Elector's Room. The Ristorante Bellotto on the upper floor has views over the Basteischlösschen – the "small Italian" (closed on Mon) also belongs to the restaurant. The Elbe terrace will tempt you to linger in summer.

➕ 196 A2 ✉ Theaterplatz 3
☎ 0351 49 81 60 🕐 Daily 10am–midnight
🚋 Tram 4, 8, 9 Theaterplatz

Kahnaletto €€

The Theaterkahn barge has been moored at the Terrassenufer, next to the Augustus Bridge, since 1994. Along with the Dresdner Brettl, a theatre for cabaret, music and literature, it also has the Kahnaletto Restaurant on board. It offers fresh Mediterranean cuisine and new dishes every day (tip: set lunch from €12.50). In the evening, have one for the road in the bar in the hull.

➕ 196 B2 ✉ Terrassenufer/Augustusbrücke
☎ 0351 4 95 30 37 🕐 Daily noon–2:30pm, 6pm–midnight, bar Tue–Sun 6pm–1am
🚋 Tram 4, 8, 9 Theaterplatz

Kastenmeiers €€€

Gourmet chef Gerd Kastenmeier made his dream of an exclusive fish restaurant come true in this gem in the painstakingly – and tastefully – renovated Kurländer

Palais. Diners can enjoy the delicacies from the creative kitchen in the beautiful arcaded courtyard in the warmer months of the year. Mon–Fri set lunch for €9.50.

➕ 196 C1 ✉ Tzschirnerplatz 3–5
☎ 0351 48 48 48 01 🕐 Daily noon–11pm
🚋 Tram 3, 7 Synagoge

Münzgasse €–€€

There is a whole string of restaurants for all tastes next to each other on Dresden's number one pub strip between the Frauenkirche and the Brühlsche Terrasse. The edelweiss Alpine restaurant is at the south end with the Hilton Bistro Ecke Frauenkirche opposite it. The Steakhaus Applaus and Bierhaus Dampfschiff, which also belong to the Hilton, follow these on the left towards the Elbe. On the other side things start off Spanish in Las Tapas, before heading down under to the Ayers Rock and ending up with traditional, down-to-earth German fare in the Kutscherschänke.

➕ 196 B2 ✉ Münzgasse 4–10
🕐 Morning to midnight or later
🚋 Tram 1, 2, 4 Altmarkt

Ogura €€

Yukio Ogura, a real master of Japanese cooking, serves his guests on the first floor of the Hilton, where sushi, sashimi and soups à la carte are complemented by a six-course set meal that changes every day. The refined Japanese decoration creates the perfect atmosphere.

➕ 196 B2 ✉ An der Frauenkirche 5
☎ 0351 8 64 29 75 🕐 Tue–Sat 11:30am–2pm, 5:30pm–10:30pm, Sun 5:30pm–9:30pm
🚋 Tram 1, 2, 4 Altmarkt

Ontario €€€

The Canadian steakhouse has a great deal of wood and leather in the chic restaurant on the first floor and the diner on the ground floor, as well as in the fireplace lounge. The menu ranges from Canadian seafood to roast caribou and bison entrecote. The Wagyu (or Kobe)

beefsteaks are very special and a real treat for meat lovers.

🏠 196 B2 ✉ An der Frauenkirche 2
☎ 0351 40 28 86 60 🕐 Daily 11am–1am
🚊 Tram 1, 2, 4 Altmarkt

Pulverturm €€

Housed in the remains of an old gunpowder tower in the cellar of the reconstructed Coselpalais, this restaurant serves rustic fare. Hardworking maidservants and snappy grenadiers serve "marching rations" (puff-pastry cannonballs) and fresh bread from the army bakery in the Turkish Vault, the Swedish Chambers or prison. The Sophienkeller, another branch in the Taschenbergpalais, is a highlight of Saxon themed gastronomy.

🏠 196 B2 ✉ An der Frauenkirche 12
☎ 0351 26 26 00 🕐 Daily 11am–1am
🚊 Tram 1, 2, 4 Altmarkt

Rossini €€€

The best restaurant in town and there is even a good view of the Frauenkirche to enjoy along with the exquisite Italian specialities served on the first floor of the Hilton. The menu, with the chef's recommendations, changes every four weeks but the delicious Fillet à la Rossini is always available.

🏠 196 B2 ✉ An der Frauenkirche 5
☎ 0351 8 64 28 55
🕐 Mon–Thu 6pm–10:30pm, Fri–Sun 5:30pm–11pm 🚊 Tram 1, 2, 4 Altmarkt

William €€ *Insider Tip*

Dresden's gourmets have had a new place to go to since 2013; it is on the upper floor of the Schauspielhaus and is named after the great playwright. Once you have made it up the stairs into the elegant restaurant, you will be able to enjoy the excellent modern cuisine served in this offshoot of the ocean & beluga gourmet restaurant.

🏠 190 B1 ✉ Theaterstraße 2
☎ 0351 44 00 88 00, 🕐 Mon–Fri 11am–11pm, Sat, Sun 10am–11pm 🚊 Tram 1, 2, 4, 8, 9, 11, 12; bus 62, 94 Postplatz

Wohnstube €€€

The restaurant in the elegant Swissôtel am Residenzschloss is one of the most interesting newcomers to Dresden's gastronomic scene. Swiss cuisine with a touch of Saxony is served in the "front living room" with its dignified but modern décor – or outside in summer – and in keeping with the times, there are also gluten-free dishes as well as options for vegetarians and vegans.

🏠 196 B2 ✉ Schlossstr. 16/Kanzleigässchen,
☎ 0351 50 12 00, 🕐 Daily 11am–11pm
🚊 Tram 1, 2, 4 Altmarkt

Where to...
Shop

What was once a shopping wasteland has come to life! The number of shops in Altstadt is also increasing as the development of Neumarkt progresses.

The Quartier an der Frauenkirche with its **QF-Passage**, which was completed in 2006, now boasts (in addition to many restaurants) an entire series of chic fashion boutiques: **Escada**, **Evelin Brandt Berlin**, **Dagmar Schreiber**, **Marina Rinaldi**, **Mode de Vie**, **Van Laack**, **Lacoste**, **Wolford** and **Prisco Shoes**. The high quality Glashütte watchmakers **A. Lange & Söhne** also have a branch here. The famous **Meissen Porcelain** can be purchased in the Meissen Outlet in the basement and in the neighbouring Hilton Hotel.

BM Geschenke & Ambiente offers arts and crafts from the Erzgebirge and has a total of three branches in Altstadt (An der Frauenkirche 18, Schlossstr. 18 and in the Hilton Hotel). Even more goods from the Erzgebirge (including many Wendt & Kühn items), as well as Herrnhuter

The Historic Altstadt

Sterne (traditional Christmas decorations) can be found in the **Galerie Tradition & Form** (Landhausstr. 6).

The **Quartier M** on the corner of Schloss- and Wilsdruffer Straße is the home of several other fashion shops including **Silbermann**, **Anderßen**, **La Donna**, **Stefanel** and **Mephisto Shoes**.

Tasteful souvenirs, books, on art and Dresden, unique toys and all kinds of knick-knacks can be purchased in the **museum shops** in the Zwinger, the Residenzschloss, the Albertinum and the Stadtmuseum in the Landhaus.

Where to...
Go Out

THEATRE/OPERA

Dresden's most famous temple of the muses is the **Semperoper**, the home of the Saxon State Opera, the Saxon Staatskapelle and the Semperoper Ballet. Classical operas, as well as contemporary musical theatre, are staged. The **Junge Szene** performs pieces for children and young people on the Probe-bühne Semper 2. The grand operas in particular are usually sold out and it is advisable to book well in advance (Visitors' Service in the Schinkelwache, Theaterplatz 2, Mon–Fri 10am–6pm, Sat 10am–5pm, Sun 10am–1pm, remaining tickets are available on the night at the box office one hour before the performance begins, tel: 0351 4 91 17 05, www.semperoper.de).

The city's most important theatre is opposite the Kronentor of the Zwinger: the **Schauspielhaus** built 1911–13. Dresden's state theatre, Staatsschauspiel, performs classic and modern plays on the main stage (box office: Theaterstr. 2/

Ostra-Allee, Mon–Fri 10am–6:30pm, Sat 10am–2pm, tel: 0351 4 91 35 55, www.staatsschauspiel-dresden.de).

Especially in spring and autumn many events are held in the **Marmorsaal** and **Zwingerhof** courtyard – from classical music concerts to open-air opera galas and waltz evenings. Tickets are available from the individual organisers or Schlösserland Sachsen (www.schloesserland-sachsen.de).

The **Theaterkahn** barge is anchored on the Elbe next to the Augustus Bridge (Terrassenufer an der Augustusbrücke, tel: 0351 4 96 94 50, www.theaterkahn.de) and has a repertoire of revue and cabaret performances.

The **Kabarett Breschke & Schuch** (Wettiner Platz 10, entrance Jahnstr, tel: 0351 4 90 40 09, www.kabarett-breschke-schuch.de) has a varied programme of political satire and musical performances.

BARS AND CLUBS

The **Karl May Bar** (Kleine Brüdergasse, tel: 0351 4 91 27 20, daily 6pm–2am) in the Kempinski Hotel Taschenbergpalais attracts with its exclusive ambience and international flair (Fri, Sat, live music). The metropolitan stylishness, unusual cocktails and view of the dome of the Frauenkirche make the Twist Skybar, on the 6th floor of the Innside Hotel, one of the hotspots for Dresden's night owls (Salzgasse 4, tel: 0351 79 51 50, daily 6pm–2am). The **m5 Nightlife** in the Hilton (Münzgasse 5, tel: 0351 4 96 54 91, www.m5-nightlife.de) is a refined dance club; the guests have all left their teenage days long behind them. The student club **Bärenzwinger** (Brühlscher Garten 1, tel: 0351 4 95 14 09, www.baerenzwinger.de) is the place to go for music, films, parties and summer theatre performances in the courtyard.

Neustadt

 **Little Treats**

Sharp View
For a breathtaking view of the city, go all the way to the front of the Libeskind Wedge in the **Museum of Military History** (➤ 108).

Picture Frame on the Elbe
It is highly unlikely that you will be alone, but the famous "**Canaletto view**" (➤ 101) will still be a great experience.

Rub Shoulders
Join the Neustadt locals on warm weekends when they head to the lawns and greenery of **Alaunplatz** (➤ 97).

Getting Your Bearings

It is just across a bridge over the Elbe from the Semperoper and Zwinger but it still remains terra incognita for many visitors to Dresden. But even if there are not as many classic sights as there are in Altstadt, Neustadt has its own unique qualities.

In 1549, Prince Elector Moritz von Sachsen united Altendresden on the right bank of the Elbe, which had been independent until then, with the Electoral residence city of Dresden – much to the distaste of the populace. After a disastrous fire in August 1685, the reconstruction of the "Neue Stadt bey Dresden" (New Town near Dresden) began following a plan drawn up by Wolf Caspar von Klengel and August the Strong made it his "New Royal City" in 1732.

The Innere Neustadt, between Haupt- and Königstraße, is one of the most beautiful quarters in Dresden. It has some of the city's last Baroque town houses, elegant shopping arcades, restaurants and several galleries. After the reunification of Germany, the Äußere Neustadt – developed in the so-called Gründerzeit, the years of rapid economic development in the late 19th century – north of the old fortifications, became a popular and trendy late-night bar district. The Colourful Republic Neustadt is proclaimed here every year in June.

TOP 10

Don't Miss

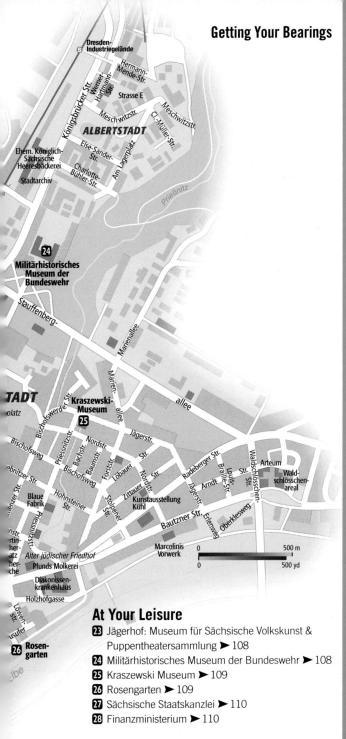

At Your Leisure

Perfect Days in...

The Perfect Day

Charming Baroque façades, fascinating museums, the world's most beautiful dairy shop and a vibrant nightlife – Neustadt offers a great deal of variety. Follow this itinerary to make sure that you don't miss any of the highlights. More info about the individual sights can be found in pages (➤ 96–116).

⏰ 9:30
Start your foray in Neustadt with what is probably the most famous view of Altstadt: the "Canaletto view" (➤ 101).

⏰ 10:00
The museums open their doors. The ⑲ **Japanisches Palais** (➤ 100) and ㉓ **Jägerhof** with the **Museum für Sächsische Volkskunst und der Puppentheater-sammlung** (➤ 108) show interesting exhibitions dealing with natural history and ethnology, as well as Saxon folk art.

⏰ Noon
Head for ⑳ **Neustädter Markt** (above; ➤ 102) and follow the Goldener Reiter into Innere Neustadt and the ⑳ **Hauptstraße** (➤ 102), which is lined with plane trees. Take time to have a look at the historic town houses on the left side of the street, with shops and studios for artists and craftsmen on the ground floor, and the Kügelgenhaus at Number 13, with the Museum of Dresden Romanticism.

⏰ 1:00
You will find the Societätstheater (➤ 115) in the courtyard behind the row of houses. The theatre restaurant L'Art de Vie (➤ 112) is a treat for the eyes, palate and nose – the herb garden terrace smells delightfully of lavender and thyme.

After your lunch break, stroll over the Obergraben and Rähnitzgasse to ㉑ **Königstraße** (➤ 105). Browse through the boutiques and galleries or simply admire the Baroque facades and beautiful courtyards. Then take in the wonderful view from the Dreikönigskirche church tower.

⏰ 3:00
After visiting the writer Erich Kästner at ㉒ **Albertplatz** (➤ 107) you continue on to ⑩ **Äußere Neustadt** (➤ 96). Go across Alaunstraße until you reach Alaunplatz. The ㉔ **Militärhistorisches Museum der Bundeswehr** (➤ 108) is

not only of interest for those with a penchant for military history. Admirers of literature can make a short detour to the Kraszewski Museum and, it is worth taking more than just a quick look at the arty Kunsthofpassage between Görlitzer and Alaunstraße.

🕔 5:00

Now go eastwards via Louisenstraße to Martin-Luther-Platz with the Martin Luther Church and the Old Jewish Cemetery next to it. Before the shops close, take a quick look at Pfunds Molkerei on Bautzner Straße, the most beautiful dairy shop in the world and then be sure you have enough time to stroll through the **26 Rosengarten** (➤ 109) on the bank of the Elbe.

🕖 7:00

Take a walk along the Königsufer past the **27 Sächsische Staatskanzlei** (➤ 110) and the **28 Finanzministerium** (➤ 110) back to where you started this morning. Or, after you have had dinner in one of the many restaurants in Äußere Neustadt, you can explore the district's nightlife.

Neustadt
★ 10 Äußere Neustadt

The Dresdeners refer to the quarter above Bautzner Straße simply as "Neustadt". In the past two decades it has become the most vibrant district in the city with countless pubs and bars, clubs, galleries and trendy shops.

The Äußere Neustadt quarter, which was created in the 19th century, was left fairly untouched by the bombings of World War II and is now one of the largest intact Gründerzeit areas in Europe. Staring in the 1970s, an increasing number of young people – students, families with children, artists and hedonists – were drawn to the area. Many of the new arrivals lived more or less illicitly but saved a large number of the over 100-year-old buildings from falling into complete disrepair. Before the fall of Communism, whole streets were threatened with demolition but later it became necessary to protect Neustadt, particularly from avaricious real-estate speculators.

ENTER AT YOUR OWN RISK?
There is a persistent rumour that Neustadt is not a very safe place. But, the quarter is no more dangerous than those in other large cities. In fact, you can actually feel safer here than in other areas because late at night there are lots of people on the streets. However, there is another "danger" lurking: watch where you tread as the Neustadt locals seem to love dogs!

Long Live the Republic!
On a weekend in June 1990, the **Bunte Republik Neustadt** (Colourful Republic of Neustadt) was proclaimed here. A cheerful yet defiant outcry against developers, it had its own provisional government, demarcation lines and its own currency. Neustadt has changed a lot since those days: most of the houses have been renovated, new pubs and shops are opening every week, and some idyllic back courtyards have had to make way for car parks. However, the free spirit of the Colourful Republic lives on and the people living in Neustadt celebrate it with a great festival every year.

From left to right: In Jacqueline Peevski's hat shop; Gründerzeit staircase

Hof der
Elemente in
the Kunsthof-
passage

Pub Culture and Courtyard Art

Launstraße, Görlitzen and Louisenstraße form the quarter's shopping and pub mile. Alaunstraße makes its way from Albertplatz past the **Scheune** (▶ 116) cultural centre up to **Alaunplatz**, a spacious green area that Neustadt locals like to use for sunbathing and relaxation. Not far from here, at Königsbrücker Straße 66, a plaque commemorates the house where the writer **Erich Kästner** was born. The **Kunsthofpassage** (▶ 115), between Görlitzer and Alaunstraße, is a gem of five artistic courtyards designed by artists from Dresden. Its shops and restaurants are great to browse, shop and while away the time.

CULTURAL HERITAGE

The Scheune was already a legendary meeting place for nonconformists in GDR days. There were punk concerts, gay discos, film evenings, readings and art performances, as well as the first trendy café – run by volunteers – in the 1980s. Since then the Scheune (▶ 113) has been Neustadt's cultural heart.

Neustadt History

The **Martin Luther Church** is located in the middle of the town house-lined Martin-Luther-Platz. Ernst Giese and Paul Weidner built the square in a melange of

World War I
memorial at
the Martin
Luther Church

Neustadt

Romanesque Revival and neo-Gothic styles from 1883–87. In front of the church chancel, on the east side, is a monument from 1928 that commemorates those who fell in World War I. There is a sandstone statue of Martin Luther in front of the the oriel of the rectory at Martin-Luther-Platz 5.

The **Old Jewish Cemetery** on adjacent Pulsnitzer Straße is overgrown with ivy. In 1751, Dresden's Jewish community was given the site, which was outside of the city gates at the time, for use as a cemetery – before that, they had had to take their dead to Teplitz. The cemetery was in use until 1869.

Pfunds Molkerei (right), the place in Neustadt that attracts the greatest number of tourist buses, is just around the corner on Bautzner Straße. The walls and ceilings of the "world's most beautiful dairy shop", which was opened in 1891, are decorated with colourful majolica tiles made by the Villeroy & Boch Company. Since reopening in 1995, the shop sells milk and cheese, cosmetics and Saxon wine, as well as all kinds of Pfunds' merchandising articles (no photographs allowed). Pfunds Restaurant is on the upper floor.

Gravestone in the Old Jewish Cemetery

Insider Tip

🎠 PLACE TO PLAY

Panama is an adventure playground in the centre of Neustadt; an oasis in the big city with a pond and ship, wooden buildings, clay oven and garden. And there are also horses, goats, chickens and rabbits. Supported by social education workers, the children from the neighbourhood can play and let off steam, do handicrafts and learn how to get on with animals. Visitors (children accompanied by parents) are very welcome (Seifhennersdorfer Str. 2; entrance Görlitzer Str., opposite the Kunsthofpassage, tel: 0351 8 03 87 48, Mon–Wed 9am–7pm, Thu, Fri 9am–2pm, Sat, Sun 9am–noon, 4pm–6:30pm; also Mar–Oct Family Sunday 1pm–6pm – donations requested, tram 13 Görlitzer Straße, www.asp-panama.de).

Even if you don't like milk, you have to see the Pfunds Molkerei

TAKING A BREAK

With its oriental cushions on the floor and 100 different kinds of tea, the tearoom in the **Feng Shui Haus** in the Kunsthofpassage is a place of tranquillity and relaxation.

➕ 191 D3 🚋 Tram 3, 6–8, 11 Albertplatz

Kunsthofpassage

➕ 191 D3 ✉ Görlitzer Straße 21–25/Alaunstraße 70
🚋 Tram 13 Görlitzer Straße or Alaunplatz, 7, 8 Louisenstraße

Martin-Luther-Kirche

➕ 191 D3 ✉ Martin-Luther-Platz 🕐 Tower ascent Apr, May, Sep Sun 2pm–6pm, Jun–Aug Fri 8–11:30pm 🎫 €1.50 🚋 Tram 11 Pulsnitzer Straße

Old Jewish Cemetery

➕ 191 D3 ✉ Pulsnitzer Straße 10/12 ☎ 0351 8 02 04 89; www.hatikva.de
🕐 Tue 9am–noon, 1pm–4pm, Thu 1pm–4pm 🚋 Tram 11 Pulsnitzer Straße

Pfunds Molkerei

➕ 191 D2 ✉ Bautzner Straße 79
☎ Shop: 0351 80 80 80; Restaurant: 0351 8 10 59 48; www.pfunds.de
🕐 Shop Mon–Sat 10am–6pm, Sun 10am–3pm, restaurant daily 10am–8pm
🚋 Tram 11 Pulsnitzer Straße/Diakonissenkrankenhaus

INSIDER INFO

Insider Tip

- The 🎯 **Nordbad** swimming pool in the courtyard of Louisenstraße 48 is over 100 years old but was modernised in the 1990s. It has pools for swimming and paddling, extensive sauna facilities and an outdoor lawn for summer sunbathing (tel: 0351 8 03 23 60, daily, times vary, www.nordbad-dresden.de).
- Those who want to visit the Old Jewish Cemetery can get information on tours in the neighbouring **HATiKVA** (Pulsnitzer Str. 10/12, tel: 0351 8 02 04 89) community centre. The small HATiKVA library also has literature on the history of Jews in Saxony.
- The Hof der Elemente (Courtyard of the Elements) in the Kunsthofpassage has a **musical façade** with pipes and drainpipes that create music when water runs through them – on the half-hour and hour.

⑲ Japanisches Palais

The Japanese Palace was acquired by August the Strong to exhibit his porcelain collection. The curved roofs, Chinese herms in the central courtyard and the name of the late Baroque-Classicist building clearly indicate its original purpose.

The Saxon Prince Elector, and lover of porcelain, purchased the former Dutch Palace on the banks of the Elbe in 1717 and commissioned his best architects – Pöppelmann, Longuelune, Knöffel and de Bodt – to convert it into a home for his ever-growing collection of porcelain. However, August died before construction was finished and with it the project, which remained unfinished.

From a porcelain palace to a public museum

It was partially destroyed in World War II and the reconstruction of the stately four-wing complex has still not been completed. There are the remains of a Baroque garden on the side to the Elbe. The city fortifications that once adjoined to the northwest were demolished at the beginning of the 19th century, but a section of the wall was preserved and included in the plans for an English-style landscaped garden.

Museum Usui Publico Patens

Today, the Museum for Public Use – a translation of the inscription in the frieze above the vestibule – houses two museums. Founded in 1875, the **Museum für Völkerkunde** (Ethnographical Museum) has now been integrated into the Saxon Ethnographic Collection and been under the

🔍 FOR YOUNG EXPLORERS

Children – decked out in an expedition helmet and armed with a magnifying glass – can set out on an excursion and solve fascinating puzzles in the dinosaur exhibition in the Natural History Collection.

CANALETTO VIEW

In 1748, Bernardo Bellotto (known as Canaletto), painted *Dresden from the Right Bank of the Elbe below the Augustus Bridge*. You can enjoy the same view if you walk along the bank below the Westin Bellevue Hotel (➤ 48). There is an empty frame that surrounds the current view and a photo of the Canaletto painting so that one can make a comparison.

auspices of the State Art Collections Dresden since 2010. The collection has around 160,000 objects and documentary photos from all around the world. The traditional focus of the collection is on Oceania, Southeast Asia and South America as well as the Middle and Far East. In 1997, a 200-year-old gem of Ottoman interior architecture was discovered in the museum's storage depot. The **Damascus Room**, with its richly decorated wall and ceiling panelling, is the highlight of an exhibition that is extremely impressive – even if it does only occupy one room. It forms the first part of what is planned to be a more extensive presentation in the future. The **Senckenberg Naturhistorische Sammlungen** was created when the Museum for Mineralogy and Geology and Museum for Animal Biology, which had developed out of the Saxon rulers' collections of art and natural history, merged. With 6.5 million items in its holdings, it is one of the largest museums of natural history in Germany. The special exhibitions on various aspects of natural history are changed every year. In 2015 the museum will present "Dinosaurs – 300 Million Years of Survival" and will followed that with "Sex and Evolution" in 2016.

Chinese herms on the Japanischen Palais – the building is named after its Japanese architectural elements

TAKING A BREAK

Relax in the garden of the neighbouring Bellevue Hotel and admire the floral splendour.

➕ 196 A4 ✉ Palaisplatz 11
🕐 Tue–Sun 10am–6pm
🚋 Tram 4, 9 Palaisplatz

**Museum für Völkerkunde
(Ethnographical Museum)**
☎ 0351 49 14 35 08; 49 14 20 00
🕐 Tue–Sun 10am–6pm; www.skd.museum
💶 €2.50 (free with the Residenzschloss ticket)

**Senckenberg Naturhistorische
Sammlungen Dresden
(Natural History Collections)**
🕐 Tue–Sun 10am–6pm
☎ 0351 79 58 41 44 08;
www.senckenberg.de/dresden 💶 €6

INSIDER INFO

The Ethnographical Museum offers **guided tours and lectures**: "Culture at Midday", "Dresden Carpet Evenings" and "Coffee in the Damascus Room".

⑳ Neustädter Markt & Hauptstraße

Neustädter Markt welcomes its visitors with outstretched arms so to speak. A few years ago, a poster on a façade at the start of the Hauptstraße stated, "This is Where Dresden Moves On" and accurately summed up Dresden's loveliest pedestrian boulevard.

Vigorous ruler – August the Strong on his steed

The square at the bridgehead of the Augustus Bridge on the Neustadt side was created to be the middle point of the Altendresden settlement on the right bank of the Elbe, which was first mentioned in a document in 1350. Over time, it developed into the Neustadt market place that had since become part of Dresden. On 13 February 1945, the buildings around the Neustädter Markt, including the 18th-century town tall, were reduced to rubble and ashes. Only the burned out **Blockhaus** (Blockhouse), the former **Neue Wache** (New Guard Post), was restored to its original appearance in 1979/1980. The Baroque building, which was constructed after 1732, by Zacharias Longuelune and Johann Christoph Knöffel, closes the square on the side to the Elbe. The building is currently empty as a result of flood damage and the State Government is working on a project for its future use. A Baroque town house at Number 15, which was already integrated into the building of the Hotel Bellevue in GDR days, was the only building preserved on adjacent Große Meißner Straße.

In the 1970s, the Neustädter Markt was reconstructed with residential buildings surrounding the square and shops, restaurants, green areas and fountains. The prefabricated buildings, which are now a bit long in the tooth, are gradually being renovated but the inconsistent façade – some of it in air-raid shelter grey – spoils the overall appearance of the ensemble.

Dresden's most famous monument, the **Goldener Reiter** (Golden Rider), has its place in the middle of the Neustädter Markt. The equestrian statue of August the Strong, a work by the canon maker Ludwig Wiedemann, was installed four years after the King's death and was regilded in 2003.

Beautifully restored old town houses line the Hauptstraße

BAROQUE HERB BEDS

Over the years, hardly anything has remained of the gardens of the town houses on Hauptstraße. However, in addition to the pavilion, the garden complex of the former property owned by the court sculptor Benjamin Thomae behind the house at Number 17 was reconstructed in the Baroque style – with herbs and quinces in beds surrounded by boxwoods.

The monarch, in the pose and garments of a Roman Emperor, is shown riding towards his Polish kingdom.

The Romantic Street

The two **Nymphenbrunnen** fountains on Neustädter Markt once decorated the town hall; together with two splendid bronze flagpoles from the year 1893, they form the start of the **Hauptstraße**, the main axis of Innere Neustadt leading to Albertplatz. After being partly destroyed in World War II, it was redeveloped along with the Neustädter Markt. Its old plane trees, sculptures and fountains makes it Dresden's most beautiful pedestrian boulevard. There are six historic **town houses** on the west side. The **Kügelhaus**, which was once also known as "God's Blessing" house due to the inscription on its façade, is now the home of the **Museum der Dresdner Romantik** (Museum of Dresden Romanticism). At the beginning of the 19th century, the house was home to Gerhard von Kügelgen, a painter of portraits and historical scenes, and the meeting place of the Dresden Romanticists including Caspar David Friedrich. The museum's everyday articles and paintings – including Anton Graff's famous

Fountains on Hauptstraße

portrait of Schiller – bring to life the cultural and intellectual history of Dresden in the years from 1785–1830. The elaborately painted wooden ceilings and a copy of Kügelgen's studio are also well worth seeing. There are **artist and craftsman** shops and workshops on the ground floor of the row of houses and the **Societaetstheater** (► 115), the first civic theatre club in Germany, which was reconstructed in the 1990s, is in the rear courtyard. Continuing on towards Albertplatz, you will see the **Dreikönigskirche** (► 106) church on the left-hand side and – on the right, between Ritter and Metzer Straße – the **Neustädter Markthalle**; the market hall was reopened in 2000 after being painstakingly renovated. However, most of the speciality shops that were originally here have since left and the market is slowly turning into a junk shop. New buildings from the late 1980s form the northern end of Hauptstraße.

From left to right: Fine shopping; Kügelgen's studio in the Museum der Dresdner Romantik

TAKING A BREAK

Insider Tip

Relax on a bench in the shade of the plane trees or enjoy the urban flair and a cappuccino in the **Schwarzmarkt Café**.

✚ 196 B3

🚋 Tram 4, 8, 9 Neustädter Markt, 3, 6–8, 11 Albertplatz

Kügelgenhaus – Museum der Dresdner Romantik
✉ Hauptstraße 13
☎ 0351 8 04 47 60; www.museen-dresden.de
🕐 Wed–Sun 10am–6pm
🎟 €4, Fri (except holidays) free after midday

POETS' LOCKS

The exhibits in the Museum der Dresdner Romantik include a few strands of hair that supposedly come from the heads of Schiller and Goethe. By the way, the latter watched the entry of the troops of the anti-Napoleon coalition from a window in Kügelgen's apartment in 1813.

INSIDER INFO

■ The **Parkhaus Hauptstraße** (Metzer Straße) is fully automated so if you leave your car there it will be mechanically transported to one of 150 parking bays and returned to you – pointing in the driving direction – when you come back (daily rate €7).

■ The **Museum Körnigreich** (Thu–Mon 11am–6pm, €3, www.koernigreich.org) at Wallgässchen 2 is dedicated to the artist Hans Körnig (1905–89) who had his studio here and became famous in the GDR for his attic exhibitions.

㉑ Königstraße

This is one of Dresden's most charming and elegant little streets. It is lined with its lovingly restored town houses with secluded courtyards, and has art galleries and chic boutiques. Together with its side streets and passageways, Königstraße is the last Baroque residential and commercial area in the city.

View of Königstraße from the Dreikönigskirche

At the beginning of the 18th century, when August the Strong had his new royal city built on the site of Altendresden, which had been razed by fire, he also demanded that a magnificent avenue be established from the middle axis of his Porcelain Palace, the later Japanischen Palais (► 100), to the Schwarzen Tor where Albertplatz (► 107) is today. The Baroque quarter around Königstraße escaped with little damage in World War II but the historic buildings progressively deteriorated in GDR times. The most beautiful part of Innere Neustadt was not saved until after the reunification of Germany.

NEW LIFE?

One of the two Classicist former gatehouses of the **Weißes Tor** still stands on the west side of Palaisplatz in front of the Japanischen Palais. It was a registry office in GDR days. An investor is now trying to breathe new life into this sleeping beauty.

Through the Baroque City

The buildings on the lower section of **Königstraße** were erected following strict building regulations and all have a uniform number of floors and size. Almost all – with the exception of the Kulturrathaus at Number 15 – have restored or redesigned inner courtyards. **Passage Königstraße** leads through to Rähnitzgasse. The Hotel Bülow Residenz (► 46) has opened its doors in the magnificent Baroque building at Number 19, which was built in 1730.

Neustadt

Just a short distance away is the **Kunsthaus Dresden**, the city's gallery for contemporary art. Going in the opposite direction, Rähnitzgasse ends at the **Dreikönigskirche**, church erected in 1732–39 and designed by Pöppelmann. The church was burned down in 1945 and in GDR days it was used as the House of the Church (entrance from the Hauptstraße) with rooms for events and meetings. The Baroque altar by Benjamin Thomae, which still shows signs of war damage, and the Renaissance relief with the *Dresden Dance of Death* on the organ gallery are highlights of the interior. The *Dance of Death* once adorned the Georgenbau in the Residenzschloss and shows the representatives of all the estates performing a round dance – led by the great leveller, Death.

From left to right: Courtyards and passage-ways on Königstraße; Rähnitzgasse with the Dreikönigs-kirche

The **Rebeccabrunnen** fountain on the square in front of the tower side was built in 1864. On the corner of Königstraße is the newly constructed Relais and Châteux Hotel **Bülow Palace** (➤ 46), Selmar Werner's **Schiller Monument** is hidden behind bushes between König and the Hauptstraße just before Albertplatz.

TAKING A BREAK

The small but excellent **Pastamanufaktur** (➤ 112) has inexpensive daily specials of fresh pasta.

➕ 196 C4 🚊 Tram 4, 9 Palaisplatz, 3, 6–8, 11 Albertplatz

Dreikönigskirche
✉ Hauptstraße 23 ☎ 0351 8 12 41 02; www.hdk-dkk.de
🕐 Mon–Fri 9am–6pm, Sat 10am–6pm, Sun 11am–4pm

INSIDER INFO

■ There is a wonderful view over the surrounding Neustadt and panorama of Altstadt, complete with Frauenkirche, from the **observation platform** of the 45m (148ft) high tower of the Dreikönigskirche (An der Dreikönigskirche, entrance D, Mar–Oct closed Mon; Nov–Feb closed Mon and Tue, times vary).

■ Numerous events are held in the House of the Church/Dreikönigskirche and the **Kulturrathaus** (Königstr. 15) exhibitions, lectures, theatre, film.

㉒ Albertplatz

This is Neustadt's central square and all the most important streets in the district – one dozen in all – converge radially here.

The neo-Baroque **Villa Eschebach** on the east side was partially destroyed in the war and reconstructed after the reunification; today, it houses the Volksbank Raiffeisenbank. On the Königsbrücker Straße corner is the Artesian Fountain, with its circular temple by Hans Erlwein, which is fed with water from a 180-year-old well. Dresden's first high-rise building – a steel-frame construction erected in 1929 by Hermann Paulick – is in the process of being converted and expanded for office and commercial use.

Browsing in the Kästner Museum

The 🏠 **Erich Kästner Museum** in the Villa Augustin is dedi-

cated to the writer who was born not far away at Königsbrücker Straße 66 in 1899 – it has an interactive micro-museum and walk-in treasure chest with letters, photos and books in the drawers and showcases. There are two stately **fountains** – *Still Water* and *Stormy Waves* – in the centre of Albertplatz, both are by Robert Dietz.

TAKING A BREAK

Neustadt locals swear by the water from the tap on the house wall behind the Artesian Fountain – even though the sign says "not suitable for drinking".

➕ 196 C5
🚋 Tram 3, 6–8, 11 Albertplatz

Erich Kästner Museum
✉ Antonstraße 1
☎ 0351 8 04 50 86;
www.erich-kaestner-museum.de
🕐 Sun–Fri 10am–6pm, Thu only for groups
🖐 €4

INSIDER INFO

■ There are regular readings, lectures and various other **events** in the Erich Kästner Museum.

■ **Temporary exhibitions** are shown in the Villa Eschebach (Volksbank Raiffeisenbank) (Mon, Wed 8:30am–4pm, Tue, Thu 8:30am–6pm, Fri 8:30am–1pm).

At Your Leisure

⏳ Jägerhof · Museum für Sächsische Volkskunst, Puppentheatersammlung

In 1568, Prince Elector August started to establish a hunting ground on the property of an abandoned Augustine monastery. After parts of the complex were demolished in the 19th century, only the west wing with its beautiful Renaissance gable and three stair towers remained intact. Oskar Seyffert, the chairman of the Society for Saxon Folklore, rescued the oldest building in Neustadt for posterity by setting up the **Museum for Saxon Folk Art** in it in 1913. The museum has now been integrated into the State Art Collections Dresden and displays folk art from Saxony over three floors: peasant furniture, wickerwork and ceramics, blue-printed fabric from the Lausitz, lacework from Vogtland and traditional Sorb costumes, as well as wooden toys and Christmas decorations from the Erzgebirge. The 🎎 **Childrens' Path** is the place to play and learn things –

and here, in contrast to most other places, the children are responsible for their parents! Special Easter and Christmas exhibitions are held each year. Since 2005 the 🎎 **Puppet Theatre Collection**, in the Jägerhof, which developed out of a private collection, has exhibitions that are changed annually. This unique museum consist of more than 50,000 individual pieces: hand puppets and marionettes, theatre figures and stage settings from Germany, other European countries and Asia.

➕ 196 C3 ✉ Köpckestraße 1
☎ 0351 49 14 20 00; www.skd.museum
🕐 Tue–Sun 10am–6pm 🚊 Tram 3, 7, 8
Carolaplatz; 4, 8, 9 Neustädter Markt 💶 €3

⏳ Militärhistorisches Museum der Bundeswehr

The Military History Museum is in Albertstadt, north of Alaunplatz, which was once the largest barracks town in Germany. Housed in the former Saxon Army arsenal, it was radically revamped in the years up to 2011. A wedge-shaped new

The Museum for Saxon Folk Art and the Puppet Theatre Collection

structure with a steel and glass facade, designed by the star architect Daniel Libeskind, now cuts through the old building. Along with the chronological exhibition of military history, this new section forms the heart of the museum with thematic installations dealing with interdisciplinary matters such as "Suffering and War", "Politics and Violence", "Animals and the Military" and "Protection and Destruction". There are also enthralling special exhibitions.

🚩 191 D4 ✉ Olbrichtplatz 2

☎ 0351 8 23 28 03; www.mhmbw.de

🕐 Thu–Tue 10am–6pm, Mon 10am–9pm

🚋 Tram 7, 8; bus 64 Stauffenbergallee 🎫 €5

25 Kraszewski Museum

Józef Ignacy Kraszewski, one of the most important Polish intellectuals of the 19th century, was forced to leave Warsaw as an opponent of the Tsar's regime in 1863 and lived in exile in Dresden for 20 years. Among the books he wrote here were *The Countess Cosel*, *Brühl* and *From the Seven Years' War* that make up his *Saxon Trilogy*. They were opulently filmed by GDR television in the 1980s as *Saxony's Shine and Prussia's Glory*. The museum in the writer's summer home in the Prussian quarter is devoted to Kraszewski's life and work, as well as the relationship between Saxony and Poland. In addition to the permanent exhibition, temporary shows, readings, lectures and concerts are on the programme and the museum also has a library and reading café.

🚩 191 E3 ✉ Nordstraße 28

☎ 0351 8 04 44 50;

www.museen-dresden.de

🕐 Wed–Sun 1pm–6pm

🚋 Tram 13 Alaunplatz, 11 Nordstraße; bus 64 Marienallee

🎫 €4, Fri, free after midday (except on holidays)

Works by Józef Ignacy Kraszewski

26 Rosengarten

The city planners reverted to an old idea of August the Strong's to create a promenade on the banks of the Elbe when they decided to completely redesign the Königsufer from the Marienbrücke upstream as far as the Waldschlösschen from 1933–38. Roughly 3ha (7.5acre) large, the Rosengarten is parallel to the Elbe and was laid out in 1935–36 as part of the overall plan of the city planner, Paul Wolf. It is now possible to admire around 100 different varieties of roses – including strains from the 1930s and GDR days with names such as *Elbe Gold*, *Magnet* and *Rocket*, along with a great variety of other trees and shrubs. The most famous sculpture

Neustadt

in the complex is in the middle of the park: it is Felix Pfeifer's bronze *Genesung (Recovery)*. The Kaffee Rosengarten at the eastern end of the sunken garden is a good place to relax after your visit.

+ 191 D2 **✉** Carusufer
🚊 Tram 6, 13 Rosa-Luxemburg-Platz

27 Sächsische Staatskanzlei

The Saxon State Chancellery lies on the right bank of the Elbe between the Carola and Albert Bridges. The neo-Baroque building was constructed from 1900–04 by Edmund Waldow and Heinrich Tscharmann as the ministry of the Kingdom of Saxony. Today, the building with the golden crown on the top of the main tower, is the home of the State Chancellery and Saxon State Ministry for the Environment and Agriculture. A few metres further upstream, you will

A Potsdamer in Dresden: the Archer near the State Chancellery

be able to admire the figure of the ***Archer***, a second cast of the statue Ernst Moritz Geyger created for the Sanssouci Park in Potsdam in 1895.

+ 190 C2 **✉** Archivstraße 1
🚊 Tram 3, 7, 8 Carolaplatz

28 Finanzministerium

The Finance Ministry on the bank of the Elbe in Neustadt, opposite the Brühlsche Terrasse, was designed in the neo-Renaissance style by Semper's pupil Otto Wanckel and built from 1890–96. Anton Dietrich created the 50m² (538ft²) picture made of colourful majolica tiles in the gable in 1896. It shows Saxonia, dressed in the country's colours, surrounded by figures representing the income and expenditure of the state. Public exhibitions are held several times a year in the **atrium** (www.smf.sachsen.de).

The staircase below the ministry, which was installed in the 1930s, as part of the restructuring of the **Königsufer**, acts as a grandstand in summer for the **Film Nights on the Banks of the Elbe** (▶ 116). From here, there is a wonderful view of **Altstadt**, from the Neue Synagoge (▶ 86) in the east, to the Yenidze (▶ 22) in the west.

+ 196 C3 **✉** Carolaplatz 1/Königsufer
🚊 Tram 3, 7, 8 Carolaplatz

Where to...
Eat and Drink

Prices
Expect to pay per person for a main course without drinks.
€ less than €12   €€ €12–20   €€€ more than €20

Bautzner Tor €

One of the last pubs in
Neustadt that has managed
to stay – more or less – as it was.
This is the place to go for a very
late lunch or – later in the evening – or to try an *Elbhang Rot* or
Lenins Hanf, local beers produced
by Schwingenheuer Brewery, a
small private brewery.
🔒 191 D2 ✉ Hoyerswerdaer Straße 37
☎ 0351 8 03 82 02 🕐 Daily from 5pm
🚋 Tram 6, 11, 13 Bautzner/Rothenburger
Straße

Insider Tip

Blumenau €

This café-bar is great for break-
fasts, or a drink, and is popular
with night owls. Warm and wel-
coming décor makes it a favourite
with the Neustadt locals. The
latest scene gossip is spread or
the next party planned over a
matcha tea latte. In summer,
people sometimes sit outside on
the pavement.
🔒 191 D3 ✉ Louisenstraße 67
☎ 0351 8 02 65 02 🕐 Mon–Thu 8:30am–midnight,
Fri 8:30am–2am, Sat 9am–2am, Sun 9am–
midnight 🚋 Tram 13 Görlitzer Straße

Böhme €€

The restaurant is named after
Jakob Böhme (1575–1624), a
mystic from Görlitz. The interior
has an assortment of old tables
and chairs, which gives the place
a homely feel. The menu changes
every day and includes imaginative
variations of local fare.
🔒 191 D3 ✉ Sebnitzer Straße 11
☎ 0351 88 94 83 54 🕐 Daily from 6pm
🚋 Tram 13 Alaunplatz

Brauhaus am Waldschlösschen €

Pork knuckles, white sausages,
Leberkäs (a kind of meatloaf) and
potato soup – the menu offers a
hearty blend of Bavarian-Saxon
dishes. Waldschlösschen beer –
dark, pale ale, wheat beer and
naturally-cloudy – is on tap and
there is live piano music every evening. Shady beer garden with chestnut trees, and a view of Dresden.
🔒 191 F3 ✉ Am Brauhaus 8b
☎ 0351 6 52 39 00 🕐 Daily 11am–midnight,
beer garden from noon, weather dependent
🚋 Tram 11 Waldschlösschen

Insider Tip

Café Neustadt €

This café is on the edge of Äußere
Neustadt, right on the lively Bautzner
Straße and not far from Pfunds
Molkerei. In spite of that, there are
usually more locals than tourists
here – enjoying a lavish breakfast
(until 3pm), chatting with friends
over a coffee or having a relaxed
dinner.
🔒 191 D2 ✉ Bautzner Straße 03
☎ 0351 8 99 66 49 🕐 Mon–Fri 7:30am–11pm,
Sat 9am–11pm, Sun 9am–8pm 🚋 Tram 11
Pulsnitzer Straße

Canaletto €€€

Even though the trees in the idyllic
garden largely rule out the chance
of admiring the famous "Canaletto
view", this elegant restaurant, in the
old section of the Westin Bellevue
Hotel, is a place where you can
dine like royalty. Exquisite ambience, modern fusion cuisine and
in summer you can dine out on the
candlelit terrace.

Neustadt

➕ 196 B3 ✉ Große Meißner Straße 15
(Westin Bellevue Hotel)
☎ 0351 8 05 16 58 🕐 Daily from 6pm
🚋 Tram 4, 9 Neustädter Markt

Caroussel €€€
One of the best restaurants in the region. Benjamin Biedlingmaier, the youngest award-winning chef in Saxony, took command in 2013. His authentic French cuisine – served on Meissen porcelain – is light, in keeping with the times, and almost playful.
➕ 196 B4 ✉ Königstraße 14 ☎ 0351 8 00 30
🕐 Tue–Sat noon–2pm and from 6:30pm
🚋 Tram 4, 9 Palaisplatz; 3, 6–8, 11 Albertplatz

Die Pastamanufaktur € *Insider Tip*
In the shadow of the Dreikönigs-kirche, this restaurant serves fresh homemade pasta every day. Daily specials at reasonable prices and tasty desserts. Monday is *Käsespätzle* (cheese noodles) night and *Maultaschen* (Swabian ravioli) are on the menu on Saturday. You can have your after-dinner espresso in the Pastamanufaktur's café next door. There is also a branch in the Festspielhaus Hellerau.
➕ 196 B4 ✉ An der Dreikönigskirche 3
☎ 0351 3 23 77 99 🕐 Daily 10am–10pm
🚋 Tram 4, 8, 9 Neustädter Markt;
3, 6–8, 11 Albertplatz

Elbsegler €
Ship ahoy! The beer garden, with its wooden railings, masts and sails, lies on the Elbe bank below the Augustus Bridge and Hotel Bellevue. People like to come here for coffee and cake on Sunday afternoon or for hearty fare and Radeberger Pilsner in the evening. A view of Altstadt is thrown in for free.
➕ 196 B3 ✉ Große Meißner Straße 15
(Westin Bellevue Hotel) ☎ 0351 8 05 17 84
🕐 From Apr, daily from noon
🚋 Tram 4, 8, 9 Neustädter Markt

Fischhaus €€
With a history that dates back more than 400 years, this restaurant (it is not a fish restaurant!) on the edge of the Dresdner Heide, is one of the oldest in the city. Guests sit in the cosy rooms or lovely garden. The variety of dishes on the menu is really impressive and ranges from simple food for hikers, to seasonal specialities and excellent game. You should definitely try one of the fabulous desserts.
➕ 194 off B5 ✉ Fischhausstraße 14
☎ Mon–Fri 11:30am–midnight, Sat 11am–midnight, Sun 11am–11pm
🚋 Tram 11 Angelikastraße

Hierschönessen €€
Sophisticated, stylish ambience and a lovely garden. All of the food is freshly prepared using locally sourced ingredients – making the menu agreeably compact. A restaurant for people who really enjoy food.
➕ 191 D3 ✉ Görlitzer Straße 20
☎ 0351 25 65 28 98
🕐 Tue–Sat 6pm–11:30pm, Sun 6pm–10pm
🚋 Tram 13 Alaunplatz

L'Art de Vie €
No matter whether it's to catch your breath after a shopping spree or after a visit to the theatre – the Societaetstheater restaurant is a good choice at any time of the day. Enjoy the Mediterranean-inspired fare in the restaurant itself, or outside on the terrace. Brunch at the weekend.
➕ 196 C4 ✉ An der Dreikönigskirche 1a
☎ 0351 8 02 73 00 🕐 Mon–Fri 9am–midnight, Sat, Sun 10am–midnight
🚋 Tram 4, 9 Palaisplatz; 3, 6–8, 11 Albertplatz

Lila Soße €–€€
This restaurant in the Kunsthof-passage serves modern German cuisine: culinary creations such as braised cucumbers with goat's cheese or Matjes herring with beetroot. The outside seating in the Courtyard of Mythical Figures is extremely popular in summer.
➕ 191 D3 ✉ Alaunstraße 70
☎ 0351 8 03 67 23 🕐 Mon–Fri 2pm–11pm, Sat, Sun noon–11pm 🚋 Tram 13 Alaunplatz

Ocakbaşi €–€€

Opened in 2013, this was the first Turkish restaurant in Dresden that did not do *Döner* and fast food. Serving original Anatolian cuisine, Ocakbaşi is the Turkish word for the way the various kebabs, lamb chops and fish are prepared on a charcoal grill. Guests can watch the meals being prepared from behind a pane of glass.

🔡 191 E3 ✉ Prießnitzstraße 18 ☎ 0351 81 13 43 85 🕐 Mon–Thu 8am–11pm, Fri–Sun to midnight 🚋 Tram 7, 8 Louisenstraße

Oosteinde €

In the underground vaults of a former public bath, this pub is full of character and even has a room for smokers. On summer evenings guests sit outside in the beer garden next to the Priesnitz Stream and enjoy their jacket potatoes with wild garlic cream or risotto Genovese with a Lößnitz Pils.

🔡 191 E3 ✉ Prießnitzstraße 18 ☎ 0351 8 02 36 22 🕐 Mon–Sat from 5pm, Sun from 10am 🚋 Tram 11 Diakonissenkrankenhaus

Planwirtschaft €

This trendy café, which opened immediately after the fall of Communism, serves dishes made with fresh meat and vegetables sourced from local suppliers. In summer, you can still enjoy a glass of wine in the garden after midnight.

🔡 191 D3 ✉ Louisenstraße 20 ☎ 0351 8 01 31 87 🕐 Mon–Fri from 5pm, Sat from 11am, Sun 9am–5pm (buffet breakfast) 🚋 Tram 7, 8 Louisenstraße

Raskolnikoff €

Restaurant in one of Neustadt's oldest houses. There are daily specials along with the "Ras" classics such as borsch or *Käsespätzle* and there's brunch on Sundays. The smokers' bar opens at 7pm and the garden in the courtyard is charming.

🔡 191 D3 ✉ Böhmische Straße 34 ☎ 0351 8 04 57 06 🕐 Mon–Fri 10am–2am, Sat, Sun 9am–2am 🚋 Tram 6, 11, 13 Bautzner/Rothenburger Straße

Scheunecafé €

The trendy café in the Scheune cultural centre is one of the oldest of Dresden's pubs. The food is Indian and mango *lassi* and Radeberger stand next to each other in perfect harmony on the list of beverages. The weekend brunch in the beer garden in summer enjoys cult status with Neustadt locals.

🔡 191 D3 ✉ Alaunstraße 36–40 ☎ 0351 8 02 66 19 🕐 Mon–Fri from 4pm, Sat, Sun from 10am 🚋 Tram 3, 6–8, 11 Albertplatz

Villandry €€ *Insider Tip*

The Haufe brothers' motto is "love your food" and they celebrate with light, Mediterranean-style meals made using produce from farms in the region. The contemporary dishes are complemented by the art on the walls and the garden completes the culinary oasis.

🔡 191 D3 ✉ Jordanstraße 8 ☎ 0351 8 99 67 24 🕐 Mon–Sat from 6:30pm 🚋 Tram 7, 8 Louisenstraße

Watzke Am Goldenen Reiter €€

Branch of the Ball- und Brauhaus Watzke (Kötzschenbroder Straße 1) Patrons polish off delicious roast chicken accompanied by unfiltered Watzke beers. A faulty casting of the Johannes Bell, which was originally intended for the Frauenkirche, takes pride of place in the centre of the room.

🔡 196 C4 ✉ Hauptstraße 1 ☎ 0351 8 10 68 20 🕐 Daily 11am–midnight 🚋 Tram 4, 8, 9 Neustädter Markt

Wenzel Prager Bierstuben €€

Garlic soup, *Svíčková* (Bohemian beef in a cream sauce with cranberry jelly) and *Powidlknödel* (dumplings stuffed with plum jam) – this restaurant serves hearty, down-to-earth Bohemian-Czech dishes. And of course a meal would not be complete without the legendary Staropramen beer.

🔡 196 B4 ✉ Königstraße 1 ☎ 0351 8 04 20 10 🕐 Sun–Thu 11am–11pm Fri, Sat 11am–11pm 🚋 Tram 4, 9 Palaisplatz

Where to…
Shop

On your shopping tour through Innere and Äußere Neustadt, you will find elegant boutiques, quirky second-hand shops, galleries and antique dealers, shops selling arts and crafts, jewellery and all kinds of knick-knacks. The opening hours vary greatly.

ANTIQUES

Neustadt has numerous antique and second-hand shops. Start your treasure hunt at **Antiquitäten am Goldenen Reiter** (Hauptstr. 17/19), **Joachim Noack** (Königstr. 5), at **Rähnitzgasse 24** or **Kunst und Trödel** (Alaunstr. 70)

GALLERIES

More than half of the around 50 galleries in Dresden are in Neustadt (information in the quarterly exhibition guide or www.dresden.de under "Exhibition Calendar").

Galerie Finckenstein (Obergraben 8a) presents art from the 1920s and 1930s, **galerie baer** (Louisenstr. 72) focuses on 21st century artists.

Female artist show their works – painting, graphics, installations, sculpture and photography – in the **Galerie Drei – Dresdner Sezession 89** (Prießnitzstr. 43).

Galerie Gebr. Lehmann (Görlitzer Str. 16) is an international dealer with artists such as Eberhard Havekost and Frank Nitsche.

The **Kunstausstellung Kühl** (Nordstr. 5) has been showcasing contemporary art since 1924. New and hip: the **Galerie M2A** features works by young artists from eastern Germany (Königsbrücker Str. 70).

ÄUSSERE NEUSTADT

There is a great variety of shops in Äußere Neustadt – especially between Alaun- and Rothenburger Straße, Louisenstraße and Görlitzer Straße. **Lindegruen** (Alaunstr. 18) and **Peccato** (Rothenburger Str. 46) have trendy fashions. Those who prefer retro styles will find what they are looking for in the **ChicSaal** (Böhmische Str. 4) second-hand shop. **Calzador** provides its clients with high-quality footwear ranging from sporty to elegant (Rothenburger Str. 32). Skateboard fashion and gear is on offer at **Black Sheep** (Louisenstr. 8). The selection at **EXX** (Böhmische Str. 18) ranges from classic to elegant, from clothes for business to evening gowns. **Tendresse** (Rothenburger Str. 44) delights its customers with pretty accessories and romantic collections made of natural fabrics. The costume designer Jacqueline Peevski can provide you with the perfect hat at **Japée** (Bautzner Str. 6). ℍ Natural fashion for childen, and accessories such as soft animals, puppets and wooden toys, are the specialty of **LouisdoOr** (Louisenstr. 4). The **Keramikwerkstatt Katarina Gnauck** (Rothenburger Str. 38) produces ceramic goods marked with a small golden crown. The **art + form** (Bautzner Str. 11) gallery shop has artworks and an extensive range of knick-knacks that make good gifts. The **ZentralOhrgan** (Louisenstr. 22) is the oldest record shop still operating in Dresden. Mainly tourists shop at **Pfunds Molkerei** (Bautzner Str. 79) for cheese, wine, soap and gifts.

HAUPTSTRASSE

The reconstructed town houses at Hauptstraße 9–19 are also the site of the **Kunsthandwerker-Passagen** with artistan workshops: unique jewellery made out of exclusive materials is produced by in the **Goldschmiede-**

werkstatt Barbara Oehlke workshop. You will be able to watch a bag maker at work in the **Lederwerkstatt**, while **Gestaltetes Metall Wolfram Ehnert** is where artistic metal craftsmanship meets modern design. The **Fachgeschäft für Plauener Spitze** offers fine lacework from the Vogtland and the **Nostalgische Maßschneiderei Goldener Schnitt** tailors romantic robes.

KÖNIGSTRASSE

Dresden's exclusive shopping area is the quiet Königstraße (and its side streets) with fashion, jewellery and design boutiques and galleries well worth exploring. There are also some well-established shops such as **Gabriele Häfner** (An der Dreikönigskirche 10) and **Cornelia Minge** (Königstr. 3) – with elegant fashion from Strenesse to Jil Sander – as well as **Leliveld Shoes** (Königstr. 12). Second-hand clothes from Armani, Escada and others hang on the racks in **Second Season** (Rähnitzgasse 22). You will find unique pieces of jewellery in the **Atelier Hennig** (Königstr. 4), from the goldsmith **Shirley Hoffmann** (Königstr. 11) and at **P'lace** (Obergraben 10).

KUNSTHOFPASSAGE

The artistically designed courtyards between Alaunstraße and Görlitzer Straße are a must on trip through Neustadt. The Kunsthofpassage, with its charming little shops, is a great place for a shopping spree well away from the everyday hustle and bustle. Stationery and calligraphy accessories are for sale at **Blue Child** and **Mrs. Hippie** has quirky clothing. The two jewellery designers at **Ultramaringelb** work with silver, gold and other materials to create unique examples of their artistry. You can purchase home accessories, jewellery, minerals and soaps – and relax on oriental cushions and sip a cup of tea – in the **Feng Shui Haus.**

Where to...
Go Out

Neustadt is Dresden's most vibrant nightlife quarter. Some of its streets are lined with bars, restaurants and clubs. And, if you don't feel like partying, you can go to the theatre or the cinema.

THEATRE

In the past, the **Kleines Haus** (Glacisstraße 28, advance sales Mon–Fri 2pm–6:30pm, tel: 0351 4 91 35 55, www.staatsschauspiel-dresden.de) served as a pub, ballroom and church. Today it houses the experimental theatre of the Dresdner Staatsschauspiel. The first post-war performance of the Staatstheater Dresden was held here on 10 July 1945. There are theatre performances, cooperative activities with the Dresden University for Music and the Fine Arts, and all kinds of guest performances on offer. This is also the home of the **Bürgerbühne** (Citizens' Theatre) where Dresdeners of any age conquer the boards as amateur thespians.

The **Societaetstheater** (An der Dreikönigskirche 1a, tel: 0351 8 03 68 10, www.societaetstheater.de) opened in 1779 as the first German theatre run by a civic club. Today it has two regular stages, and one in the garden in summer, that provide the venue for contemporary plays.

The **projekttheater** (Louisenstr. 47, tel: 0351 8 10 76 00, www.projekt theater.de) is an experimental theatre for guest performances by independent theatre groups. In the **Carte Blanche** (Prießnitzstr. 10, tel: 0351 20 47 20, www.carte-blanche-dresden.de) there are revues and drag shows and if you feel like a laugh you can go downstairs in the

Neustadt

Kügelgenhaus where the Dresdner Comedy & Theater Club has opened its – still relatively new – venue in the cellar (Hauptstr. 13, tel: 0351 4 64 48 77).

CLUBS AND DISCOS

The **Scheune** cultural centre (Alaunstraße 36/40, tel: 0351 32 35 56 40, www.scheune.org), in the heart of Äußere Neustadt, is the home of rock, hip-hop, electronica and poetry. In summer, it also hosts the two-week Schaubudensommer festival. Next door is **Katy's Garage** *Insider Tip* (Alaunstr. 48, tel: 0351 6 56 77 01, www.katysgarage.de) with theme evenings such as Rock Friday, Neustadt Disco and Wednesday "older evening" for those over 25. Beer garden in summer.

Concerts – usually, jazz, funk or soul – are held almost every evening in the **Blue Note** (Görlitzer Str. 2b, tel: 0351 8 01 42 75, www.bluenote-dresden.de). The first Thursday in the month is open mic night.

Disco beats pound in the **Downtown** (Katharinenstr. 11–13, tel: 0351 8 11 55 92, www.downtown-dresden.de) on Friday and Saturday. One floor higher up, the **Groove Station** (Katharinenstraße 11–13, tel: 0351 8 02 95 94, www.groovestation.de) has rock 'n' roll evenings and parties.

The **Jazzclub Tonne** in the cellar vaults of the Kulturrathaus (Königstraße 15, tel: 0351 8 02 60 17, www.jazzclubtonne.de) showcases contemporary jazz.

Every weekend a whole row of clubs of all kinds attracts thousands to **Strasse E** (Industriegelände/Werner-Hartmann-Straße, www.strasse-e.de) in a former industrial complex north of Äußere Neustadt. House, reggae, dark wave, rock and disco can be experienced right next to each other in the **Reithalle**, **Spinnerei** and **Bunker**.

BARS

First-class cocktails are served in **Frank's Bar** (Alaunstr. 80, tel: 0351 65 88 83 80, daily from 7pm, franksbar.de). The boss, Frank Ulbrich, is a real master of his trade and in addition to all the classics, there are also many new prize-winning creations on offer.

The gay community gathers in the **Boys Bar** next door for the various weekly special events and theme evenings (Alaunstr. 80, tel: 0351 5 63 36 30, www.boys-dresden.de, Fri, Sat 8pm–5am, to 3am on other days). With its comfortable leather couches, American diner-style and opening hours until the early morning, the **SideDoor** (Böhmische Str. 38, tel: 0179 6 85 64 40, www.sidedoor-dresden.de, daily from 8pm till late) has found a huge following in Dresden. The **Pinta** (Louisenstraße 49, tel: 0351 8 10 67 61, pinta-cocktails.de, daily from 7pm) has also entered the race with a touch of Caribbean flair, dim lighting and an endless list of drinks.

CINEMAS

The **Schauburg** (Königsbrücker Straße 55, tel: 0351 8 03 21 85, www.schauburg-dresden.de) is Dresden's oldest and most popular cinema: three screens with sophisticated cinematic fare. "Cinema, Coffee and Cigarettes" is the motto of the **Thalia** art-house cinema (with bistro, Görlitzer Str. 6, tel: 0351 6 52 47 03, www.thalia-dresden.de).

The **Filmnächte am Elbufer** (Film Nights on the Banks of the Elbe, Königsufer, tel: 0351 89 93 20, dresden.filmnaechte.de) are held on the Königsufer in July and August: this is where you will be able to experience blockbusters and audience favourites, as well as concerts by top international stars in front of the breathtaking backdrop of Dresden Altstadt.

City Centre to Großer Garten

 **Little Treats**

Through the Park on Two Wheels

It's great fun to glide along the avenues of the **Großer Garten** on a Segway (► 122; e.g. www.seg-tour-dresden.de).

Through the Park on a Miniature Train

Or you can take a ride on the 5.6km (3.5mi) long **rail circuit** (► 124). Fun for adults too.

An Evening at the Met…

…or maybe the Moscow Bolshoi? You can do this without buying a plane ticket in the Rundkino or **UFA Kristallpalast** cinema (► 136).

Getting Your Bearings

There is a Dresden away from the tourist crowds, to experience it all you need to do is venture away from the magical "Zwinger – Semperoper – Frauenkirche" triangle. The new, post-war Dresden developed out of a wasteland of rubble; it has its centre immediately to the south of the historic Altstadt.

There were only ruins between Wilsdruffer Straße and Hauptbahnhof in 1945 and, a few years later, even they were gone. A large-scale clearing programme turned what was once the lively city centre into several square kilometres of meadow. Only four buildings – the Kreuzkirche, town hall, Gewandhaus and a bank – remained standing. Change began in 1953, first the Altmarkt and the neighbouring quarters were "reinvented", followed by Prager Straße in the 1960s and 1970s. Although these new buildings cannot take

Prager Straße from the Borowski Restaurant terrace

Rollerbladers on the Palaisteich in the Großer Garten

the place of old Dresden they are still fine examples of city planning of the period and have since become part of Dresden's urban identity.

Today, Dresden's centre is characterised by the hustle and bustle of a large modern city with shopping centres and department stores, cafés and restaurants, cinemas and theatres. The largest park in the city – the Großer Garten – adjoins to the east. After sightseeing and shopping, the park is an ideal place to catch your breath.

TOP 10
⭐ Großer Garten ➤ 122

Don't Miss
㉙ Altmarkt ➤ 126
㉚ Prager Straße ➤ 130
㉛ Deutsches Hygiene-Museum ➤ 132

At Your Leisure
㉜ Bürgerwiese & Blüherpark ➤ 133
㉝ Georg-Arnold-Bad ➤ 133

The Perfect Day

Visit modern Dresden: there may not be many historic buildings but there is a wonderful park and several good shopping possibilities. The following route will help you make sure that you don't miss any of the highlights. The individual sights are described in more detail on pages (➤ 122–136).

🕘 9:00

Start with a stroll across the **㉙Altmarkt** (above; ➤ 126). There is always already plenty of activity here at this time of the morning on market days. On other days, you can go browsing at the Altmarkt Galerie, which opens its doors at 9:30am.

🕥 10:30

If you don't feel up to the stress of spending money so early in the morning, you can treat yourself to a few minutes of peace in the Kreuzkirche (➤ 127). The tower's observation platform also offers a wonderful view over the city centre. Stroll through the narrow streets between the Altmarkt and Pirnaischer Platz and go to the **Rauschenbach Deli** for a "quickie" – in Dresden, that's a butter croissant and a coffee. Go past the Gewandhaus (now a hotel) and around the town hall and you arrive at Prager Straße.

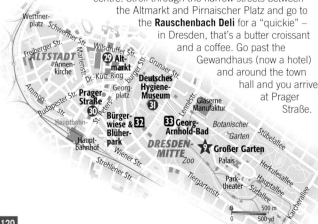

🕚 11:30

Some aesthetes might turn up their noses at the prefabricated buildings from GDR days on ㉚ **Prager Straße** (► 130) and quite a few Dresdeners do the same. No matter: those in the know appreciate them, and not just as a place to shop or stroll. At lunchtime you can have a snack in one of the fast food restaurants in the Centrum Galerie.

🕧 12:30

Past the Rundkino, which is hidden behind some post-reunification buildings, you will find yourself in front of the Kristallpalast. The avant-garde building housing this cinema is very controversial but it has also been awarded many prizes. Go across St Petersburger Straße and then through the ㉜ **Bürgerwiese & Blüherpark** (► 133).

🕐 1:00

Pay a visit to the transparent men in the ㉛ **Deutsches Hygiene-Museum** (right; ► 132). And, in addition to the permanent exhibition Human Adventure, take a look at the – usually fascinating – temporary exhibits. The **Lingner Café-Restaurant** is another option for lunch.

🕒 3:00

Do you have your swimming costume with you? Then it's off to the pool at the ㉝ **Georg-Arnold-Bad** (► 133). Another way to spend the afternoon – but only on Friday – is to stroll across the Sachsenmarkt, a weekly market with mainly regional products, on Lingnerallee. And then you will see the

DIE GLÄSERNE MANUFAKTUR

⭐ **Großer Garten** (► 122) in front of you. Depending on your interests, take a tour of the Gläserne Manufaktur (left; ► 24) (best to book in advance), stroll through the zoo or botanical garden, go for a ride on the park railway or just relax on one of the benches and take in the greenery.

🕖 7:00

Stop for refreshments at the **Carolaschlösschen** (► 134) and wait there until the fountain in the Carolasee lights up.

⭐9 Großer Garten

Just 1km (0.6mi) to the east of the Frauenkirche is Dresden's largest and most beautiful park. The Großer Garten (Great Garden) is a popular recreation area with straight avenues and winding paths, sculptures and ponds, open-air stages and garden restaurants, botanical garden, zoo and railway. And even a factory.

In 1676, Prince Elector Johann Georg III commissioned a garden for pleasure and hunting, in the French Baroque style, to be created outside of the city's gates. It experienced a chequered history over the centuries – from large expansions to being devastated in war on several occasions. The approximately 2km² (.7mi²) large park has Lennés pupil Friedrich Bouché to thank for the way it looks today. His designs transformed large sections of the park into an English landscaped garden from 1873 onwards.

Palais in the Großer Garten with the *Time abducts Beauty* statue

The **Palais Großer Garten** is at the intersection of the Haupt- and Queralle. It was built from 1678–83 as Saxony's

GROSSER GARTEN AS A THEATRE OF WAR

The bombing of Dresden in February 1945 was not the first time that the Großer Garten was destroyed by war. The Prussians plundered the park in the Seven Years' War and in August 1813 the park once again became a theatre of war when Napoleon had his last victory over the Russian, Austrian and Prussian forces in the Battle of Dresden. A few months later, Prince Repnin-Wolkonski, the Russian Governor General of occupied Saxony, ordered that the Großer Garten be rehabilitated and opened to the people of Dresden.

Full steam ahead through the Großer Garten

first Baroque palace and was designed by Johann Georg Starcke. The ground floor houses a collection of original Saxon Baroque sculptures that can be seen on a guided tour or when concerts and other events are being held. Only five of the original eight **Kavaliershäuser** from 1794 survived World War II. A pond was added on the east side of the palace in 1715. Not far away from it is the **Parktheater**, which was erected in 1719 for the celebrations of the marriage between Friedrich August II and Maria Josepha, the daughter of the Austrian Emperor. It is occasionally used for theatre performances and concerts in summer. The **Junge Garde open-air stage**, which was built in 1955, is mainly used for rock, Dixieland and comedy performances and the **Sonnenhäusel Puppet Theatre** is located to the north of Herkulesallee.

The Carolasee (Carola Lake) was created out of a former gravel pit in 1881. Today, you can watch people enjoying themselves rowing from the Carolaschlösschen Restaurant (► 134) beer garden. Poelzig's Expressionism-inspired **mosaic fountain** was set up near the Torwirtschaft Restaurant (► 135) in 1926.

On a guided tour for the "Friends of Dresden Zoo"

City Centre to Großer Garten

Flora, Fauna and a Railway

The **Botanical Garden of the Technical University of Dresden**, which was established here in 1893, now has Volkswagen's Gläserne Manufaktur as its neighbour. Around 10,000 different varieties of plants, from different climate zones and regions of the world, are on display outdoors or in glasshouses in the 12ha (32 acre) garden grounds.

The **Dresden Zoo,** founded in 1861, is the fourth-oldest in Germany. It is especially famous for its orang-utan breeding programme. Many improvements have been made over the past decade including a savannah for lions and caracals, a giraffe and zebra complex, as well as the Prof. Brandes-Haus for animals from tropical regions where koalas also have their new home. The Africa House is currently being renovated to satisfy the newest standards for keeping animals in a zoo.

The **Dresdner Park Eisenbahn railway** (known as the Pioneer Railway from 1951–1991) has a gauge of 381mm (15 inches) and covers a 5.6km (3.5mi) route through the park. The miniature steam trains, which were built in 1925 and huff and puff through the Großer Garten at 30kph (18mph), are very popular. The round trip takes half an hour and you can get on and off at five stops. The staff is made up of children – with the exception of the engine drivers!

> ### 🎪 FUN IN THE PARK
> A trip on the park railway and a visit to the petting zoo are absolute musts. The zoo's Punch welcomes children on the puppet stage from Easter to October. In addition, the **Sonnenhäusel Puppet Theatre** gives regular performances in the summer months.

Gläserne Manufaktur

The steel and glass building, designed by Gunter Henn, was built in 2001 on the former exhibition grounds at the northwest corner of the Großer Garten. Volkswagen has its luxury sedan, the *Phaeton,* assembled in this **transparent factory** – work becomes something of an event. Visitors taking part in a guided tour will get to see all of the production areas and get a closer look at – and even sit in – the exclusive vehicles in the VW Lounge. The Kugelhaus, a spherical building, is a tribute to the world's first spherical house by Peter Birkenholz that was erected here for the 1928 "Technical City" exhibition which was torn down by the National Socialists in 1938. Those who buy cars here are treated like VIPs in the exclusive clients' lounge.

You can even take a little boat trip on the Carolasee

Großer Garten

VW's luxury sedan, the *Phaeton*, is assembled in the Gläsernen Manufaktur

TAKING A BREAK

A park bench and an ice cream, a picnic under a shady tree – what more could you want? Perhaps a coffee and cake on the terrace of the **Carolaschlösschen** Restaurant?

➕ 193 D/E 2/3

Botanischer Garten (Botanical Garden)
➕ 193 D3 ✉ Stübelallee 2 ☎ 0351 4 59 31 85; http://tu-dresden.de/bot-garten
🕐 Apr–Sep daily 8am–6pm, Mar, Oct 10am–5pm, Feb, Nov 10am–4pm, Jan, Dec 10am–3:30pm; glasshouses year-round from 10am
🚃 Tram 1, 2, 4, 10, 12, 13 Straßburger Platz 💶 Free

Gläserne Manufaktur (Transparent Factory)
➕ 193 D3 ✉ Lennéstraße 1 ☎ 0351 4 20 44 11; www.glaesernemanufaktur.de
🕐 Mon–Fri 8:30am–7pm, Sat, Sun 9am–6pm, 75-minute tours, on the hour (bookings advisable) 🚃 Tram 1, 2, 4, 10, 12, 13 Straßburger Platz 💶 €7

Parkeisenbahn (Park Railway)
➕ 193 D3 ✉ 5 Stops include Straßburger Platz ☎ 0351 4 45 67 95; www.parkeisenbahn-dresden.de 🕐 Mid-Apr–Oct usually Tue–Sun 10am–6pm, Jul, Aug, also Mon, shorter in Oct; special trips on Museum Night, St Nicholas Day and on other occasions 🚃 Tram 1, 2, 4, 10, 12, 13 Straßburger Platz 💶 €1–5

Zoo Dresden
➕ 193 D2/3 ✉ Tiergartenstraße 1 ☎ 0351 47 80 60; www.zoo-dresden.de
🕐 Apr–Oct daily 8:30am–6:30pm, spring/autumn to 5:30pm, winter to 4:30pm
🚃 Tram 9, 13; bus 75 Zoo 💶 €12

INSIDER INFO

■ See the whole car production process on a tour through VW's transparent factory. There are also special architecture tours and 👨‍👧 **tours for children**. Reservations are recommended. During opening hours, there is free admission to the Visitors' Centre piazza and the Orangery exhibition area. Guests who have brunch in the Restaurant Lesage (➤ 134) have a tour of the plant included in the price.

■ A visit to the botanical garden is free.

■ After Duisburg, the Dresden Zoo is only the second German zoo to keep koala bears (since 2013). If you want to see the cute – but, usually rather drowsy – marsupials in action, you should be at their enclosure at around 10:30am when they are fed fresh eucalyptus leaves.

㉙ Altmarkt

The Altmarkt is the centre of the city and its oldest square; records date it back to 1370. It was the venue of court festivities and civil revolutions, famous people such as Heinrich von Kleist and Carl Maria von Weber lived here and the Striezelmarkt has been held on the square since 1434.

The square already had shops and cafés in the 19th and early 20th centuries, such as the Löwenapotheke pharmacy, the Renner department store (with the Dresden's first escalator) and the **Konditorei Kreutzkamm** (▶ 136), which was founded in 1825. The Altmarkt's darkest hour was in 1945. The bombs that fell on 13 February reduced all of the buildings in its vicinity to ash and rubble. In the following days, the bodies of many victims of the attacks were brought to the square and cremated there.

The area of the square was more than doubled when it was rebuilt after 1953. Seven-storey residential and commercial buildings with prestigious shops were erected on the west and east sides. Dresden managed to avoid the Soviet-style monumental buildings that were common in other East German cities at the time. In contrast to the prevailing concept of building, attempts were even made to adapt some of the stylistic elements from 17th century Dresden – this soon led to the practice being described as "Socialist Baroque". Many new shops have moved into the

View of the Kreuzkirche and Altmarkt from the Rathaus tower

area around the Altmarkt in recent years. The **Altmarkt Galerie** between the Altmarkt and Wallstraße was opened in 2002 and doubled in size when it was expanded in 2011. It now has about 200 shops, restaurants and cafés and is Dresden's largest and most popular shopping centre. In addition to the Striezelmarkt (▶ 36), the Altmarkt (with an underground car park since 2008) is also where the autumn and spring markets are held.

Culture for the People

The first plans for a "House of Socialist Culture" on the north side of the Altmarkt

The Altmarkt-Galerie offers you plenty of scope for a shopping spree

originally showed a multi-storey tower in the gingerbread style of the Stalinist era. However, 15 years later, a building in a more modern international style, with a glass façade and copper roof, was built. Since its inauguration in 1969, the **Kulturpalast,** with a main hall with seating for almost 2,500 people, studio theatre and various salons, has been the venue for congresses, balls and concerts. It was also the home of the Dresden Philharmonic and the place where the Dresden Music Festival and Dixieland Festival took place. The façade on Schlossstraße is adorned with Gerhard Bondzin's painting *The Path of the Red Banner*. Since 2013 the Kulturpalast has been undergoing work to convert it into a multifunctional building with a concert hall for the Dresden Philharmonic. The plan includes preserving the external appearance as much as possible. The reopening is planned for 2017.

Kreuzkirche

The church, which was built in the 12th century, has been Dresden's main Evangelical church since the first Lutheran service was held in it in 1539. It was destroyed by fire and suffered war damage many times in its 800-year history but was always rebuilt. The Prussians have the Renaissance tower, which is well known from Canaletto's paintings, on their conscience: it was damaged when it came under fire from Friedrich II's troops and collapsed in 1765. The church's nave was destroyed by fire in 1897 and it was gutted once again during the bombing on 13 February 1945. The renovated church was consecrated in 1955 and given a new organ, made by the Dresden Jehmlich Company, in 1963. The simple interior design we see today was originally a provisional

City Centre to Großer Garten

arrangement but proved to be a suitable permanent solution. The altar painting *Crucifixion* was created by Anton Dietrich in 1900, the *Cross of Nails* in the Schütz Chapel is a token of reconciliation presented by Coventry Cathedral in 1986. If you climb up to the **observation platform** of the church tower, you will pass the second-largest (after the Cologne Cathedral) church bells in Germany. A memorial plaque next to the main portal honours the city's Jews who were murdered by the National Socialists; in front of the church is a monument to Julius Otto (1828–75) who was the Kreuzkirche cantor and the *Swords to Ploughshares* sculpture on the south side pays homage to the peace movement.

Civic Pride

The **Rathaus** town hall to the east of the church is currently being renovated. An entire block of town houses and a Baroque church had to make way when it was built in the early in 20th century. In 1910, the new town hall, designed by Karl Roth and Edmund Bräter, replaced the old one in Altmarkt, which had become too small. Destroyed in the war, it was rebuilt on a smaller scale. The town hall's tower

The Art Nouveau painting in the Rathaus staircase is the work of Otto Gussmann

Kreuzkirche and Rathaus tower

(with an observation platform that will, unfortunately, be closed until 2016) rises up almost 100m (328ft) above the building and its six courtyards. On the top of the tower is the **Goldener Rathausmann**, a 5m (16ft) high – recently gilded – statue of Hercules holding a cornucopia over the city. The golden gate is guarded by two lions and in front of it is a monument to the women who cleared Dresden of rubble after the war, the so-called **Dresdner Trümmerfrau**.

In recent years, several new restaurants have opened their doors in the quarter between Altmarkt and Pirnaischer Platz. Robert Diez created the **Gänsediebbrunnen** fountain on Weiße Gasse in 1878. The **Gewandhaus,** which was built in 1768–70, was once the domicile of the butchers and cloth merchants and has now been converted into a hotel. The **Dinglinger-Brunnen** was installed behind the late-Baroque-Classicist building when it was rebuilt after the war.

TAKING A BREAK

There is a selection of fast foods in the basement of the Altmarkt Galerie – burgers, tapas, *bami goreng* and freshly pressed fruit juices – while the 🍴 **Laden Café aha** (➤ 134) on Kreuzstraße is ideal for families with children.

➕ 196 B1 🚊 Tram 1, 2, 4 Altmarkt, 8, 9, 11, 12; bus 62 Prager Straße

Kreuzkirche
🕐 Mon–Fri 10am–6pm, Sat 10am–3pm, Sun noon–6pm, Nov, Jan, Feb shorter, last ascent of the tower 30 minutes before closing 💶 Tower €3

INSIDER INFO

On your way from Altmarkt to Prager Straße, you will pass a stairway to the underworld at the Dr.-Külz-Ring/Seestraße crossing. The Berlin artist Franka Hörnschemeyer designed the controversial **Trichter** (funnel) installation. Stairs lead from street level down to a thick pane of glass that offers an unusual view into Dresden's sewerage system. The media soon dubbed it the "toilet cinema".

Insider Tip

㉚ Prager Straße

The "Prager" was once Dresden's most famous shopping and entertainment hub but it was almost completely destroyed in World War II and then rebuilt twenty years later as a "Socialist pedestrian boulevard".

The inauguration of the Saxon-Bohemian railway line in 1851 made a connection between the old Bohemian station (the current main station) and the historic Altstadt a top priority. As a result, starting in the middle of the 19th century, a densely populated quarter developed with Prager Straße as the central axis. Today, venerable Dresdeners still recall the boulevard's numerous pastry shops, its elegant boutiques and large cinemas; they have fond memories of elaborately decorated Gründerzeit facades, of the Victoriahaus and Residenz department store.

The firestorm on 13 February 1945 destroyed all of that old glory. In hindsight, many of the buildings could have been saved but the limited financial resources of the post-war years and the ideologically driven desire for liberation from the ballast of the past led to their complete demolition.

ARRIVE IN STYLE

The **Hauptbahnhof** main station at the southern end of Prager Straße was inaugurated in 1898. It was given a modern facelift by the prominent British architect Sir Norman Foster – this included a new dome for the entrance, as well as a transparent roof made with Teflon-coated fibreglass membranes.

New Objectivity

In 1965 the new Prager Straße started emerging as a composition of hotels, pavilions with shops and restaurants, a 240m (787ft) long row of housing, a department store and a cinema. Although it does not replace the old

The *Friendship between Nations* sculpture on Prager Straße

Prager Straße

"Prager", the new street is now regarded as an outstanding example of GDR post-war modernism.

New office and commercial buildings have gone up at the ends of the street in recent years. At the northern end are mainly department stores and the **Centrum Galerie,** a shopping mall with a variety of shops and restaurants, which replaced the old Centrum department. The southern

Futuristic building: the UFA-Kino Kristallpalast

end now has the Prager Spitz and a small shopping centre, designed to be reminiscent of the Dresdner Kugelhaus (spherical house) of 1928.

The exemplary open spaces – with trees, green spaces and fountains placed along the course of the street – fell victim to a revamp in 2004. The popular **Pusteblumenbrunnen** (Dandelion Fountain) created by the sculptress Leonie Wirth was rearranged and Wolf-Eike Kuntsche's metal sculpture *Völkerfreundschaft (Friendship between Nations),* which was removed in 1994, was installed once again.

Round or Angular

The most striking building is the Filmtheater Prager Straße, which is popularly referred to as the **Rundkino**, was built in 1970–72 as a two-screen cinema – one of them with more than 1,000 seats. This is the home of the **Cineplex-Kino** a cinema for 2- and 3-D films and the **Dresden Puppet Theatre.** The **Kristallpalast**, designed by the Viennese firm of architects, CoopHimmelB(l)au, was built behind the block of flats on the east side and opened in 1998. The angular architecture of the Multiplex cinema divided public opinion.

TAKING A BREAK

From the **Borowski Restaurant** (➤ 134) terrace you can watch the hustle and bustle going on down below or you can have a snack on the Prager – almost everything – from *Dönor* to bratwurst – is available here.

✚ 192 B3

🚆 Tram 8, 9, 11, 12; bus 62 Prager Straße; bus 3, 7–9, 11, Walpurgisstraße and Hbf-Nord; S-Bahn, tram 3, 7, 8, 10; bus 66 Hauptbahnhof

INSIDER INFO

The 👥 **Dresden Puppet Theatre** (reservations: tel: 0351 4 96 53 70, Visitors' Service: tel: 0351 4 29 12 20, www.tjg-dresden.de) gives performances for children and adults in the Rundkino's former studio theatre.

③① Deutsches Hygiene-Museum

The name provokes visitors to ask questions, and the staff to try and give imaginative answers. Maybe that is the reason why this is one of Dresden's most fascinating exhibitions.

Since its overhaul in 1991, the museum presents itself as a **universal museum of mankind.** It was founded in 1912 on the initiative of the Dresden-based Odol mouthwash manufacturer Karl August Lingner. The goal at that time was to educate the public. In 1930, the museum building was a melange of monumental and Bauhaus styles; it was then severely damaged in the air attack on Dresden in 1945, rebuilt after the war and extensively renovated again in 2001. The new permanent exhibition, **Human Adventure**, has seven main themes about the human race and health. They include exhibits on sexuality, memory, and death. Special exhibitions – quite often with controversial questions about life – complete the profile. There are numerous activities for people with disabilities.

Informative insights in the German Hygiene Museum

TAKING A BREAK
The **Café-Restaurant Lingner** (➤ 135) serves fresh food; in summer you can sit outside on the terrace with a view of the greenery.

➕ 192 C4 ✉ Lingnerplatz 1
☎ 0351 4 84 64 00; www.dhmd.de
🕔 Tue–Sun 10am–6pm 🚋 Tram 10, 13 Großer Garten; 1, 2, 4, 12 Dt. Hygiene-Museum
🎟 €7, Fri free after 3pm

🚸 FOR YOUNG EXPLORERS
■ The **Kindermuseum** takes 4 to 12 year old children on interactive courses where they can learn a lot about their five senses – with a hall of mirrors, a dark room, smelling boxes and other activities.
■ The **Transparent Man**, which was first exhibited in 1930, is a see-through model that shows the skeleton, blood vessels, nerves and organs of the human being.

INSIDER INFO

The **tickets** are valid for two consecutive days.

At Your Leisure

The monument to Mozart on the Bürgerwiese

32 Bürgerwiese & Blüherpark

Since 1945 these two areas have been in a kind of no man's land between the city centre and Großer Garten. The Bürgerwiese was laid out as a city park in 1838 and was later redesigned by Peter Josef Lenné and others. Hermann Hosaeus' monument to Mozart – three women dancing – from 1907 was destroyed in 1945 and restored in 1991. To the east the Bürgerwiese joins up with the Blüherpark. Its southern section, bordering on the Hygiene Museum, was redesigned in 2005, including the remains of the Sekundogenitor Palace that was destroyed in 1945. The neighbouring **glücksgas stadium** is the home of the traditional football club SG Dynamo Dresden.

➕ 192 C3
🚊 Tram 9, 10, 11, 13; bus 62, 75 Lennéplatz; tram 8, 9, 11, 12; bus 75, 82 Prager Straße; tram 10, 13 Großer Garten

33 🏊 Georg-Arnhold-Bad

These public swimming pools were opened in 1926 and named after their donor, the Jewish banker Georg Arnold. The complex includes an indoor swimming pool with outdoor facilities, four-seasons pool with jet stream canal, whirlpool and an 86m (282ft) slide. If you don't have your swimming costume with you, you can relax at Willy Vanillis Softeis-Milchbar near the entrance: delicious soft serve ice cream made in original GDR machines using ingredients from the time-honoured Anona and Komet firms (in the bathing season daily 11am–8pm).

➕ 192 C3 ✉ Helmut-Schön-Allee 2
☎ 0351 4 94 22 03
🕐 Outdoor pool May–mid-Sep daily 9am–10pm, early morning swims in the outdoor pool Mon–Fri 6am–8am, indoor pool, various opening times
🚊 Tram 10, 13 Großer Garten
💶 From €5

Where to…
Eat and Drink

Prices
Expect to pay per person for a main course without drinks.
€ less than €12   €€ €12–20   €€€ more than €20

Altmarkt-Galerie €–€€
Shopping gives you an appetite and happily there are numerous fast food eateries in the mall: burgers, pizzas, tapas, Asian soups, hot dogs, sushi and more.
✚ 192 B4 ✉ Webergasse 1
◉ Mon–Sat 9:30am–9pm
🚋 Tram 1, 2, 4 Altmarkt; tram 8, 9, 11, 12; bus 62, 75 Prager Straße

Barococo €€
The restaurant is on the first floor with views of Altmarkt; it is affiliated to the Hein Mück fish dealers and naturally serves all sorts of good things from the lakes and seas, as well as meat and vegetarian dishes. In the café on the ground floor smoking is permitted after midday.
✚ 192 B4 ✉ Altmarkt 10
☎ 0351 8 62 30 40 ◉ Daily from 9am
🚋 Tram 1, 2, 4 Altmarkt; tram 8, 9, 11, 12; bus 62 Prager Straße

Borowski €
The Borowski is on the first floor of the Wöhrl Plaza complex and it is a great place to sit and watch the Prager Straße activity while you enjoy a meal, coffee or a cocktail. In summer, the seating area on the terrace is very popular – guests sitting there hover above Dresden's traditional shopping strip.
✚ 192 B3 ✉ Prager Straße 8a
☎ 0351 4 90 64 11 ◉ Sun–Thu 9am–midnight, Fri, Sat 9am–1am 🚋 Tram 8, 9, 11, 12; bus 62, Prager Straße; tram 3, 7–9, 11 Walpurgisstraße

Carolaschlösschen €–€€
This popular park restaurant has been open since 1895. Choose between the Grand Café and the Galerie-Restaurant on the upper floor. Of course, the most beautiful place to sit is on the lakeside terrace (balcony or beer garden under the trees).
✚ 193 E2 ✉ Großer Garten (off Tiergarten-/Oskarstraße) ☎ 0351 2 50 60 00
◉ Mon–Fri from 11am, Sat, Sun from 10am
🚋 Tram 9, 13; bus 75 Querallee; bus 61, 63, 75, 85 Strehlen

Kreutzkamm €
In 1825, 25-year-old Jeremias Kreutzkamm opened a pastry shop that was to become a real Dresden institution. The main house on Altmarkt was destroyed in World War II and Kreutzkamm moved to Munich but a café was opened once again in Dresden in the 1990s. It has had its home in the Altmarktgalerie since 2011.
✚ 192 B4 ✉ Altmarkt 25 ☎ 0351 4 95 41 72
◉ Mon–Sat 9:30am–9pm, Sun noon–6pm
🚋 Tram 1, 2, 4 Altmarkt

Laden Café aha €–€€ *Insider Tip*
Eat healthy food and have a clean conscience. This café serves mainly wholefoods, vegetarian and organic dishes. The coffee is Fair Trade and there is a children's play corner as well as a children's menu. There is a one-world shop on the lower floor.
✚ 192 B4 ✉ Kreuzstraße 7
☎ 0351 4 96 06 73 ◉ Daily 9am–midnight
🚋 Tram 1, 2, 4 Altmarkt

Lesage €€–€€€
The restaurant, bistro and bar in the Gläsernen Manufaktur are affiliated with the Dresden Kempinski-

Hotel Taschenbergpalais and the menu is correspondingly upmarket. Sunday brunch includes a tour of the factory. Weekdays from noon–3pm two-course set lunch for €17.

⊞ 193 D3 ⊠ Lennéstraße 1
☎ 0351 4 20 42 50 🕓 Restaurant: Mon noon–3pm, Tue–Sat noon–3pm, 6pm–10pm, Sun 11am–3pm (brunch), bistro/bar: Sun, Mon 10am–6pm, Tue–Sat 9am–10pm
🚊 Tram 1, 2, 4, 10, 12, 13 Straßburger Platz

Lingner €–€€

This is a successful balancing act between a museum café and smart restaurant. It is named after Karl August Lingner, the manufacturer of Odol mouthwash and founder of the German Hygiene Museum and is done out in the timeless style of the 1930s when the museum was opened; the kitchen uses regional ingredients.

⊞ 192 C3 ⊠ Lingnerplatz 1
☎ 0351 4 84 66 00 🕓 Tue–Sun 10:30am–midnight; reservations are requested after 9pm
🚊 Tram 10, 13 Großer Garten

Markthalle Café Prag €

The impressive premises of the Café Prag, which was opened in 1956 and served as a variety theatre and dance hall in GDR times, is now a food market with around 30 restaurants. Here, you can take a culinary trip around the world and taste foods from Turkey, Russia, Syria, India, Vietnam and Japan.

⊞ 192 B4 ⊠ Seestraße 10 🕓 Mon–Thu 9:30am–8:30pm, Fri, Sat 9:30am–11pm
🚊 Tram 8, 9, 11, 12; bus 62 Prager Straße; tram 1, 2, 4 Altmarkt

Rauschenbach Deli €–€€

A popular spot in Altstadt – chic but not over the top. This is the place to discuss the state of the world while tucking into your salad or pizza. Weekdays 11am–2pm lunch, breakfast to 4pm, Sat, Sun 9am–2pm brunch.

⊞ 196 B1 ⊠ Weiße Gasse 2
☎ 0351 8 21 27 60 🕓 Daily from 9
🚊 Tram 1, 2, 4 Altmarkt

Torwirtschaft Großer Garten €–€€

This pub, at the western end of the main avenue in the Großer Garten, has a very popular beer garden. In good weather the pork knuckles are washed down with a Feldschlösschen Pilsner and there is often live music. For Dynamo fans: this is the meeting place for home games and away matches are shown in a tent.

⊞ 193 D3 ⊠ Lennéstraße 11
☎ 0351 4 59 52 02 🕓 Restaurant daily from 11am; beer garden, depending on the weather, Mar–Nov Mon–Fri from 4pm, Sat, Sun from 11am
🚊 Tram 10, 13 Großer Garten

Vapiano €

Franchise restaurant where pasta, pizza and antipasti are freshly made to order. You place your order at the counter and receive a chip that buzzes when your meal is ready. You then pay when you leave.

⊞ 192 B3 ⊠ St Petersburger Straße 26 (entrance from Prager Straße)
☎ 0351 4 82 48 64 🕓 Thu–Sat 10am–1am, Sun–Wed 10am–midnight
🚊 Tram 3, 7–9, 11 Walpurgisstraße

Weiße Gasse €–€€

The pedestrian street leading off Wilsdruffer Straße has developed into a real pub district. Around 20 restaurants, cafés and bars are now grouped around the Gänsediebbrunnen fountain and on neighbouring Kreuz- and Gewandhausstraße. In addition to the trendy Rauschenbach Deli (► left column), there is also the Agra, Aroma, Cuchi Lounge, Förster's, Tapas Barcelona, Capetown's, Mangoo and SchnitzelGarten (all listed under: www.weissegasse.de). You can enjoy traditional fare such as Dresdner *Sauerbraten* and potato soup, as well as tapas, sushi, couscous and even crocodile fillet.

⊞ 196 B1 ⊠ Weiße Gasse 1–7
🕓 Daily from 9am–11am onwards
🚊 Tram 1, 2, 4 Altmarkt

Where to...
Shop

PRAGER STRASSE AND ALTMARKT

The "Prager" is Dresden's traditional shopping street. This is where the large department stores and main chains (including **Peek & Cloppenburg**, **Wöhrl**, **H&M**, **Esprit**) are located. One of the most attractive **Karstadt** stores in Germany, with a delicatessen and a **Meissener Porzellan-Manufaktur** section, opened its doors at the north end of Prager Straße in 1995 (Prager Straße 12). Diagonally across the street is the **Centrum Galerie** with shops and restaurants while **C & A** (Seestraße 7), **Strauss Innovation** (Altmarkt 10a/10b) and **Sportarena** (Kramergasse 4) can all be found on Seestraße, which leads to Altmarkt.

Kunsthandwerk an der Kreuzkirche (An der Kreuzkirche 6) has the largest collection of folk art from the Erzgebirge in Dresden. Spring and autumn markets are held on the **Altmarkt**, as is the Striezelmarkt from the end of November to Christmas Eve. Following the opening of the extension in the spring of 2011, the **Altmarkt Galerie** (between Altmarkt and Wallstraße) is now Dresden's largest and most attractive shopping centre. It has **Zara, Tom Tailor, Boss** and **Tommy Hilfiger** branches, as well as a wide range of food and cosmetics shops, a Saturn electrical goods market and the first Apple shop in eastern Germany. The traditional pastry shop **Kreutzkamm** is next to the Altmarkt entrance. Next door is a curved staircase that leads up into a pink, Nougat paradise: the shop and café run by **Viba**, a confectionery manufacturer from Thuringia.

Where to...
Go Out

A great variety of events were formerly held in the **Kulturpalast**: concerts with the Dresden Philharmonic, Dixieland and also folk music, rock and pop, and comedy. The extensive renovation work should be completed by 2017 (Altmarkt, Ticketcentrale, tel: 0351 4 86 66 66, www.kultur palast-dresden.de).

The **Herkuleskeule** ensemble, which was founded in 1961, presents classic political cabaret. Book tickets in advance as performances are often sold out (Sternstr. 1, tel: 0351 4 92 55 55, www.herkuleskeule.de).

The ⚊ **Puppet Theatre** of the Theater Junge Generation (➤ 131) has performances for both children and adults in its repertoire. Classical and modern light entertainment, comedy and revues are on the programme of the **Comödie Dresden** (Freiberger Str. 39, tel: 0351 86 64 10, www.comoedie-dresden.de) and **Boulevardtheater Dresden** (Maternistraße 17, www.boulevardtheater.de). The latest blockbusters, live broadcasts of sporting events and performances from world-famous opera houses are shown in the **UFA Kristallpalast** (St Petersburger Str. 24a, tel: 0351 4 82 58 25, www.ufa-dresden.de) and the neighbouring **Cineplex Rundkino** (Prager Str. 6, tel: 0351 4 84 39 22, www.cineplex.de/dresden/).

The biggest club discotheque, the **Musikpark Dresden**, is not far from Prager Straße right at Hauptbahnhof. Starting at 10pm, the three dance floors resonate to pop, house, soul and party hits from Thursday to Saturday (Wiener Platz 9, tel: 0351 48 52 51 30, www.mp-dd.de).

The Elbhang

 ## Little Treats

Historic Ride

Go on a trip back in time with a funicular ride up to the elegant villas of the **Weißer Hirsch** (▶ 152) district.

Stylish Eating

The Sunday brunch in the **Lingnerterrassen** (▶ 155) is very popular – both for the extensive buffet and the view.

Waldbühne

Beer garden, concerts and ice-skating in winter – the **Weißer Hirsch** (▶ 152) outdoor concert venue has a lot on offer.

Getting Your Bearings

Anyone who really wants to get to know Dresden has to experience the Elbhang, the banks and slopes of the Elbe. This is where the Dresdeners celebrate their way of life: from the castles along the Elbe with their vineyards, to the villas on the "Hirsch", the rural peace and quiet between Körnerplatz and Pillnitz, to the summer residence of the Saxon court.

You will be able to experience the cheerful, laid-back attitude towards life that almost inevitably sets in here in a great number of ways. Possibly from the deck of a steamer or peddling a bicycle along the Elbe Cycle Route. But, you will feel the full pleasure this idyllic place when you take in the view from the terrace of the Lingnerschloss, enjoy a trip on the funicular, or a glass of wine in the summer garden of the Gare de la lune, or if you watch the squirrels and robins in the Schloss Pillnitz Park.

The Dresdeners even have a special festival celebrating their Elbhang; it is held every year on a weekend in June and takes over the entire area from the eastern border of the city on the right bank of the Elbe to the "Blue Wonder" bridge. The bridge is an icon of the Elbhang, and the entire city, and the beer gardens in its vicinity are among the locals' favourite places. If you sit here on a warm summer evening, you will find out what Dresden is all about.

View of the Elbe and the "Blue Wonder" from Schloss Albrechtsberg

Getting Your Bearings

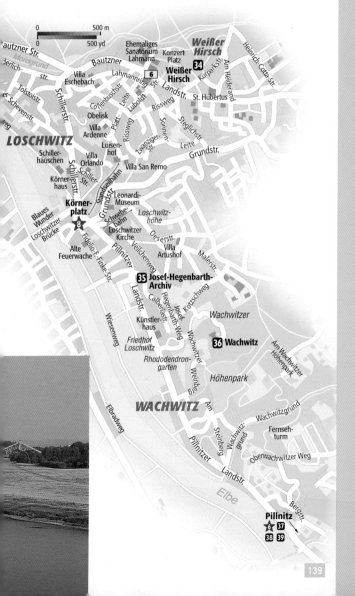

The Perfect Day

Make sure that you do not set out too late on this excursion into the countryside. Along the way you will pass magnificent castles, elegant villas, charming half-timbered houses and two Baroque churches. And you will experience the "Blue Wonder". The following route will help you make sure that you do not miss out on a single highlight. The individual sights are described in pages (➤ 142–156).

🕘 9:00

Take tram 11 towards Bühlau and get off at the Wilhelminenstraße stop. Just a few steps further on, at the corner of Brockhausstraße, go through the gate into Schloss Albrechtsberg's park (above). You can only visit the largest of the three ★Elbe castles (➤ 146) when events are being held or on one of the rare guided tours. As compensation, you will be able to enjoy the phenomenal view over the Elbe Valley from the garden terrace and this will stay with you as you proceed on your way to the Lingner and Eckberg castles.

🕥 10:30

Take tramline 11 again, go from the Elbschlösser stop (in front of the Schloss Eckberg gatehouse, 200 m towards the city) to the Plattleite stop. Plattleite Street leads, via ❸❹Weißer Hirsch (➤ 152), where a station building known as "Dresden's balcony" has wonderful views over the city. You then take the funicular (right) – the station is opposite – down to ★❽Körnerplatz (➤ 148).

🕚 11:00

Time for some nourishment – there are plenty of options around Loschwitz the old village centre: baguettes, pasta, Dresdner *Sauerbraten*, cakes and ice cream. After that, it is a good idea to take a constitutional through the adjacent streets.

🕐 1:00

Take bus line 63 from Körnerplatz to Pillnitz. There are some interesting stops on the way: the **35 Josef-Hegenbarth-Archiv** (➤ 152), the old fishing and winegrowing village of **36 Wachwitz** (➤ 152) and the Elbwiesen (Elbe meadows) between Wachwitz and Niederpoyritz. The Dresden Fernsehturm tower is also visible along the route (left).

🕒 3:00

Everyone is immediately captivated by ⭐ **Schloss Pillnitz** (➤ 142), a castle with fanciful flourishes in a fairytale setting on the Elbe with a beautiful old park. Take your time and stroll through the castle complex and along the shady paths that run through the park. You might like to visit the Kunstgewerbemuseum (Museum of Applied Art) in the Upper and Riverside Palaces (only May–Oct Tue–Sun) or the castle's museum. Those who have time and feel so inclined can also visit the **37 Weinbergkirche Vineyard Church** (➤ 152) or the **38 Maria am Wasser** church (below; ➤ 153). Lovers of classical music should definitely look in at the **39 Carl Maria von Weber Museum** (➤ 153).

🕕 6:00

You can either dine in the restaurant in **Schloss Pillnitz** (➤ 155) or take the bus back to Körnerplatz and end the day in a restaurant or beer garden with a view of the "Blue Wonder" bridge.

⭐ 6 Schloss & Park Pillnitz

One of the most beautiful castle complexes in Saxony lies on the eastern outskirts of the Dresden, idyllically located between vineyards and the Elbe. Here, nature and architecture form a perfect symbiosis that has created a slice of paradise.

It was originally intended for Countess Anna Constantia von Cosel, the most famous mistress in Saxon history. But, things turned out differently. Although the Saxon regent August the Strong presented her with the property in 1706, she had to return it when their liaison ended. While Countess Cosel spent the rest of her life – all 49 years – in exile at nearby Castle Stolpen, the pleasure palace in Pillnitz became the summer residence of the Dresden court and sent visitors – then and now – into raptures.

The New Palace, Schloss Pillnitz

🐾 FURRY FRIENDS

The youngsters will have a lot of fun with the numerous – rather cheeky – squirrels. However, they should not be fed, that way the wildlife will stay wild.

Serene Architecture

In 1720 construction began on the **Bergpalais** (Upper Palace) and the **Wasserpalais** (Riverside Palace) to the west of the 16th century Renaissance palace, based on plans by Daniel Pöppelmann. A Gothic church had to make way for a wooden ceremonial hall (Temple of Venus) with adjacent pavilions. About 70 years later, additional wings were built on to the Upper- and Riverside Palace under the direction of the master builder Christian Friedrich Exner. The old palace and Temple of Venus were razed by fire in 1818 and the three-wing **Neues Palais** was built on the site in the years up to 1826. Christian Friedrich Schuricht's plans with a Classicistic domed hall, Catholic chapel and utility rooms referenced Pöppelmann's architectural style. The **palace museum** opened in this part of the complex in 2006. The only section remaining from August the Strong's days is the **Löwenkopfbastei** (Lion's Head Bastion) consisting of the foundation of a stone pleasure pavilion and a lion's head on the side to the Elbe.

Schloss Pillnitz is one of Dresden's architectural treasures. Built in Chinoiserie style, the buildings were intended to convey the impression of an "Indian pleasure palace". The double-curved roofs, the vestibules with ornately decorated columns on the garden side, and the extremely colourful Chinoiserie painting invest the complex with a serene, oriental character. Conceived as the main entrance, an **outside staircase**, with stone sphinxes on its surrounding walls, designed by Zacharias Longuelune, lead up to the front of the Riverside Palace facing the Elbe. This is where the royal parties coming from the Dresden court used to moor their gondolas.

Kunstgewerbemuseum

Today, the Upper- and Riverside Palace now house the
Museum of Decorative Arts, which is part of the State Art
Collections Dresden. The reason that it has always –
completely without reason – been overshadowed by its
more famous sister museums in the city centre is possibly
due to the fact that, as there is no heating in this summer
residence, it is only open from May to October and not
year-round. Here, visitors can see unique examples of
regional and international arts and crafts from five centuries.
The displays include precious objects made in the Saxon
court workshops, Art Nouveau items and machine-made
furniture produced by the Deutsche Werkstätten in Hellerau,
as well as creations by modern designers from all over the
world. One of the most famous exhibits is August the Strong's
audience throne from 1718/19.

Art Garden

The pleasure garden between the Riverside and Upper
Palaces, which was redesigned by Peter Joseph Lenné in
the middle of the 19th century, merges with the palace's
28ha (70 acre) park. The garden reflects the influences of
a number of different commissioners and garden designers.
Countess Cosel already had hedged gardens – so-called
charmilles – planted here. During August the Strong's reign,
the Jousting Building was added on the uphill side for
courtly entertainment. The **Orangery** has functioned as
the winter home for several hundred potted plants since it
was expanded in 1879–88. The **Palm House**, which opened
in 1861, was once the largest greenhouse in Germany.

CERTAINLY NO WALLFLOWER

The main botanical attraction in the castle's park is the **Pillnitz Camellia** (Camellia japonica L.) It was probably brought to Dresden from Japan, via England, at the end of the 18th century and was then planted where it is today in 1801. In January 1905, its wooden shelter was destroyed by fire when it was −20 °C the water used to put out the blaze created a veil of ice over the plant but the camellia survived. The almost 9m high plant has spent its winters in a mobile, air-conditioned glasshouse since 1992. It bears about 35,000 crimson blossoms from mid-February to April (in the winter season, greenhouse ticket €2).

Over the years, the property was expanded as additional land was acquired. In this way, the **English Garden,** complete with pond and pavilion, was established in 1778–1804, as was the **Chinese Garden** named after the Chinese Pavilion.

TAKING A BREAK

The gastronomy in the **Schlosshotel Pillnitz** has something for all tastes: take-away ice cream, bratwurst in the beer garden, cake in the café and dinner in the restaurant.

Visitor Information Alte Wache

➕ 195 off F1 ☎ 0351 2 61 32 00; www.schloesserland-sachsen.de
🕐 Apr–Oct 9am–6pm, Nov–Mar 10am–4pm 🚌 Bus 63 Pillnitzer Platz
🎫 Ticket for both museums, park and glasshouses €8, garden Apr–Oct (without museums) €2, Nov–Mar park, free access

Palace Park

➕ 195 off F1 🕐 Daily 6am until nightfall

Palace Museum

➕ 195 off F1 ☎ 0351 2 61 32 60 🕐 May–Oct Tue–Sun 10am–6pm, Nov–Apr Sat, Sun 11am–3pm, guided tours every hour 🎫 €6

Kunstgewerbemuseum

Decorative Arts Museum ✉ Schloss Pillnitz ☎ 0351 49 14 20 00; www.skd. museum 🕐 Upper Palace May–Oct Tue–Sun 10am–6pm; Riverside Palace Wed–Mon 10am–6pm 🎫 €8

INSIDER INFO

- The staff in the Alte Wache provide information on the entire range of theme **tours** on offer in the castle and park, as well as on other events. The visitors' information service also sells Meissen porcelain, **souvenirs**, books, Saxon wine and cuttings of the Pillnitz Camellia, when it is in bloom.
- Many different bird species have their home in the **castle's park** so it is a good idea to have an field guide with you!
- You will almost have the estate to yourself if you visit **early in the morning**. Just make your tour of the Elbhang in the opposite direction. *Insider Tip*
- If you want to spend more than a day in Pillnitz, you can **stay overnight** in the Schlosshotel Pillnitz, or in one of the estate's two holiday homes.

☆ Elbe Castles

Between the city centre and "Blue Wonder" bridge are three magnificent mid 19th-century castles, nestled along the parkland slopes of the Elbe. The view from here, down the Elbe Valley is incredibly picturesque.

Prince Albrecht of Prussia had the impressive **Schloss Albrechtsberg** erected here in 1845. Schinkel's pupil Adolph Lohse designed the three-storey castle with its square corner towers in the style of a late-Classicist villa. Extensive staircases lead from the garden terrace on the Elbe side to the Roman bath with covered walk and pool (currently being renovated).

The castle was the "Walter Ulbricht Pioneers Palace" from 1951– 90 and now houses Dresden's youth art academy and other institutions. The interior of the castle, with its coffered ceilings, damask wall coverings and Venetian chandeliers, is only open to the public when events, conferences and other celebrations are being held, or as part of one of the occasional guided tours. There is an exhibition about the castle's history in the gatehouse (daily 10am–6pm, free admission).

Only 200m away from Prince Albrecht's castle is the more modest **Lingner Castle.** Formerly the Villa Stockhausen, it was owned by the prince's chamberlain, Baron von Stockhausen, and designed by the same architect, Alfred Lohse, and built around the same time. When the Dresden industrialist Karl August Lingner purchased the property in 1906, the Villa Stockhausen became Lingner Castle. The Odol mouthwash manufacturer and founder of the Hygiene Museum is buried in a mausoleum in the vineyard below

The vineyards below the Lingner Castle stretch down to the banks of the Elbe

From left to right: Schloss Albrechtsberg was modelled on the Villa d'Este near Rome; Schloss Eckberg in neo-Gothic Tudor style

the palace. A foundation with the aim of saving the building, which had been neglected for many years, was formed in 2003. In the meantime, a few sections of the estate – such as the main staircase, rooftop terrace and cinema – have been restored and some rooms are used for various events.

Schloss Eckberg, which Semper's pupil Christian Friedrich Arnold built for the prominent merchant John Daniel Souchay, is located next to this, on a spur over the Elbe. Today, the fanciful neo-Gothic building is a luxurious hotel (➤ 47, 155).

TAKING A BREAK

The **Lingnerterrassen**, the restaurant and terrace in the east wing both open at 11am; the beer garden opens at 10am on weekends from April to October. Early risers touring the Elbe castles should simply enjoy the view – and maybe a packed snack.

➕ 194 C5 ✉ Bautzner Straße 130–134
🚋 Tram 11 Wilhelminenstraße or Elbschlösser

Schloss Albrechtsberg
☎ 0351 8 11 58 21; www.schloss-albrechtsberg.de 🕐 Tours by arrangement

Lingnerschloss
☎ 0351 6 46 53 82; www.lingnerschloss.de 🕐 Guided tours Apr–Oct Wed 3pm

INSIDER INFO

■ The vintner Lutz Müller cultivates the vineyards below the Elbe castle. The main varieties grown here and at other sites in Pillnitz are Riesling, Müller Thurgau and Pinot Blanc. Wine seminars are held in the **cellar** of the Kavaliershaus at Schloss Albrechtsberg. In addition, wine tastings are held on the banks and – on fine weekends in summer – a wine tavern opens at 11am (tel: 0351 3 28 92 17, www.winzer-lutz-mueller.de).

■ The magnificent Crown Hall is often used for **classical music concerts** – including performances by the Dresden Philharmonic (tickets: www.schloss-albrechtsberg.de). The Garden Hall (Dresden Registry Office, tel: 0351 4 88 88 14) is a wedding venue.

■ The Lingner Salons in the Lingner Castle has an exhibition about the Odol founder (daily 11am–5pm, free admission, donation welcome) and, depending on the weather, you can visit the **rooftop terrace**, which has a phenomenal view over the Elbe Valley. Only during the Salon's opening hours.

■ The **night-time view** of the Elbe castles from the Käthe Kollwitz embankment is quite something, a fairy tale come to life!

Insider Tip

⭐8 Körnerplatz

Named after Christian Gottfried Körner, the father of the poet Theodor Körner, whose family lived nearby, the former village square of the community of Loschwitz is the heart of the Elbhang today.

The rural buildings on Körnerplatz had to make way for four-storey blocks of flats at the end of the 19th century. This was due to a new transport link between Blasewitz and Loschwitz to the east of Dresden, which were both independent communities at the time. When it was inaugurated in 1893, the bridge over the Elbe in Loschwitz bore the name of King Albert but it soon became known as the **Blaues Wunder** or the "Blue Wonder". The steel suspension bridge – at the time, a great technical achievement – has its blue paint to thank for this nick-name. The claim that the original colour was actually green and that it changed to blue when the yellow pigments faded is a myth.

Footpaths were added to both sides of the bridge in the 1930s. If you cross over to the Blasewitz side, you will be able to admire the view of the Elbwiesen and the Elbe castles not quite one mile further downstream. A plaque on the bridgehead on the left side of the Elbe commemorates two brave men who prevented the bridge from being blown up in 1945. **Schillerplatz** is surrounded by the SchillerGalerie – a shopping centre and Multiplex cinema – and many shops and restaurants, including three of Dresden's gastronomic institutions: the SchillerGarten (➤ 155), the Café Toscana (➤ 154) and the Villa Marie (➤ 155).

The Blaues Wunder connects Schillerplatz in Blasewitz to Loschwitz's Körnerplatz

"Joy, bright spark of divinity"

Today, **Körnerplatz**, which is lined with stately Gründerzeit buildings, on the Loschwitz side of the Elbe, has to deal with a great deal of traffic. Take a stroll through the neighbouring streets as there are a number of historically interesting places along the way. The poet Theodor Körner

ONE OF SCHILLER'S CHARACTERS
Friedrich Schiller, whose name crops up wherever you turn near the "Blue Wonder" bridge, immortalised Blasewitz innkeeper's daughter Justine Segedin in his drama *Wallensteins Lager (Wallenstein's Camp)* in the character of Gustel von Blasewitz. That he had an affair with the beautiful lass is just a persistent rumour. Justine survived the poet by 50 years and died in 1856 – at almost 94 years of age – as the widow of Senator Renner in Dresden.

spent his childhood summers in his parent's vineyard house at Körnerweg 6. Friedrich Schiller stayed several times from 1785–1801 in the Körnerhaus and in the family's garden house on today's Schillerstraße. This is where he (supposedly) wrote *Don Carlos* and the legendary *Ode to Joy*. Dresden's smallest museum – the **Schillerhäuschen** – is in the summerhouse where the poet's stayed on the Elbhang. A memorial fountain showing reliefs of Friedrich Schiller, Christian Gottfried Körner and his son Theodor Körner – who died in the war against Napoleon in 1813 – was erected on the opposite side of the street by Oskar Rassau and Martin Pietzsch in 1912–13.

Going up Grundstraße from Körnerplatz, you will see a striking half-timbered house on the right-hand side. Eduard Leonhardi – ink manufacturer, landscape artist and patron of the arts – bought the disused Hentschel Mill sometime around 1880, had it converted into a studio house and rechristened it the "Red Blackbird". The pupil of Ludwig Richter also provided support for young artists such as Robert Sterl and Max Pietschmann. The façade

eonhardi
Museum above
Körnerplatz

The Elbhang

is decorated with mottos and ornaments and is the work of Charles Palmié. In addition to the permanent exhibition, the **Leonhardi Museum** – as a city gallery – mainly presents contemporary Saxon art. The memorial in the garden, which was set up in 1884, honours the painter Ludwig Richter who had close ties to the Elbhang in Loschwitz.

The Baroque Loschwitzer Kirche was rebuilt after reunification

There are several half-timbered houses on Friedrich-Wieck-Straße, which runs off from Körnerplatz, with galleries and craft shops. Further towards the Elbe, a 1869 marble relief on the interior of a pavilion – which the locals call the "mustard tin" – is dedicated to the father of the sculptor Josef Herrmann, who once saved two people from drowning in the Elbe. Friedrich Wieck, Clara Schumann's father, lived in the house diagonally across the street at Number 10 from 1840–73. At the old ferry house, which dates back to 1697, at Number 45 (today, a restaurant) you reach the Elbe with a view of the "Blue Wonder".

Up High

The **funicular**, which was inaugurated in 1895, takes its passengers up 95m (312ft) to the Weißer Hirsch district. The building opposite the top station is known as "Dresden's balcony" as the views over the city and the Elbe are breathtaking.

The **suspension railway** opened in 1901 – one of the first in the world – and takes you from Pillnitzer Landstraße to Oberloschwitz 84m (275ft) higher up. Johann Christian Fehre and George Bähr's **Loschwitzer Kirche**

FEAST FOR THE SENSES

The **Elbhangfest** is held annually on the last weekend in June between Loschwitz and Pillnitz. Along with thousands of guests, locals celebrate their dolce vita in the streets and village squares, in gardens and pubs. The festival includes concerts and open-air theatre performances, suckling pig and Saxon wine, processions, a boat parade and fireworks.

Half-timbered house on Friedrich-Wieck-Straße

built between 1705–08, is on the slope next to the valley station 2.5m (8ft) above street level. The Baroque village church was gutted by fire on 13 February 1945 but was restored, faithful to the original, after German reunification. In 2002, the famous **Nosseni Altar** from Dresden's Sophienkirche, which was damaged in the war and demolished in 1962, found a worthy place here.

TAKING A BREAK

The cakes in the **Wippler** bakery are delicious – to take away or to enjoy with a cup of coffee in the café.

Insider Tip

➕ 195 E4 🚋 Tram 6, 12; bus 63, 65, 85 Schillerplatz; bus 61, 63; funicular, suspension railway (Körnerplatz)

Schillerhäuschen

➕ 195 E4 ✉ Schillerstraße 19 🕐 Easter–Sep Sat, Sun 10am–5pm, special tours tel: 0351 31 58 10; www.museen-dresden.de
💶 Free, donations welcome

Leonhardi Museum

➕ 195 E4 ✉ Grundstraße 26 ☎ 0351 2 68 35 13; www.leonhardi-museum.de
🕐 Tue–Fri 2pm–6pm, Sat, Sun 10am–6pm
💶 €4 (Fri after midday, free, except holidays)

Loschwitzer Kirche

💶 195 E4 ✉ Pillnitzer Landstraße 9
☎ 0351 2 15 00 50; www.loschwitzer-kirche.de
🕐 Daily 8am–6pm (to sunset in winter)

INSIDER INFO

There is an **observation platform** on the roof of the suspension railway's top station. Take the glass panorama lift up and when you get to the top you will feel very close to the sky!

At Your Leisure

34 Weißer Hirsch

The upmarket district above the "Blue Wonder" bridge – named after a restaurant that no longer exists – became famous as a spa and residential area for the upper class about 100 years ago. Today, most of the people living in the numerous villas are business people, artist and academics. The scientist Manfred von Ardenne headed the only private research in the GDR on the "Hirsch". The former Lahmann Psychiatric Sanatorium, which was used as a Soviet military hospital

Josef-Hegenbarth-Archiv with exhibitions

after 1945, it is currently being converted into a residential park with exclusive apartments. The neighbouring – once fashionable – Parkhotel (► 156) is now a party location. The upper station area is also a spectacular lookout that offers panoramic views over Dresden and the Elbe Valley.

➕ 195 F5 🚋 Tram 11 Plattleite, funicular

35 Josef-Hegenbarth-Archiv

The painter and graphic artist Josef Hegenbarth lived and worked on the Elbhang from 1921–62. His widow bequeathed the house and artistic estate to the Dresdner Kupferstich-Kabinett. Exhibitions of works by the artist are displayed in the rooms on

the first floor. All of the drawings have been digitalised and can be seen on the www.josef-hegenbarth. de website.

➕ 195 E3 ✉ Calberlastraße 2
☎ 0351 49 14 32 11 or 0351 49 14 20 00;
www.skd.museum 🕐 Thu only by appointment, May–Oct also Sat, Sun 3pm–6pm
🚌 Bus 63 Calberlastraße 💳 €3

36 Wachwitz

Around 2km (1mi) upstream from Körnerplatz the Pillnitzer Landstraße approaches the Elbe and leads to Wachwitz. The village has characteristic frame- and half-timbered houses and pleasant beer gardens, with views of the Elbe, and was incorporated into Dresden in 1930. On the Elbhang slope north of the village is **Wachwitz Castle**, a royal villa built in the 1930s by Dresden's last monarch for his son Friedrich Christian. The rhododendron garden, which was established in 1970, is one of the most important of its kind in Europe and attracts countless visitors during May and June. The **Künstlerhaus** (Artists' House), with flats and studios in the style of reform architecture, built by Martin Pietzsch in 1897–98 is right next to the bus stop on Pillnitzer Landstraße.

➕ 195 F2 🚌 Bus 63 Künstlerhaus, Josef-Hermann-Straße, Altwachwitz

37 Weinbergkirche Zum Heiligen Geist

In 1723 August the Strong had the Vineyard Church of the Holy Spirit, designed by Matthäus Daniel Pöppelmann, erected in the vineyards above Schloss Pillnitz to replace the demolished Castle Church. The baptismal font and late-Renaissance altar from the old church were used in the new construction. The Baroque building with its high windows, steep roof and bell tower was restored in the 1990s. It is now used for church services, exhibitions and other events.

🕂 195 off F1 ✉ Bergweg 3

☎ 0351 2 61 85 77; www.weinbergkirche.de

🕐 May–Oct Fri–Sun 1pm–5pm

🚌 Bus 63 Rathaus Pillnitz

38 Schifferkirche Maria am Wasser

This church, which has been renovated several times, has stood on the banks of the Elbe for more than 600 years, where it was often used for prayer by sailors and haulers working on the river. The church

is popular as a wedding venue and was given its present appearance, with the roof turret and onion tower, in 1774. It is also the venue for exhibitions and concerts.

🕂 195 off F1 ✉ Kirchgasse 6

☎ 0351 2 61 83 30; www.maria-am-wasser.de

🕐 To visit the church ring the parsonage bell

🚌 Bus 63 Van-Gogh-Straße

Carl Maria von Weber Museum

39 Carl Maria von Weber Museum

Carl Maria von Weber, the composer and music director of the Dresden Opera, was out for a stroll with his wife in spring 1818, when he discovered the vintner's house in Hosterwitz. It became his family's summerhouse from 1822–24 and is where *Invitation to the Dance* and the operas *Der Freischütz*, *Euryanthe* and *Oberon* were composed.

The small museum has exhibits about his life and work, concerts and other events are held in the music room and garden.

🕂 195 off F1 ✉ Dresdner Straße 44, Dresden-Hosterwitz

☎ 0351 2 61 82 34; www.museen-dresden.de 🕐 Wed–Sun 1pm–6pm

🚌 Bus 63 Van-Gogh-Straße

🎫 €4, Fri from midday, free (except on holidays)

The Maria am Wasser sailors' church near Pillnitz

Where to...
Eat and Drink

Prices
Expect to pay per person for a main course without drinks.
€ less than €12   €€ €12–20   €€€ more than €20

bean & beluga €€€

Award-winning chef Stefan Hermann's domain is not a classic gourmet restaurant but rather a magnificent experience for the senses in which modern and traditional elements merge to form a unique culinary style. Wine bar, delicatessen and Tuesday to Saturday, the "bean & beluga to go" meal for €17.

➕ 195 F5 ✉ Bautzner Landstraße 32
☎ 0351 44 00 88 00; www.bean-and-beluga.de
🕐 Tue–Sat 6:30pm–10pm, wine bar & delicatessen Tue–Fri 1pm–11pm, Sat 10am–11pm 🚊 Tram 11 Plattleite

Café Toscana €

The classic among Dresden's cafés. It was named – more than 100 years ago – after Luise of Tuscany, a Saxon princess who had fallen out of favour. The Radeberger family enterprise Eisold took over the café three years after it had closed in 1989 and once again made it one of the best places for cakes and exquisite chocolates.

➕ 195 D3 ✉ Schillerplatz 7
☎ 0351 3 10 07 44 🕐 Mon–Sun 9am–7pm
🚊 Tram 6, 12; bus 61, 63, 65 Schillerplatz

Clara das WeinCafé €

Warm colours, simple furniture and the aroma of coffee: this small café is an oasis of good taste. If it starts to rain while you are out on a stroll, this is the perfect place to have a glass of wine and wait for the sun to shine.

➕ 195 E4 ✉ Friedrich-Wieck-Straße 20
☎ 0351 2 66 67 04 🕐 Tue–Sat 6pm–1am, Sun 2:30pm–10pm 🚊 Bus 61, 63 Körnerplatz

Demnitz-Elbegarten € *Insider Tip*

This legendary beer garden, not far from the Blaues Wunder, attracts a younger crowd that gather here under shady chestnut trees. On offer is beer and cider, goulash and *Mutzbraten* (spiced pork roasted in a birch wood fire) with *Sauerkraut*. There is also a children's playground.

➕ 195 E4 ✉ Friedrich-Wieck-Straße 18
☎ 0351 2 10 64 43
🕐 During the season Mon–Fri noon–11pm, Sat, Sun 11am–11pm
🚊 Bus 61, 63 Körnerplatz

Elbterrasse Wachwitz €€

Popular tourist restaurant on the road to Pillnitz that mainly serves hearty fare: *Sauerbraten*, knuckle of lamb, smoked pork knuckle and fish. Vegetarian and vegan food is prepared for those who request it. In summer, guests sit outside in the beer garden on the Elbe.

➕ 195 off F1 ✉ Altwachwitz 14
☎ 035126 96 10 🕐 Mar–Oct daily 10am–midnight, Nov–Feb Wed–Mon noon–10pm
🚊 Bus 63 Altwachwitz

Erbgerichtsklause €

Here, you can watch the ferry plying its way tirelessly across the river while enjoying the homemade brawn in aspic, *Rostbrätl* (marinated pork neck), farmer's breakfast or a bratwurst.

➕ 195 off F1 ✉ Pillnitzer Landstraße 170
☎ 0351 2 63 11 50 🕐 Mar–Oct daily from noon
🚊 Bus 63 Moosleite

Körnergarten €

The name has no connection with the local dynasty of poets but refers to the Körner family that took over in 1897. Today, the restaurant and beer garden has become one of the fixtures on the Elbhang. The food is down-to-earth and the prices reasonable.

➕ 195 E4 ✉ Friedrich-Wieck-Straße 26
☎ 0351 2 68 36 20 🕐 Daily 11am–midnight
🚌 Bus 61, 63 Körnerplatz

Lingnerterrassen €€

A tasty meal, stunning view and affordable prices – when Karl August Lingner bequeathed Lingner Castle to the city, he did so with the proviso that it was to be a place for all the city's citizens. His wishes are honoured in the castle's Lingnerterrassen restaurant and beer garden where everyone can enjoy pasta, or more traditional potato soup and calf's liver, at very reasonable prices. The wonderful view of Dresden and the Elbe Valley is entirely free.

➕ 194 C5 ✉ Bautzner Straße 132 (Loschwitz)
☎ 0351 4 56 85 10; www.lingnerterrassen.de
🕐 Mon–Sun 11am–11pm
🚌 Tram 11 Wilhelminenstraße or Elbschlösser

SchillerGarten €–€€

Named after Friedrich Schiller, this is believed to be the place where he met "Gustel von Blasewitz" (▶ 149). After the flood damage in 2002, this Dresden institution was once again under water in 2013 – but is now back on track again with a bar, fireside lounge, winter garden and beer garden that seats 850. The Feldschlösschen Brewery started making Männel beer, which was so popular in GDR days, once again exclusively for the SchillerGarten.

➕ 195 D3 ✉ Schillerplatz 9
☎ 0351 81 19 90 🕐 Daily 11am–1am
🚌 Tram 6, 12; bus 61, 63, 65 Schillerplatz

Schloss Eckberg €€€

Chef de cuisine Martin Tomas' innovative, Mediterranean-inspired, creations are served in the historic garden hall or the beautiful, bright winter garden conservatory. There

is a splendid view over the city from here and from the terrace.

➕ 195 D5 ✉ Bautzner Straße 134
☎ 0351 8 09 91 93 🕐 Daily 11am–11pm
🚌 Tram 11 Elbschlösser

Schlosshotel Pillnitz €–€€€

The castle hotel offers a winter garden café, a wine cellar and the elegant Kaminrestaurant. The restaurant serves international cuisine made with regional produce and wine produced by Klaus Zimmerling from Pillnitz. The beer garden is very popular in summer.

➕ 195 off F1
✉ August-Böckstiegel-Straße 10
☎ 0351 2 61 40 🕐 Café daily 10am–10pm; Kaminrestaurant Mon–Sat 6pm–10pm
🚌 Bus 63 Pillnitzer Platz

Villa Marie €€

Tuscan flair with a view of the Elbhang and the Blaues Wunder – the Villa delights with an unfussy Mediterranean ambience and the simple pleasures of Italian cooking. A popular meeting place for brunch on Sunday.

➕ 195 D4 ✉ Fährgässchen 1
☎ 0351 31 54 40
🕐 Mon–Sat 11:30am–1am, Sun 10am–1am
🚌 Tram 6, 12; bus 61, 63, 65 Schillerplatz

Where to...
Shop

FRIEDRICH-WIECK-STRASSE

If you are looking for gifts to take back home with you, you are guaranteed to find them in the area around Körnerplatz. The charming shops at Friedrich-Wieck-Straße 3, 5 and 7 sell **arts and crafts and ceramics**, exquisite jewellery is the speciality of the goldsmith **Constanze Maria Makolies** (Friedrich-Wieck-Str. 11) and

Titanblau (Körnerplatz 10). Stylish living home décor items are offered by **Lampenmanufaktur** (Am Körnerplatz 1) with historical lamps and furniture accessories, in the **Kleinod** and the **Loop** (both Dammstr. 1), as well as **Antiques & Garden** (Schillerstraße 1). The **Sweetwater Record-store** (Friedrich-Wieck-Str. 4) is *the* jazz specialist among Dresden's record shops. Several galleries have works by contemporary artists on display: **Galerie am Blauen Wunder** (Pillnitzer Landstraße 2), **Galerie am Damm** (Körnerplatz 10) and **Galerie Hieronymus** (Friedrich-Wieck-Str. 11). You can stock up on tasty goodies at **Kleinert's Spezialitäten** (Friedrich-Wieck-Str. 45b), a delicatessen shop and small café decorated with great attention to detail. Friedrich-Wieck-Straße is transformed into an atmospheric **Christmas market** during Advent.

SCHILLERPLATZ

The opening of the **SchillerGalerie** (Loschwitzer Str. 52a) shopping centre in 2000 seems to have woken up the sleeping beauty and it is now once again developing into a good shopping destination. In the side streets there are shops for clothing, jewellery, toys and books.

WEISSER HIRSCH

There are a few shops worth taking a closer look at around the old Parkhotel. The **Kunsthandlung Kühne** (Plattleite 68) has works by Dresden artists from the 18th to 20th century and furniture from the Baroque to Biedermeier eras.

Insider Tip **Grünschnabel** (Bautzner Landstr. 20) is an attractive shop, with old tiles on the walls, which sells delicatessen products, fragrant bath accessories and charming table and kitchen items. And, last but not least, Foto Wolf (Bautzner Landstr. 11b), the best specialist photo shop in the city, is also on the "Hirsch".

Where to...
Go Out

Concerts featuring the Dresden Philharmonic and master concerts under the auspices of the Moritzburg Festival are held at **Schloss Albrechtsberg** (► 147). In summer, there is a unique opportunity to visit the castle when it participates in the so-called "Night of the Palaces" (www.dresdner-schloesser nacht. de) and there are also occasional **picnics with music**.The Förderverein Lingerschloss (tel: 0351 6 46 53 82, www.lingnerschloss.de) has information on events at **Lingner Castle** – concerts, lectures, readings, exhibitions, and films.

From May to October the restaurant **Saloppe** (Brockhausstraße 1, tel: 0172 3 53 25 86, www.saloppe. de) is an outdoor party venue with concerts, beer garden and more. The house crowd gets together in the Blauer Salon in the **Parkhotel** (Bautzner Landstr. 7) at weekends; sometimes international stars spin the turntables – and sometimes local heroes. The highlight is the **Hutball** (www.hutball.de) in March for which the ballroom is opened.

The **Kakadu Bar** (www.kakadu bar.de) was already legendary in GDR times and has recently come back to life but is, unfortunately, only open for special events. A tango night is held once a week in the ballroom of the **Gare de la lune** (Pillnitzer Landstraße 148, tel: 0351 2 67 85 54, www.gare-de-la-lune.de).

Readings, concerts and film evenings are on the programme of the **KulturHaus Loschwitz** (Friedrich-Wieck-Str. 6, tel: 0351 2 66 66 55, www.kulturhaus-loschwitz.de), and an art and culture society organises exhibitions and concerts in the **Alte Feuerwache** (www.feuerwache-loschwitz.de).

Excursions

Excursions

Dresden lies in the centre of an historically cultural region. In less than one hour, you can drive to mediaeval towns, magnificent castles and one of the loveliest low mountain ranges in Germany.

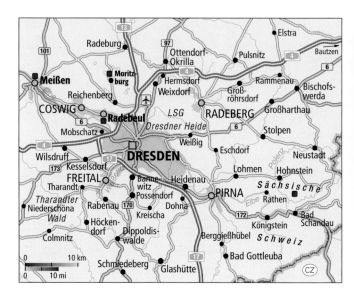

Saxon Switzerland

The Elbe Sandstone Mountains is an exceptional landscape. It has table mountains, rugged rock faces, deep gorges, clear streams, spectacular views and peaceful spa towns that attract and captivate hundreds of thousands of visitors every year.

In the summer of 1766, the Swiss artists Anton Graff and Adrian Zingg wandered upstream along the Elbe from Dresden. The unspoilt mountainous world behind Pirna reminded them of the their homeland – and that is how Saxon Switzerland got its name. Together with Bohemian Switzerland on the other side of the border in the Czech Republic, it forms the Elbe Sandstone Mountains. The unique rocky landscape originated in the Cretaceous Period when the area lay under a chalk sea on the bottom of which there was a huge 600m (1969ft) sandstone plate. Over millions of years the rivers and streams created rugged rocky reefs and jagged crests.

Saxon Switzerland is a climber's paradise; the first conquest of a rock face was documented in 1864. Today, an estimated 15,000–17,000 ascents lead to more than 1,000 peaks. Since 1910, free climbing – without any artificial aids, ropes are only used for safety – has been practised here. Hikers and nature lovers enjoy the regions

Saxon Switzerland

flora and fauna and the more than 1,000km (620mi) network of hiking trails. It is also possible to cycle through Saxon Switzerland along the Elbe Cycle Route (www.elberadweg.de).

Pirna

Pirna is the gateway to Saxon Switzerland. The historic old town is a mediaeval gem and visitors can still experience the *Market Place in Pirna* in almost the same way as Canaletto did when he painted it 250 years ago. Dating back to 1396 is the **Rathaus** town hall, with its Gothic portals, Renaissance curved gables and Baroque tower, taking pride of place in the middle of the square. Pirna's Tourist Service has its office in the **Canalettohaus** in the house Am Markt 7. The 500-year-old architectural monument is over shadowed by the **St Marien** church, a late-Gothic church with delicate reticulated vaults and original preserved painting, which was built in 1502–46. There are many stately town houses with gables, oriels, porches with seating alcoves and delightful courtyards on the neighbouring streets. **Sonnenstein Castle**, high above the city, was first documented in 1269. It has been a fortress, prison and sanatorium and during the National Socialist regime the Nazis murdered 15,000 people here. A memorial site honours the victims of the crime. The terrace garden on the slopes of the castle hill has been accessible to hikers since 2012.

Column with decorated capital in the St Marien church in Pirna

The market square in Pirna provides the setting for the annual Christmas market

Bastei and the Spa Town of Rathen

The rock formation in Saxon Switzerland that attracts the most visitors, the Bastei (Bastion), rises 190m (624ft) above the Elbe. Coming from Lohmen or Rathewalde, it can be

reached via the Basteistraße or – in peak periods – by shuttle bus. The 🏰 **SteinReich**, a theme park of wood and sandstone, with legends, puzzles, play areas and animals awaits young and old explorers at the entrance to the Basteistraße. No visit to the Bastei would be complete without admiring the view from the observation platform, having refreshments in the Panorama Restaurant (tel: 035024 77 90, Apr–Oct Daily 10am–10:30pm, Nov–Mar daily 10am–5pm) and walking across the stone **Bastei Bridge** – the symbol of Saxon Switzerland that was built in 1851. A tour of **Neurathen Castle**, which was first documented in 1261, provides a review of the early history of the region and a spectacular view of the nearby rocks with imaginative names such as the *Mönch* (Monk), *Lokomotive* and *Höllenhund* (Hellhound).

If you have enough time, a visit to Rathen is more than worthwhile. The small spa town – only 500 inhabitants – on the Elbe has two paths that connect it to the Bastei. The shorter route leads past the Bastei Bridge and Neurathen Castle to several spots with fine views down to the valley; the somewhat longer one takes you through the wild and romantic **Schwedenlöcher** gorge. The Grünbach stream forms the Amsel Falls and Amsel Lake in the **Amselgrund** Valley. The Saxon State Theatre performs in Europe's "most beautiful natural theatre", the outdoor **Felsenbühne Rathen**. The repertoire includes Carl Maria von Weber's *Freischütz*, plays based on Karl May's yarns and the musical *Three Hazelnuts for Cinderella*. Those day-trippers who want to go to Rathen via the Bastei without taking any detours will have to head for Oberrathen on the left bank of the Elbe by S-Bahn or car and then take the ferry across to Niederrathen.

The Bastei Bridge – the symbol of Saxon Switzerland

Picturesque gorges and pristine nature await you in the Schwedenlöcher gorge

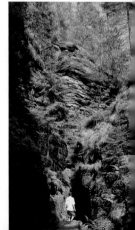

Königstein Fortress

At the end of the 16th century, work began to turn what was a Bohemian castle into the Wettin's state fortress. Over the centuries, Königstein – which was never taken by military force – has served as a defence complex, place of refuge for the Saxon rulers along with the treasury, prisoner of war camp and state prison. Tsar Peter I, Friedrich Wilhelm I and Napoleon all stayed here and Johann Friedrich Böttger, Michail Bakunin and August Bebel were three of the "involuntary" guests. The 9.5ha (23 acre) fortress grounds have been an open-air museum of military history since 1955. Take to time explore the castle buildings and arsenals, the garrison church, casemates and the oldest barracks building in Germany dating from 1589/90. A walk around the 2.2km (just over 1mi) long parapet offers breathtaking views of the surrounding countryside and leads past

the Hungerturm and Friedrichsburg to the reconstructed "wishing table". Bread and cakes are still baked in the **fortress bakery** and visitors can take a **culinary journey** back in time in the theme restaurant In Den Kasematten (reservations required; tel: 0350216144). An atmospheric **Christmas market** is held on the weekends in Advent.

The town of Königstein that lies at the foot of the fortress, at the confluence of the Biela and Elbe rivers, is an ideal starting point for short trips into the picturesque Biela Valley and to some of the most famous rock massifs in Saxon

Königstein Fortress – a unique example of the European fortress architecture

Switzerland – the **Quirl**, the **Pfaffenstein** with the 43m (141ft) high, free-standing, **Barbarine** pinnacle and the majestic **Lilienstein** on the other side of the Elbe.

Bad Schandau

Since the beginning of the 19th century people have enjoyed the spa in this tranquil little town on the right bank of the Elbe. The **St Johannes** church, which was built in 1709 at the market place, has a Renaissance altar that was originally created for the Kreuz Church in Dresden. In 1904, the hotelier Rudolf Sendig had a 50m (164ft) high tower erected; the **historic lift** in it takes visitors up to the **Ostrauer Scheibe** with its magnificent wooden villas. The interactive exhibitions in the **National Park Centre** provide information on the Saxon Switzerland National Park.

Insider Tip

Excursions

The electric **Kirnitzschtalbahn** tramway (approx. 9am–7pm, every half an hour, in the winter approx. every hour), which links Bad Schandau to the **Lichtenhain Waterfall**, has been in operation since 1898. There is also a restaurant of the same name (tel: 035971 5 37 33, Easter–Oct daily 9am–10pm; earlier in closing times winter, or temporarily closed). Bad Schandau is also the starting place for hikes and climbing tours in the **Schrammstein area** and excursions to **Bohemian Switzerland** across the border (take ID with you).

SAXON SWITZERLAND NATIONAL PARK

In 1990, while the last GDR government was still in power, two separate areas of Saxon Switzerland on the right side of the Elbe were proclaimed a national park; a neighbouring section of Bohemian Switzerland was added in 2000. Hiking is only permitted on marked trails in the central zone of the park.

Saxon Switzerland National Park
✉ An der Elbe 4, Bad Schandau ☎ 035022 90 06 00; www.nationalpark-saechsische-schweiz.de

Saxon Switzerland National Park Centre
✉ Dresdner Straße 2b, Bad Schandau ☎ 035022 5 02 40; www.lanu.de
🕐 Apr–Oct daily 9am–6pm, Nov–Mar Tue–Sun 9am–5pm; Jan closed 🎫 €4

SteinReich
☎ 035975 84 33 96; http://steinreich-sachsen.de
🕐 Easter–Oct 10am–8pm 🎫 €4.50

Felsenbühne Rathen
✉ Wehlgrund ☎ 0351 8 95 42 14, 035024 77 70; www.landesbuehnen-sachsen.de
🕐 Box office during the season Tue–Sun 11am–5pm and before all performances

Königstein Fortress
☎ 035021 6 46 07; www.festung-koenigstein.de 🕐 Apr–Oct 9am–6pm, Nov–Mar 9am–5pm, last admission, 1 hour before closing 🎫 €8

Historic Lift Bad Schandau
✉ Rudolf-Sendig-Straße 🕐 May–Sep daily 9am–7pm, Apr, Oct 9am–6pm, Nov–Mar 9am–5pm 🎫 €1.80

Getting there: 20–40km (12–25mi) southeast of Dresden city centre; by car, via the A 17 and B 172; S-Bahn S 1 Pirna, Königstein, Kurort Rathen, Bad Schandau; steamer. To Königstein Fortress: with the Festungsexpress from Königstein (Reißiger Platz) or by car to the car park below the fortress and from there on foot or with the narrow-gauge railway to the entrance (lift).

Bizarre rocky landscapes and breathtaking views

Meißen

What is today a porcelain and wine town was the birthplace of Saxony. While on a campaign against the Slavs in 929, King Heinrich I founded Misni Castle here on the Elbe. 160 years later, the margraviate of Meißen fell to the Wettins who then ruled over Saxony until 1918.

Albrechtsburg and the Cathedral above the Elbe

The **Meißen Cathedral** and **Albrechtsburg** stand proudly on the castle hill high above the town and river. In 1470, the brothers Ernst and Albrecht von Wettin, who were ruling together at the time, commissioned the master builder Arnold von Westfalen to construction a residence with sufficient space for two royal courts. After the land was divided into an Ernestine and Augustine line, the newly constructed residence lost its importance. In 1710, August the Strong quartered the first European porcelain factory in the rooms of the Albrechtsburg. After the porcelain production moved, the castle was opened to the public as a museum in 1881.

The late-Gothic architecture with the so-called arched curtain windows and elaborate vaulting survived the centuries without any significant alterations being made. The **Große Wendelstein** a stair tower in front of the courtyard façade is especially impressive; the decoration with paintings of historical scenes dates from the 19th century. Three floors are devoted to a permanent exhibition with five themed areas dealing with the history and architecture of the castle, the House of Wettin and the former use of the architectural monument for manufacturing porcelain.

Excursions

Special exhibitions, tours focusing on specific subjects, concerts and mediaeval festivities make up the varied programme of events.

The **Meißen Cathedral**, which was erected around 1250, is a masterwork of Gothic architecture. The two 87m (285ft) high west towers, which are also the main landmarks of the city, were not completed until 1908. The Wettin family funeral chapel was added in front of the west facade with the richly decorated portal in the 15th century and the cloisters, with the beautiful ceiling vaults, are located to the south of the high choir. The altar triptych from the workshop of Lukas Cranach the Elder and the seven sculptures – including the founders of the Meißen diocese Empress Adelheid and Emperor Otto I – by the Naumburg Master are of outstanding artistic quality. If you have the urge to feel like Quasimodo, you should take part in one of the tours of the tower. The 500m (1640ft) long tour along the outer walls of the Albrechtsburg and the Cathedral offers charming views of the Elbe Valley and the old town of Meißen.

Known throughout the world: Meissener Porcelain

Old Houses, Wine and Porcelain

Of course, no visit to Meißen would be complete without a long stroll through the narrow, winding streets and stairways of the mediaeval city. The late-Gothic **Rathaus** town hall, with its high roof and three transverse gables, stands alongside renovated Renaissance town houses at the market square. The world's oldest porcelain glockenspiel chimes out from the tower of the **Frauenkirche**, which was erected in 1457. The Vincenz Richter Restaurant next to the church is a real institution in Meißen; it has a history as a guild house and tavern that goes back almost 500 years. The restaurant serves hearty food and wine from its own vineyards in Meißen – and sometimes shows the guests the instruments in its own torture chamber.

The marketplace in Meißen, seen from the tower of the Frauenkirche

Meissen Porcelain® is one of the oldest and most famous brands in the world. Just two years after the

In the courtyard of the Vincenz Richter Restaurant

apprentice chemist Johann Friedrich Böttger and scientist Ehrenfried Walther von Tschirnhaus had "invented" European hard porcelain in 1708, August the Strong established the **Porzellan Manufaktur Meissen** in 1710. Since the company left the Albrechtsburg, the "white gold" with the crossed blue swords has been produced in Triebischtal in the district of Meißen. The **Erlebniswelt Haus Meissen** acts as a visitors' centre. The **Museum of MEISSEN® Art** shows the world's most comprehensive collection of Meissener porcelain from the beginnings to the present day. The **MEISSEN art-CAMPUS®** presents contemporary international porcelain art. Visitors can watch the production of traditionally hand-made Meissener porcelain in the exhibition workshops. The **MEISSEN® Boutique, Outlet Store** and **Museum Shop** offer the world's largest selection of MEISSEN® – from porcelain to accessories. And, of course whatever you eat or drink in the café and restaurant is served on the restaurant's own porcelain.

Albrechtsburg
✉ Domplatz 1 (parking deck below the castle hill, lift)
☎ 03521 4 70 70; www.albrechtsburg-meissen.de
🕐 Mar–Oct Daily 10am–6pm, Nov–Feb daily to 5pm 💶 €8

Meißen Cathedral
✉ Domplatz 7 ☎ 03521 45 24 90; www.dom-zu-meissen.de
🕐 Apr–Oct 9am–6pm, Nov–Mar daily 10am–4pm; tower tours Apr–Oct 1pm–4pm every hour; organ music Apr–Oct Mon–Sat noon–12:20pm, sacred evening music May–Oct Sat 5pm; for information on other concerts, see the website
💶 €4 (without tour or music)

Vincenz Richter Restaurant
✉ An der Frauenkirche 12 ☎ 03521 45 32 85; www.vincenz-richter.de
🕐 Tue–Sun from noon

Staatliche Porzellan-Manufaktur Meissen
✉ Talstraße 9 ☎ 03521 46 82 08; www.meissen.de
🕐 May–Oct daily 9am–6pm, Nov–Apr daily 9am–5pm 💶 €9

Getting there: 25km (16mi) west of Dresden city centre; by car via the B 6 (parking places near the Elbe); S-Bahn S1, steamer.

FUMMEL PASTRY
There is a legend that the electoral courier who once travelled between Meißen and Dresden was a little too fond of Meißen wine and therefore had a hard time staying in the saddle. The Prince Elector ordered that the bakers' guild in Meißen produce a fragile pastry that the aforementioned courier had to be able to deliver in one piece – the **Meißner Fummel** was born. Today, this delicate speciality, which consists mainly of air, is still prepared by the Konditorei Zieger (Rote Stufen 5).

Moritzburg

Moritzburg, one of the Dresdeners most popular excursion destinations, lies at the heart of a charming landscape of gently rolling hills, tranquil forests and artificial lakes.

Schloss Moritzburg, with its four imposing round towers, rises up majestically in the middle of the castle lake. From 1723 onwards, August the Strong commissioned his court architect Pöppelmann to transform the castle erected by Duke Moritz of Saxony in the 16th century into this Baroque hunting and pleasure castle. The castle museum's rooms are, to a large degree, preserved in their original state, and visitors can admire the costly historic leather wall coverings and large collection of hunting trophies. August the Strong's **Moritzburger Federzimmer** (Feather Room) is a prime exam-

ple of European craftsmanship. The magnificent bed and tapestries contain than 1 million chicken, duck, peacock and pheasant feathers and was returned to its original site in 2003 after almost two decades of restoration work. There is a collection of original Meissen porcelain in one of the four corner towers that can be seen on a guided tour (Apr–Oct daily).

Schloss Moritzburg lies in the centre of an artificial lake

From Advent to February part of the castle is transformed into a fairy tale by the 🎭 **Three Hazelnuts for Cinderella exhibition**. This is dedicated to the German-Czech cult film of the same name – some of the scenes were shot in Moritzburg Castle in the winter of 1972/1973.

The terrace around the castle is decorated with numerous sandstone sculptures and a Baroque park with cavaliers' houses follows to the north. The **Fasanenschlösschen** (Little Pheasant Castle) around 3km (2mi) to the east was built in the Chinoiserie style under Friedrich August II, the great

Little Pheasant Castle

grandson of August the Strong, in 1770–76 (visits on guided tours: May–Oct daily from 11am). The large lake nearby was turned into a harbour complete with **jetty and lighthouse** for the court's maritime festivities. (information on the Fasanenschlösschen and lighthouse; tel: 035207 87 36 10).

Culture and Nature

The graphic artist and sculptress Käthe Kollwitz spent the last months before her death in April 1945 in Moritzburg. The **Käthe Kollwitz House** commemorates her with an exhibition of cycles of graphic works, sculptures, photographs and documents.

At the end of the 17th century, Prince Elector Johann Georg IV had a hunting park laid out not far from Moritzburg Castle. Today, around 30 indigenous species of animals – including fallow deer, wolves, elks and lynxes – live in the spacious, almost natural, environment of the **Wildgehege game enclosure** (remember your binoculars!) There is another enclosure where you can pet baby animals and a show with birds of prey in flight. The **Adventure Park** in the game enclosure (abenteuerpark-moritzburg.de) and **high-rope course** at the Mittleteich (www.hochseilgarten-moritzburg.de) offer even more outdoor excitement.

Over three weekends in September, more than 20,000 spectators visit the Moritzburg **Hengstparaden** stallion parade, with historical scenes, fanfare players on horseback, dressage quadrilles and post coaches drawn by 16 horses. The **Moritzburg Festival,** an internationally renowned chamber music festival, takes place every August (www.moritzburg festival.de).

Schloss Moritzburg
☎ 035207 8 73 18;
www.schloss-moritzburg.de
🕐 Baroque exhibition and Feather Room: Apr–Oct daily 10am–5pm; winter exhibition mid-Nov–Feb Tue–Sun 10am–5pm 💶 €7

Käthe Kollwitz House
✉ Meißner Straße 7
☎ 035207 8 28 18;
www.kollwitz-moritzburg.de
🕐 Apr–Oct Mon–Fri 11am–5pm, Sat, Sun 10am–5pm, Nov–Mar Tue–Fri noon–4, Sat, Sun 11am–4pm 💶 €4

Wildgehege Moritzburg
✉ Radeburger Straße 2
☎ 035207 8 14 88; www.wildgehege-moritzburg.sachsen.de

🕐 Mar–Oct daily 10am–6pm, Nov, Dec daily 9am–2pm, Jan, Feb Sat, Sun and in the winter holidays daily 9am–4pm 💶 €4

Landgestüt Moritzburg (Hengstparade)
✉ Schlossallee 1/Hengstparadeplatz
☎ Tel: 035207 89 01 06; www.saechsische-gestuetsverwaltung.de
💶 Seating from €18 (advance booking recommended)

Getting there: 13km (8mi) north of Dresden city centre; by car, via the Großenhainer Straße/ Moritzburger Landstraße (parking area at the castle lake); bus 326, 457; small-gauge railway.

Bautzen (Budyšin)

This 1000-year-old town in the centre of the Oberlausitz district has its unique character from its German and Sorb culture and history. The historic old town, high above the Spree River, is one of the most beautiful mediaeval towns in Germany.

The ideal starting point for a tour of the town is the main market square with the town hall. The Baroque building is dominated by the **St Petri Cathedral**, a three-nave Gothic hall church with an 83m (272ft) high tower topped with a 17th-century Baroque dome (the cathedral is undergoing renovations due to be completed at the end of 2015). St Petri has been an ecumenical church since the Reformation; both Catholic and Protestants celebrate their services here. The St Petri **Domschatzkammer,** the treasury of the Dresden-Meißen diocese in the neighbouring monastery, is well worth visiting. The **Nicolai Cemetery**, with the ruins of the Nicolai Church that was destroyed in the Thirty Years' War, is not far away. There is a lovely view of the countryside around Bautzen from the battlements. You enter the **Schloss Ortenburg** courtyard through the 500-year-old Matthias Tower. This was erected by Otto I on the site of the Slavic Budissin fortress, which was taken in the 10th century – the Renaissance gable is from 1698. The castle's former salting house is now the home of the **Sorb Museum**. The **castle's theatre** – the puppet and cabaret stage of the **Deutsch-Sorbisches Volkstheater** – was opened next door in 2003; in the foyer is the Rietschel gable from the first Semperoper in Dresden, which was destroyed by fire.

Princes' box in the St Petri Cathedral

The **Alte Wasserkunst** water tower, the city's landmark, was built in 1558 and served as a fortress and also supplied the city with water – right up until 1965. Today, the tapered tower is used as a technical museum, observation tower, gallery and café all rolled into one.

Portal to the cathedral chapter

The **Reichenturm** or "Leaning Tower of Bautzen" on the eastern edge of the old town is 56m (184ft) high and tilts 1.44m (almost 5ft). The **Gedenkstätte Bautzen** is a memorial site at the old Bautzen II prison that commemorates the victims of political oppression during the National Socialist period, the Soviet occupation and years of Social Unity Party rule.

WITAJĆE K NAM – WELCOME

You will see road signs in two languages only a few miles to the east of Dresden. Here in the Lausitz, 60,000 Sorbs, the smallest of the Slavic nations, have their home. While the Upper Sorbs live around Cottbus, Bautzen – Budyšin – is considered the capital of the, predominantly Catholic, Upper Sorbs. Institutions such as the Sorb Museum, the German Sorb People's Theatre and the Sorb National Ensemble devote themselves to the cultivation of their rich cultural heritage. Every year, Sorb Easter customs – from the artistic decoration of Easter eggs to procession with Easter riders – attract thousands of visitors. In 2008, a Sorb – Stanislaw Tillich – became Saxony's Prime Minister.

View of
Schloss
Ortenburg

Domschatzkammer in the Cathedral Monastery
✉ An der Petrikirche 6 ☎ 03591 35 19 50
🕐 Mon–Fri 10am–noon, 1pm–4pm 💰 Donations welcome

Serbski muzej – Sorb Museum
✉ Ortenburg 3–5
☎ 03591 2 70 87 00; www.museum.sorben.com
🕐 Apr–Oct Tue–Fri 10am–5pm, Sat, Sun 10am–6pm,
Nov–Mar Tue–Fri 10am–4pm, Sat, Sun 10am–5pm 💰 €5

Alte Wasserkunst
✉ Wendischer Kirchhof 12 ☎ 03591 4 15 88
🕐 Apr–Oct daily 10am–5pm, Nov, Dec, Feb, Mar daily
10am–4pm, Jan Sat, Sun 10am–4pm 💰 €2.50

Reichenturm
✉ Reichenstraße 🕐 Observation platform: Apr–Oct daily
10am–5pm 💰 €1.40

Gedenkstätte Bautzen
✉ Weigangstraße 8a ☎ 03591 4 04 74; www.stsg.de
🕐 Mon–Thu 10am–4pm, Fri 10am–8pm, Sat, Sun
10am–6pm, guided tours Fri 5pm, Sat, Sun 2pm 💰 Free

The
Reichenturm
is Bautzen's
own "Leaning
Tower"

Getting there: 60km (37mi) east of Dresden city centre:
by car via the A 4 or B 6; Deutsche Bahn

Radebeul

The vineyards on the slopes of the Lößnitz and an author of adventure stories have made this small town just outside of Dresden famous.

The author Karl May lived in Radebeul from 1896 until his death in 1912. The **Villa Shatterhand,** the author's former home, is now the 🎫 **Karl-May-Museum.** An exhibition in the **Villa Bärenfett,** in the property's garden, provides information on the lifestyle and culture of North American Indians (his favourite subject). Karl May's grave is in the Radebeul-Ost Cemetery. Karl May Festivals are held in Radebeul every year in May.

The **Weinbaumuseum Hoflößnitz** (Viticulture Museum) and Saxon's State Vineyard at **Schloss Wackerbarth** provide information about the viticulture tradition of the Saxon Wine Route (► 33) and also get to taste the local wines. The village green in **Altkötzschenbroda,** which is lined with pleasant taverns, is always worth visiting, not only during the **Autumn and Wine Festival** in September or the annual Christmas Market.

The 🎫 **Lößnitzdackel,** a steam-driven, small-gauge railway links Radebeul-Ost and Radeburg (tel: 035207 8 92 90, www.loessnitzgrundbahn.de). A visit to a performance in the **Saxon State Theatre** (Meißner Straße 152, tel: 0351 8 95 42 14, www.dresden-theater.de) is a good way to spend the evening.

Top to bottom: Karl May Festival; Saxon's State Vineyard at Schloss Wackerbarth

---

Karl-May-Museum
✉ Karl-May-Straße 5 ☎ 0351 8 37 30 10; www.karl-may-museum.de
🕐 Mar–Oct Tue–Sun 9am–6pm, Nov–Feb Tue–Sun 10am–4pm 🎟 €8

Weinbaumuseum Hoflößnitz (Viticulture Museum)
✉ Knohllweg 37 ☎ 0351 8 39 83 41; www.hofloessnitz.de 🕐 Apr–Oct Tue–Sun
10am–5pm, Nov–Mar Tue–Fri noon–4pm, Sat, Sun 11am–5pm 🎟 €3

Schloss Wackerbarth
✉ Wackerbarthstraße 1 ☎ 0351 8 95 50; www.schloss-wackerbarth.de
🕐 Visitors' Centre Apr–Dec 9:30am–8pm, shorter in winter
🎟 €11–16 (guided tours)

Getting there: Northwest of Dresden, just beyond the city limits, by car:
via Leipziger Straße; tram 4, S-Bahn S 1 Radebeul-Ost, -Weintraube, -West

Walks & Tours

1 GARDEN CITY OF HELLERAU
Walk

DISTANCE 3km (2mi) **TIME** 2 hours
START/END POINT Deutsche Werkstätten Hellerau at Moritzburger Weg
By car via Königsbrücker Str./Moritzburger Weg; tram 8 Am Hellerrand

Developed north of Dresden in 1908, this is one of the first German garden cities. It was initiated by the furniture manufacturer Karl Schmidt, who was inspired by the English garden city movement. The architects, and Werkbund members, Richard Riemerschmid, Hermann Muthesius and Heinrich Tessenow, built it.

1–2

Start your walk at the **Deutsche Werkstätten Hellerau** (you can also start at the market if you come by tram ► 173). In 1909, the carpenter Karl Schmidt built his furniture factory here; it soon became famous for mass-produced "machine" furniture. Richard Riemerschmid provided the plans for the building complex with a layout that looks something like a screw clamp. Today, mainly office furniture is produced there. The gatehouse and adjoining garage building now house Schmidt's, a stylish restaurant.

Leave the grounds through the archway and turn left. **Karl Schmidt's home** at Moritzburger Weg 69, as well as the decorative wrought-iron gate, is also Riemerschmid's work.

2–3

Riemerschmid was also responsible for the overall concept of the garden city. Starting in 1909, he designed the row of terraced houses – with a 45m² (485ft²) living area and 80m² (860ft²) garden – for the **Kleinhausviertel** along Grüne Zipfel Street. This is where the workers of the Deutsche Werkstätten lived. The historic Waldschänke Hellerau on the corner of Moritzburger Weg is now a community centre.

Stylish restaurant in the Deutsche Werkstätten Hellerau courtyard

Karl Schmidt's home designed by Riemerschmid

3–4

Grüne Zipfel ends at the **market**. The only buildings by Riemerschmid are the impressive row of houses with apartments and shops on the southwest side; the others were constructed in 1929/1930.

4–5

Most of the Beim Gräbchen houses (as well as the **small houses** on An der Winkelwiese and Am Dorffrieden) are by Hermann Muthesius. Pay special attention to the elaborately decorated **foremen's homes** on the upper section of the street. Heinrich Tessenow developed the wood-and-brick construction of the workers' houses along Am Schänkenberg.

5–6

When you reach Am Sonnenhang, have a look at the **model home settlement** of the Deutsche Werkstätten buildings planned for serial production. Number 6 was a project of the Hygiene Museum's architect Wilhelm Kreis.

6–7

Walk along Talkenberg past a small park and then follow Heideweg until you reach the **Festspielhaus Hellerau** built in 1911/1912. Heinrich Tessenow designed the building for the music pedagogue Émile Jacques-Dalcroze, who established a school for rhythmic gymnastics here. Before the First World War, the Festspielhaus was meeting place for the European avant-garde: Kokoschka, Kafka and Stravinsky. Today, this is the home of **HELLERAU** – the European Centre of the Dresden Arts.

7–8

Turn back and stroll through the Landhaus quarter until you reach the Deutsche Werkstätten again. Riemerschmid's **Jaques-Dalcroze-Villa** (Auf dem Sand 10), **Tessenow's home** (Tännichtweg 2), which he designed himself, and **Haus Dohrn** (Tännichtweg 9a) by Theodor Fischer are particularly noteworthy. Tessenow's design of the two houses at **Heideweg 24** and **26** was modelled on Goethe's garden house.

Festspielhaus Hellerau 7

HELLERAU

Karl-Liebknecht-Str.

Auf dem Heideweg

Am Talkenberg

Am Sonnenhang

Am Schänkenberg

Beim Gräbchen

Am 5

Markt 4

6 Deutsche Werkstätten Hellerau

8 Moritzburger Weg

Heideweg

An Grünen Zipfel

1 2

3

0 500 m
0 500 yd

2 ALONG THE ELBE

Cycle Tour, Boat Tour

DISTANCE 14km (9mi) (cycle hire ➤ 43; steamer ➤ 84)
TIME ½–1 day **START POINT** Marienbrücke, right Elbe
bank ✚ 190 B2 🚋 Tram 4, 9 Palaisplatz
END POINT Pillnitz 🚌 Bus 63 Pillnitzer Platz, steamer

The Elbe flows in a wide curve
through Dresden and is lined with
broad meadows, castles and vineyards until it reaches the centre
of the city. You can experience
all that this unique landscape has
to offer when you cycle along the
Elbe Cycle Route – and, you can
go back by bus, train or steamer.

1–2

Starting on the right bank of the
Elbe below the **Marienbrücke**, the
cycle tour heads upstream through
the centre of Dresden. Those who
do not want to cycle can walk the
first part of this tour. First of all,
you pass the remains of Bastion VI
of the old Neustadt
fortifications and the
Baroque garden at the
Japanisches Palais (➤ 100).
The opposite bank is dominated by the **Yenidze** in the west,
the International Congress
Center, the converted Erlwein reservoir that is now part of the Maritim
Hotel and the **Saxon Parliament**.
You will be able to admire the
famous "**Canaletto view**" (➤ 101)
below the Westin Bellevue Hotel.

2–3

The Altstadt panorama lies in
front of you in all its glory behind
the Augustus Bridge – with the
Neue Synagoge (➤ 86), the
Brühlsche Terrasse (➤ 80), with
the **Residenzschloss** (➤ 70),
Hofkirche (➤ 78) and **Semperoper**
(➤ 77, towered over by the
Frauenkirche (➤ 58). The best
place to enjoy the view is from the
stairway below the **Finanzministerium**
(Finance Ministry, ➤ 110). In
summer, you will pass through
the location of the Film Nights

**The tour along the Elbe starts with a view
of Dresden's Altstadt**

Rosengarten is an idyllic rose garden

ITZ on the Elbe Bank (➤ 116) here. You continue along the Königsufer (➤ 110), pass beneath the Carola Bridge and past the **Sächsische Staatskanzlei** (State Chancellery, ➤ 110) and the larger-than-life bronze statue of the *Archer*.

3–**4**
If you have walked this far, you can end your stroll at the **Rosengarten** (➤ 109) – or stay on this side of the Elbe and go on a bit further, the "Blue Wonder" is only about 5km (3mi) away.

4–**5**
After you have had a look at the Rosengarten and/or enjoyed an ice cream in the Kaffee Rosengarten (➤ 109), cycle back, cross the Albert Bridge and continue along the cycle path on the left side of the Elbe. If you make this trip on Saturday, you will be able to browse around in the gigantic flea market (8am–2pm) near the Albert Bridge. You pass the Streuobstwiese near the Johannstädter Fährgarten, a popular beer garden.

Walks & Tours

The "Wiese" was an allotment garden site until 2002 but it was destroyed by the floodwaters of the Elbe and later cleared. You pass the controversial **Waldschlösschen Bridge** after river kilometre 53. The **Elbwiesen** now become more spacious and are almost 300m (1000ft) wide for the next 3km (2mi). Along the way, you may spot some sheep taking care of the mowing.

5–6

You will have a wonderful view of the 19th-century **Elbe castles** (➤ 146) from the Elbe Cycle Route. From left

The Elbe Cycle Route passes right by the "Blue Wonder" bridge

to right, you can see the Lingner and Eckberg castles. Make a short stop to enjoy the biodiversity of the **Glatthaferwiese am Elbufer Johannstadt**, a nature conservation

area, between the cycle path and Käthe-Kollwitz-Ufer. The impressive **"Blue Wonder"**, Dresden's most beautiful bridge, now rises up in front of you; above it, you glimpse the Weißer Hirsch (➤ 152) with the Luisenhof and **funicular railway** (➤ 150). Three of Dresden's gastronomic highlights are located right at the bridgehead in Blasewitz: the Villa Marie (➤ 155), the Café Toscana (➤ 154) and the Schiller-Garten (➤ 155).

6–7

You will see the **suspension railway** (➤ 150) on the Loschwitzhöhe on the other side – its top station also functions as an observation tower – and the **Loschwitz Church** (➤ 151) below it. The Elbe Cycle Route now runs right next to the river and you head towards Pillnitz. After 2km (1mi), the route passes by the – also protected – **Alttolkewitz** Elbe meadow. Wachwitz, with its lovely village centre, lies waiting for you on the other side of the river; the ferry at the end of the meadow can take you across to Niederpoyritz. Dresden's **television tower** is above the Wachwitzer Elbhang. In the years before reunification, the 252m (827ft) high television tower, which was inaugurated in 1969, was a popular excursion destination with an observation platform and café. It is now only used as a transmitter.

7–8

The Volkshaus Laubegast on the Laubegaster Ufer is, unfortunately, no longer used as a ballroom. There is a monument to Friederike Caroline Neuber, the famous German actress and theatre pioneer who lived in Laubegast and died here in 1760. **Laubegast**, which was first mentioned in 1408, is one of those suburbs that was incorporated into Dresden in the early 20th century but has still managed to preserve some of its village structure. Make a short detour into

En route on the Elbhang

the side streets where you will find some lovely half-timbered house and a few rustic pubs. After going around the Laubegast shipyard, the route once again returns to the Elbe bank. You will notice the **Maria am Wasser** church (➤ 153) above the meadows on the right side of the Elbe.

Downstream, you will see the **Pillnitzer Elbinsel**, the last of the Elbe islands, which was placed under protection in 1924. It is a resting and wintering place for migratory birds and the home of the Elbe beaver. Take the ferry

across to Schloss Pillnitz, the destination of this excursion and visit the **castle and park** (➤ 142).

You have two options for your return trip: you can always pedal back or you will get a completely new perspective if you make your journey back to the city on board a steamer and admire the Elbe Valley from the water. If there is enough space, you can take your cycle for free with you on the boat.

TAKING A BREAK

There are many beer gardens and pleasant restaurants with views of the Elbe along the route.

On the ferry to Pillnitz

Walks & Tours

3 THROUGH FRIEDRICHSTADT
Cycle Tour

DISTANCE 4km/2.5mi (cycle hire ➤ 43)   **TIME** 2–3 hours
START POINT Volksfestgelände at the Marien Bridge
END POINT Yenidze ✚ 190 A2 ▣ Tram 6, 11 Kongresszentrum

Bronze steer in front of the old abattoir

Friedrichstadt, named after Friedrich August II, borders on Altstadt in the west and was incorporated into Dresden in 1835. Although the historically significant district suffered severe damage on 13 February 1945, and was only partially reconstructed, there are still many interesting things to see: historic industrial architecture, old cemeteries and Baroque buildings that attest to a glorious past.

1–2

Start you tour at the **Volksfestgelände** downstream on the Elbe behind the Marien Bridge; this is where the Vogelwiese and spring and autumn festivals have been held since 2004. Opposite is the **Sportpark Ostragehege** with the Heinz-Steyer-Stadion, the new EnergieVerbund Arena for ice sports and ball games and other sports complexes. Turn right onto Pieschener Allee, after around 800m (half a mile) it leads

into the Schlachthofring. The **Pieschener Allee** natural conservation area consists of a four-row avenue of lime trees, planted in August the Strong's days, which leads down to the Elbwiesen.

In 1906–10, Germany's most modern and largest livestock yard and abattoir of the time was established in the **Ostragehege** – the former hunting grounds of the Saxon Prince Electors. The complex, which was designed by Hans Erlwein, is laid out like a village and astounds with its peaceful, rural atmosphere. The chimney of the power plant was covered by a bulky construction reminiscent of a Baroque church. A fountain with a bronze steer and the inscription "To the Health of our Beautiful City of Dresden" was installed in front of the main entrance, which is lined with houses with mansard roofs.

Sections of the abattoir, which was shut down in 1995, were converted to the fairgrounds of the **Messe Dresden** (www.messe-

with the floodwater of the Elbe. The Alberthafen, which was built in 1891–95 and named after King Albert, forms the southern end of the Ostragehege; the harbour basin is 1100m (3600ft) long and 150m (492ft) wide. The mountain of rubble deposited on the east side of the harbour after World War II now makes a fine viewing hill. There is another striking industrial building next to the **Alberthafen**: the **Hafenmühle** mill, with its 64m (210ft) high silo tower, was commissioned by the Dresden Bienert dynasty of millers, and built in 1913.

dresden.de) at the end of the 1990s. The halls are used for fairs, as well as rock and pop concerts, and official functions, congresses and meetings are held in the Börse Dresden at the old abattoir entrance.

2–3

The Schlachthof Bridge leads over the meadow of the Altstädter Flutrinne, the bypass channel installed 100 years ago to cope

Many famous people found their final resting place at the Innerer Matthäusfriedhof

3–4

You now go from Magdeburger Straße to **Friedrichstraße**. What was once the most important street in **Friedrichstadt** has seen better days but is still interesting from a cultural history point of view. The Evangelical Lutheran **Matthäuskirche** church was designed by Matthäus Daniel Pöppelmann, and built in 1728–30, he was buried in the crypt in 1736. Among the important people buried at the neighbouring **Innerer Matthäusfriedhof** cemetery are Johann Andreas Schubert, builder of the first German locomotive, Wilhelm Walther, creator of the Fürstenzug, and Ludwig Bramsch, whose famous liquor factory had its headquarters at Friedrichstraße 56 for more than 170 years.

> **ART**
>
> In 1832, Caspar David Friedrich captured what was still a wild and romantic area in the west of the Saxon residence in his painting: *The Große Gehege near Dresden.*

Walks & Tours

Insider Tip

TAKING A BREAK
Go to the **Fischhaus Alberthafen** restaurant to get your strength back while enjoying the view of the harbour basin. During the week, reasonably priced lunch meals are served in the affiliated harbour canteen.

Today, the Friedrichstadt Hospital is located in the **Marcolini Palais** next door. It was built in 1736 as the countryseat of Count Brühl and later altered for the Electoral Chamberlain Camillo von Marcolini following plans by Johann Daniel Schade and Johann Gottfried. The most important Baroque fountain in Dresden – the **Neptunbrunnen** created in 1744 by Lorenzo Mattielli and designed by Longuelune – can be seen in the hospital's garden.

There are many culturally significant and artistically important Baroque and Classicist tombs in the **Alter Katholischer Friedhof**, the Old Catholic Cemetery, established in 1721, diagonally opposite. Gottfried Semper created the tomb for the family of the composer Carl Maria von Weber; the sculptor Balthasar Permoser's monument, which is in the chapel today, is his own work. You will find traces of

Carl Maria von Weber's grave in the Alter Katholischer Friedhof

famous people wherever you go on Friedrichstraße. Napoleon had his quarters in the Marcolini Palais in 1813 and that is also where Richard Wagner composed his *Lohengrin*. The painter Adrian Ludwig Richter was born at Number 44 and the inventor and engineer Johann Andreas Schubert lived at Number 46.

4–5

The final highlight of the tour is the most original building in the district. The **Yenidze** was commissioned by the Dresden industrialist Hugo Zietz and created in the form of a mosque in 1907–09. Built for the Orientalische Tabak- und Zigarettenfabrik, the factory was adorned with a colourfully glazed dome and with a smokestack disguised as a minaret. At the time, Martin Hammitzsch's building was extremely controversial. In GDR days, the Yenidze functioned as a storehouse for the state-run cigarette industry and is now used for offices, as well as a restaurant with a terrace and lovely panorama view. Fascinating 🎭**fairy tale readings** take place in the dome.

Tales from the Arabian Nights in the Yenidze

Practicalities

Practicalities

WHAT YOU NEED

		UK	USA	Canada	Australia	Ireland	Netherlands
● Required ○ Suggested ▲ Not required	Some countries require a passport to remain valid for a minimum period (usually at least six months) beyond the date of entry – check beforehand.						
Passport/National Identity Card		●	●	●	●	●	●
Visa (regulations can change – check before booking)		▲	▲	▲	▲	▲	▲
Onward or Return Ticket		▲	●	▲	▲	▲	▲
Health Inoculations (tetanus and polio)		▲	▲	▲	▲	▲	▲
Health Documentation (► 186, Health)		●	▲	▲	▲	●	●
Travel Insurance		○	○	○	○	○	○
Driving Licence (national)		●	●	●	●	●	●
Car Insurance Certificate		●	●	●	●	●	●
Car Registration Document		●	●	●	●	●	●

WHEN TO GO

High season   Low season

JAN	FEB	MAR	APRIL	MAY	JUNE	JULY	AUG	SEP	OCT	NOV	DEC
1°C	3°C	8°C	14°C	18°C	23°C	24°C	24°C	20°C	14°C	7°C	3°C
34°F	37°F	46°F	57°F	64°F	73°F	75°F	75°F	68°F	57°F	45°F	37°F

☼ Sun   ☁ Cloud   ⛅ Sun/Showers

The temperatures indicated are the average monthly **daytime temperatures**. The peak tourist season is May to October and December. Its location in a valley gives Dresden a mild climate but there can be rather humid days in the middle of summer. The best months are May and June when the city is in full bloom – in the real sense of the phrase – and when life moves out doors and the beer gardens and city festivals are in full swing. The golden autumn days and wine festivals in the surroundings attract many visitors in September and October and the festively decorated city with the Striezelmarkt and other Christmas markets has a very special atmosphere.

GETTING ADVANCE INFORMATION

Dresden Tourist Information
✉ Prager Str. 2b, 01069 Dresden Service Center ☎ 0351 50 15 01
ℹ www.dresden.de (Official site of the Saxon capital with information on accommodation, calendar of events, city map and many useful additional links.)

GETTING THERE

By plane: There are many international flights to Dresden operated by Lufthansa, Air Berlin, Germanwings, easyJet and other airlines. There are also domestic flights from Berlin, Frankfurt, Düsseldorf, Munich, Cologne/Bonn, Stuttgart, Hamburg and other cities to the Dresden-Klotzsche Airport, 9 km (5.5mi) north of the centre.

By train: There are Eurostar connections to Germany from London and elsewhere in Europe and several daily inter-city express (ICE) trains to Dresden from all other major cities in Germany. Long-distance trains stop at the impressive **Hauptbahnhof** main station, which was completed in 1898, and/or the **Dresden-Neustadt Station**.

By car: Autobahns (motorways) to Dresden: the A 13 from Berlin, the A 4 from Görlitz and Jena, Eisenach and Aachen and the A 17 from Prague. Coming from the west, drivers should take the Altstadt exit, from the north, Hellerau, from the southeast Südvorstadt. Dresden is on the B 6 (to Bautzen or Meißen), B 170 (to Zinnwald/Czech Republic), B 172 (to Pirna and Saxon Switzerland) and B 173 (to Freiberg).

By bus: Long-distance buses have regular services from cities such as Berlin, Hamburg, Cologne and Munich to the Dresden Bus Terminal on the north side of the Hauptbahnhof.

CURRENCY & FOREIGN EXCHANGE

Currency: The official abbreviation for the euro is EUR. Euro notes are available in denominations of €5, €10, €20, €50, €100, €200 and €500. Coins come in 1 and 2 euros and 50, 20, 10, 5, 2 and 1 cents.

An **exchange rate calculator** is available on the Internet: www.oanda.com.

ATMs: Cash machines (ATMs) are found all over the city.

Credit cards are accepted in larger hotels, restaurants and shops.

Blocked Credit/Debit cards: Have the emergency number of your bank handy just in case your credit or debit card is blocked while you're abroad – banks sometimes view spending away from home as suspicious activity. To help prevent this from happening, you can contact most banks ahead of time to let them know the dates of your trip.

TOURIST INFORMATION (see also ➤ 40)

www.banq.de Up-to-date information on events, concerts, clubs, nightlife, alternative music and the nightlife scene in Neustadt; **www.cybersax.de** Online version of the *SAX* city magazine with the latest events and information on city and cultural politics; **www.dresden-nightlife.de** Gastronomy, culture, parties, tickets; **www.elberadweg.de** Cycle guide for the Elbe Cycle Route from Bad Schandau to Cuxhaven with advice on the route, accommodation and sightseeing; **www.kneipensurfer.de** Gastronomy, pub and club guide; **www.skd.museum** Museums, exhibitions and events of the State Art Collections Dresden; **www.sz-online.de** News from all over the world, Saxony and Dresden, ticket service and map of the city; on Thursday also the PluSZ event magazine; **www.vvo-online.de** City and public transport information with timetables and latest details on traffic conditions.

GERMAN NATIONAL TOURIST OFFICE: www.germany.travel

In the UK	In the US	In Canada
60 Buckingham Palace Road	122 East 42nd Street, 52nd	480 University Avenue
London SW1W 0AH	Floor	Toronto, Ontario M5G 1V2
☎ 020/7317-0908	New York, NY 10168	☎ 416/968-1685
	☎ 800-651-7010	

Practicalities

ELECTRICITY

 The power supply in Germany is 220 volts. Travellers from outside continental Europe should use an adaptor.

TIPS/GRATUITIES

People generally round up bills for restaurants, drinks and taxis. If in doubt, you tip 10%.

Hotel Porters	€1–€2 per bag
Housekeeping (hotels, etc.)	€1–€2 per day
Tour Guides	at own discretion
Toilets	50 cents

OPENING HOURS

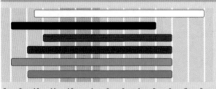

8am 9am 10am 11am 12 noon 1pm 2pm 3pm 4pm 5pm 6pm 7pm 8pm

⬜ Daytime　　　🟩 Midday　　　⬜ Evening

○ Shops
● Offices
● Museums/Monuments
● Post offices
○ Pharmacies
○ Banks

Shops: Most of the shops in the city centre are open Mon–Sat 9:30/10am–8pm, some to 9pm. There are variations in Neustadt: Mon–Fri 10am/noon–6/8pm, Sat 10am/noon–4/6pm. Legal opening hours are Mon–Sat 6am–10pm.

Banks: Banks and Sparkassen (savings banks) have varying opening hours. The Am Altmarkt branch of the Ostsächsische Sparkasse Dresden (Dr.-Külz-Ring 17) is open Mon–Fri 9am–7pm and Sat 9am–4pm.

Museums: Most museums in Dresden are open 10am–6pm but closed on one day in the week (usually Mon or Tue in the city centre).

TIME

 Dresden lies within the Central European time zone (CET), i.e. one hour ahead of Greenwich Mean Time (GMT). Clocks are adjusted forwards one hour for summer time in March. They're put back again in October.

NATIONAL HOLIDAYS

1 Jan	New Year's Day
March/April	Good Friday, Easter Sunday/Monday
1 May	Labour Day
May/June	Ascension Day, Pentecost, Whit Monday
3 Oct	Day of German Unity
31 Oct	Reformation Day
mid-Nov	Day of Prayer and Repentance
25/26 Dec	Christmas
31 Dec	New Year's Eve

TIME DIFFERENCES

Dresden (CET) 12 noon	← London (GMT) 11am	← New York (ET) 6am	← Los Angeles (PT) 3am	→ Sydney (AEST) 8pm

STAYING IN TOUCH

Post The number of branches of the German Post Office in Dresden has been greatly reduced in recent years. The gap has been partially filled by points of sale and DHL Packet Shops.
The Main Post Office at Königsbrücker Straße 21–29 is open Mon–Fri 9am–7pm and Sat 10am–1pm, the branch in the basement of the Karstadt department store Mon–Sat 10am–8pm. You can buy stamps from vending machines outside of these hours.

Public telephones The traditional yellow telephone boxes have almost completely disappeared and been replaced by the pink-coloured booths operated by Deutsche Telekom. These work with coins or telephone cards – however, they are rarely needed on account of the widespread use of mobile telephones. For overseas calls, dial the country code followed by the number (omit the first "0" from the area code.)

International Dialling Codes:

United Kingdom:	0044
Republic of Ireland:	00353
USA/Canada:	001
Australia:	0061
Germany:	0049

Mobile providers and services: Making local calls and phoning other European countries is no longer very expensive for EU visitors thanks to European roaming tariffs. Check the prices and T&Cs with your operator in advance. Costs may be higher for non-EU travellers. Network providers in Germany include E-Plus, O$_2$, Vodafone and T-Mobile.

WiFi and Internet: Most hotels provide Internet access and it is sometimes even free. It is also frequently possible to log in with a smartphone or tablet. There are also WiFi hotspots in many cafés and public institutions. Internet cafés are gradually disappearing from the city.

PERSONAL SAFETY

Dresden is considered to be a safe city. In spite of what some people say, Äußere Neustadt, with its numerous bars, pubs and clubs, is no more dangerous that the other parts of town.

There is neither a red-light district nor an open drug scene.

Although pickpocketing is far less widespread than in other large German cities, you should take to protect yourself from thieves in crowds such as those at the Stadtfest city festival and Strietzelmarkt:

■ Never put your wallet in your hip pocket.
■ Don't put your handbag down on the ground next to you.
■ Don't leave valuables in your car or hotel room. You can either rent a safe or leave your things at the reception desk in most hotels.

Police assistance:
☎ 110 from any phone

LOST & FOUND

Städtisches Fundbüro Dresden: Ordnungsamt, Theaterstraße 13, tel: 0351 4 88 59 96, Mon–Fri 9am–noon; closed Wed

EMERGENCY	110
POLICE	110
FIRE, AMBULANCE	112
POISON EMERGENCIES	1 9240

Practicalities

HEALTH

 Insurance: In case you have to see a doctor, it's recommended that Non-EU visitors obtain special travel health insurance. You'll find doctors' addresses in telephone directories' yellow pages. For emergency on-call doctors *(Ärtzlicher Bereitschaftdienst)* call 0351 1 92 92.

 Dental services: Dental treatments for non-German visitors can be expensive. Patients are given a bill which can be claimed against health insurance on arrival back home. For the emergency dental service *(Zahnärztlicher Bereitschaftsdienst)* call 0351 4 58 36 70.

 Weather: Dresden can be hot in the middle of summer. Protect yourself against the sun and drink plenty of fluids.

 Drugs: There are numerous pharmacies *(Apotheke)* in Dresden selling prescription and non-prescription drugs, homeopathic remedies, medicinal herbs and drugstore products. For the Emergency Pharmacy Service *(Apothekennotdienst)* call 0351 8 04 22 51.

 Safe water: All tap/faucet water is readily drinkable. The water from historic green pumps should not be consumed.

CONCESSIONS

Many cultural and tourist institutions offer concessions for students, unemployed, severely disabled persons and senior citizens. The **Dresden City Card** (1 day €9.90, 2 days €29.90) entitles you to unlimited travel on the ÖPNV (except cable railways) and you will receive reductions from many partners. The two-day card also includes free admission to the museums of the State Art Collections Dresden (except the Historisches Grünes Gewölbe). The **Dresden Regio Card** (4 days €79.90) has a similar offer but also includes public transport in the VVO alliance territory. The **Schlösserland-Karte** is valid for ten days (€20).

TRAVELLING WITH A DISABILITY

The "Dresden without Barriers" brochure is available from the Tourist Information Offices (▶ 40). They can also organise city tours in **sign language**. **Tourists with reduced mobility** will find information, including **city map** and **online city guide** complete with information on the accessibility to several hundred institutions at www.dresden.de in the disablity section under "Living & Working". Good tips for wheelchair users: **www.rollpfad.de**

CHILDREN

Information on activities for children can be found in the *SAX* city magazine (▶ 51) or under www.dresden.de. Special attractions for children are also marked with the logo shown above.

CUSTOMS

EU citizens may import and export goods for their personal use tax-free (800 cigarettes, 90L of wine). The duty-free limits for non-EU citizens are: 50g perfume, 2L of wine, 1L of spirits and 200 cigarettes. Non-EU citizens require a visa (valid up to 90 days) or a residence or settlement permit.

EMBASSIES AND CONSULATES

UK (Berlin)
☎ 030 20 45 70
www.ukingermany.fco.gov.uk

USA (Berlin)
☎ 030 8 30 50
germany.usembassy.gov

Ireland (Berlin)
☎ 030 22 07 20
www.dfa.ie/irish-embassy/Germany

Canada (Berlin)
☎ 030 20 31 20
www.canadainternational.gc.ca

Useful Words and Phrases

You'll often see the German "sharp S" (ß) in words like Straße (street) etc. on signs throughout the city. It's pronounced (and also frequently written) as a double 'ss'. Str. is an abbreviation of Straße. In German addresses, the house number comes after the name of the street (e.g. Musterstraße 12/Musterstr. 12). The following German terms have been used throughout this book:

U-Bahn underground railway (subway)
S-Bahn overground (often overhead) local and regional railway
Bahnhof railway station
Reichstag the Federal German Parliament

SURVIVAL PHRASES

Yes/no **Ja/nein**
Good morning **Guten Morgen**
Good afternoon **Guten Tag**
Good evening **Guten Abend**
Goodbye **Auf Wiedersehen**
How are you? **Wie geht es Ihnen?**
You're welcome **Bitte schön**
Please **Bitte**
Thank you **Danke**
Excuse me **Entschuldigung**
I'm sorry **Es tut mir Leid**
Do you have...? **Haben Sie...?**
I'd like... **Ich möchte...**
How much is that? **Was kostet das?**
I don't understand **Ich verstehe nicht**
Do you speak English?
  Sprechen Sie Englisch?
Open **Geöffnet**
Closed **Geschlossen**
Push/pull **Drücken/Ziehen**
Women's lavatory **Damen**
Men's lavatory **Herren**

OTHER USEFUL WORDS & PHRASES

Yesterday **Gestern**
Today **Heute**
Tomorrow **Morgen**
Could you call a doctor please?
  Könnten Sie bitte einen Arzt rufen?

Do you have a vacant room?
  Haben Sie ein Zimmer frei?
with a bath/shower **mit Bad/Dusche**
Single room **Das Einzelzimmer**
Double room **Das Doppelzimmer**
One/two nights **Eine Nacht/Zwei Nächte**
How much per night? **Was kostet es pro Nacht?**

DIRECTIONS & GETTING AROUND

Where is...? **Wo ist...?**
  the train/bus station **die Bahnhof/Busbahnhof**
  the bank **die Bank**
Where are the nearest toilets? **Wo sind die nächsten Toiletten?**
Turn left/right **Biegen Sie links ab/rechts ab**
Go straight on **Gehen Sie geradeaus**
Here/there **Hier/da**
North **Nord**
East **Ost**
South **Süd**
West **West**

DAYS OF THE WEEK

Monday **Montag**
Tuesday **Dienstag**
Wednesday **Mittwoch**
Thursday **Donnerstag**
Friday **Freitag**
Saturday **Samstag**
Sunday **Sonntag**

NUMBERS

1 **eins**	12 **zwölf**	30 **dreißig**	102 **ein hundert zwei**
2 **zwei**	13 **dreizehn**	31 **einunddreißig**	
3 **drei**	14 **vierzehn**	32 **zweiunddreißig**	200 **zwei hundert**
4 **vier**	15 **fünfzehn**	40 **vierzig**	300 **drei hundert**
5 **fünf**	16 **sechszehn**	50 **fünfzig**	400 **vier hundert**
6 **sechs**	17 **siebzehn**	60 **sechzig**	500 **fünf hundert**
7 **sieben**	18 **achtzehn**	70 **siebzig**	600 **sechs hundert**
8 **acht**	19 **neunzehn**	80 **achtzig**	700 **sieben hundert**
9 **neun**	20 **zwanzig**	90 **neunzig**	800 **acht hundert**
10 **zehn**	21 **einundzwanzig**	100 **ein hundert**	900 **neun hundert**
11 **elf**	22 **zweiundzwanzig**	101 **ein hundert eins**	1,000 **tausend**

Useful Words and Phrases

EATING OUT

A table for... please **Einen Tisch für... bitte**
We have/haven't booked **Wir haben/haben nicht reserviert**
I'd like to reserve a table for... people at...
Ich möchte einen Tisch für... Personen um... reservieren
I am a vegetarian **Ich bin Vegetarier**
May I see the menu, please?
Die Speisekarte bitte?
Is there a dish of the day, please?
Gibt es ein Tagesgericht?
We'd like something to drink
Wir möchten etwas zu trinken
Do you have a wine list in English?
Haben Sie eine Weinkarte auf Englisch?
This is not what I ordered
Das habe ich nicht bestellt
Could we sit there? **Können wir dort sitzen?**
When do you open/close?
Wann machen Sie auf/zu?
The food is cold **Das Essen ist kalt**
The food was excellent
Das Essen war ausgezeichnet

Can I have the bill, please?
Wir möchten zahlen, bitte
Is service included? **Ist das mit Bedienung?**

Breakfast **Das Frühstück**
Lunch **Das Mittagessen**
Dinner **Das Abendessen**
Starters **Die Vorspeise**
Main course **Das Hauptgericht**
Desserts **Die Nachspeisen**
Fish dishes **Fischgerichte**
Meat dishes **Fleischgerichte**
Fruit **Obst**
Vegetables **Gemüse**
Dish of the day **Das Tagesgericht**
Wine list **Die Weinkarte**
Salt **Das Salz**
Pepper **Der Pfeffer**
Knife **Das Messer**
Fork **Die Gabel**
Spoon **Der Löffel**
Waiter **Kellner**
Waitress **Kellnerin**

MENU A–Z

Äpfel Apples
Apfelsaft Apple juice
Apfelsinen Oranges
Aufschnitt Sliced cold meat
Austern Oysters
Belegte Brote Sandwiches
Birnen Pears
Blumenkohl Cauliflower
Brathähnchen Roast chicken
Bratwurst Fried sausage
Brokkoli Broccoli
Brötchen Bread roll
Creme Cream
Eintopf Stew
Eisbein Pork knuckle
Ente Duck
Erbsen Peas
Erdbeeren Strawberries
Fasan Pheasant
Fenchel Fennel

Flunder Flounder
Forelle Trout
Frühstücksspeck Grilled bacon
Gans Goose
Gekochtes Ei Boiled egg
Gulasch Goulash
Grüne Bohnen Green beans
Heilbutt Halibut
Hering Herring
Himbeeren Raspberries
Honig Honey
Hummer Lobster
Kabeljau Cod
Kaffee Coffee
Kalbsleber Calf's liver
Karotten Carrots
Karoffeln Potatoes
Käse Cheese
Käsekuchen Cheesecake
Kasseler Smoked pork loin

Kirschen Cherries
Krabben Shrimps
Kohl Cabbage
Konfitüre Preserves
Kopfsalat Lettuce
Lachs Salmon
Lammbraten Roast lamb
Lauch Leeks
Mais Sweet corn
Milch Milk
Obsttorte Fruit tart
Obstsalat Fruit salad
Orangensaft Orange juice
Paprika (Bell) Pepper
Pfirsiche Peaches
Pflaumen Plums
Pilze Mushrooms
Rinderbraten Roast beef
Rotkohl Red cabbage
Rührei Scrambled egg

Schinken Ham
Scholle Plaice
Schokoladentorte Chocolate cake
Schweinebraten Roast pork
Schweinekotelett Pork chop
Seezunge Sole
Spargel Asparagus
Spiegelei Fried egg
Spinat Spinach
Suppen Soups
Tee Tea
Tomaten Tomatoes
Vanillepudding Custard
Wiener Schnitzel Veal escalope
Weintrauben Grapes
Wild Game
Zucchini Courgettes/ Zucchini
Zwiebeln Onions

Street Atlas

For chapters: See inside front cover

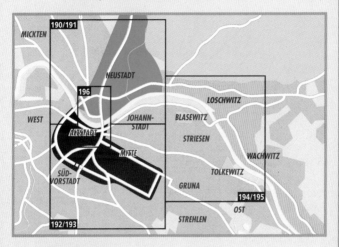

Key to Street Atlas

Information		Post office
Museum		Taxi rank
Theatre / Opera house		Peak
Monument		Sight / Attraction
Church / Chapel		Zoo
Synagogue		S-Bahn line/station
Tower		Park Eisenbahn railway
Hospital		Funicular
Car park		TOP 10
Open air pool		Don't Miss
Indoor pool		At Your Leisure

1 : 21 000

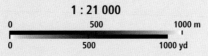

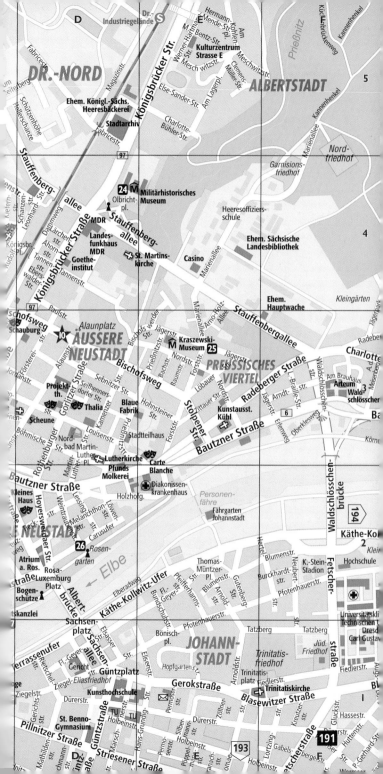

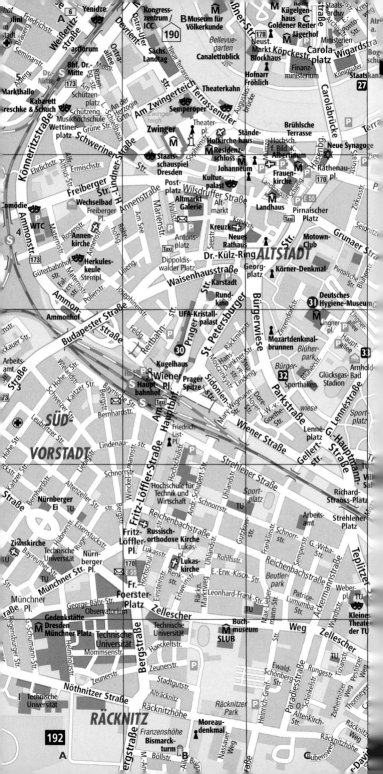

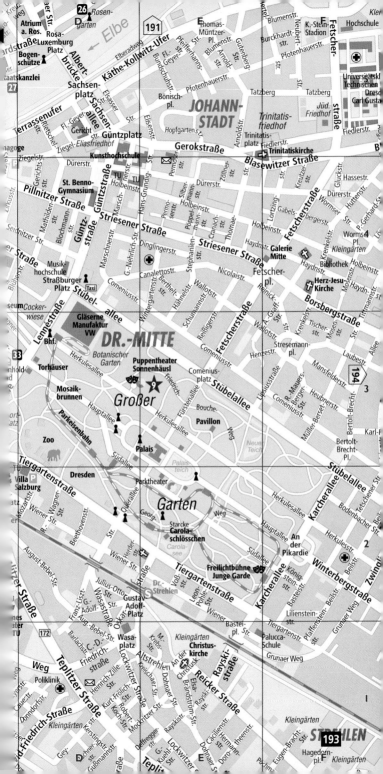

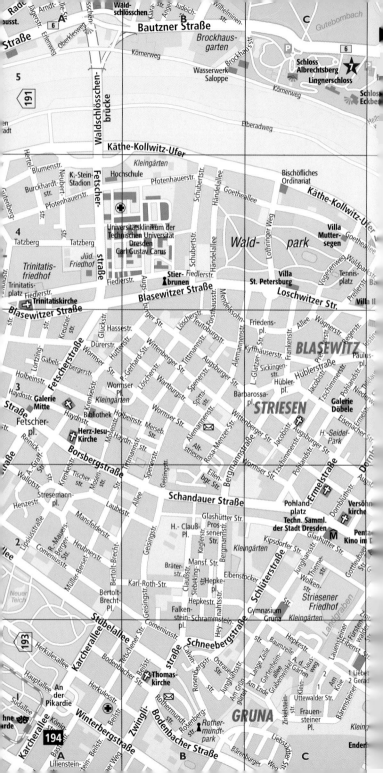

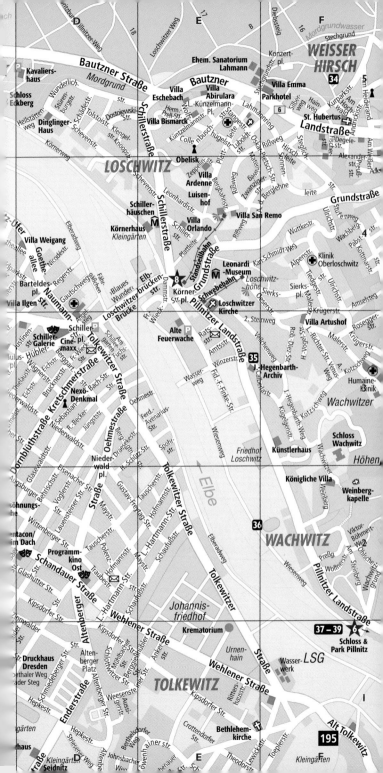

Street Index

Street Index

Street Index / Index

Index

Index

Index

Index

Events Throughout the Year

JANUARY/FEBRUARY

SemperOpernball: A glittering evening and a feast for the eyes and ears (www.semperopernball.de).

FEBRUARY

Erich Kästner Museum Festival: Dresden pays homage to its famous writer (www.erich-kaestner-museum.de, www.ekm-festival.de).

MARCH

Hutball: *The* social event of the Dresden spring. Everybody wears their best headgear to go to the ball in the Parkhotel – and, on the following evening, there's more fun at the "Party zum Hutball" (www.hutball.de).

APRIL

Osterreiten: The processions of the Easter riders in Bautzen are the highlights of the Catholic Sorb Easter festivities.
Filmfest Dresden – International Short Film Festival: Filmmakers from all over the world present their works in the Schauburg and other cinemas (www.filmfest-dresden.de).
Tanzwoche Dresden: Ten days of modern dance and physical theatre, performances and cross-genre projects (www.tanzwoche.de).

MAY

Dampferparade: The historic paddle steamers and boats of the Sächsische Dampfschiffahrt lift their anchors to take part in the parade of the fleet on 1 May (www.saechsische-dampfschiffahrt.de).
Dixieland-Festival: Every year in May, since 1971, Dresden becomes the capital of Dixieland. The brass band parade through Altstadt is the crowning event (www.dixieland.de).
Karl May Festtage: Real and wannabe Indians, cowboys and cowgirls get together in Radebeul on the weekend after Ascension for a powwow, country shows and plenty of action (www.karl-may-fest.de).
Dresdner Musikfestspiele: There is not only classical music but also jazz and world music at this festival. Legendary: "Dresden singt & musiziert" (Dresden sings and makes music) on the Brühlsche Terrasse with thousands taking part (www.musik-festspiele.com).

JUNE

Nacht der Kirchen: Dresden's churches open their doors for all those who are interested. On even years (www.nacht-der-kirchen-dresden.de).
Bunte Republik Neustadt: Äußere Neustadt locals and their guests celebrate their weekend-long, lively district festival with concerts, art and parties on the streets and squares, in pubs and courtyards.
Elbhangfest: On the last weekend in June, the Elbe banks between Loschwitz and Pillnitz becomes a gigantic festival area with around 200 different events, markets, parades and dragon-boat races (www.elbhangfest.de).
Film Nights on the Banks of the Elbe: There are open-air cinema and concerts on the Königsufer from the end of June – early September (dresden.filmnaechte.de).

JULY

Long Night of the Sciences: Universities and research institutes open their laboratories and rooms (www.wissenschaftsnacht-dresden.de).
Museum Summer Night: The city's museums are open until 1am. Historical trams and buses connect the individual locations (www.dresden.de).
Schaubuden-Sommer: The rediscovery of the show booth: ten days of attractions and sensations – theatre, music and installations – in the Scheune courtyard in Äußere Neustadt (www.schaubudensommer.de).
Ostrale – International Exhibition of Contemporary art: Modern art in the Ostragehege and the city (www.ostrale.de).

AUGUST

Moritzburg Festival: One of the most renowned chamber music festivals; in the Moritzburg church, castle and other venues (www.moritzburgfestival.de).
Stadtfest: The entire city centre is transformed into festival area for a whole weekend (www.dresdner-stadtfest.com).

SEPTEMBER

Dresden Potters' market: Some 70 ceramicists display their goods around the Goldenen Reiter (www.toepfermarkt-dresden.de).
Autumn & Wine Festival and International Travelling Theatre Festival in Radebeul: On the last weekend in September the Altkötzschenbroda village green

Events Throughout the Year / Picture Credits

transforms into a gigantic wine village (www.weinfest-radebeul.de).

OCTOBER

Tonlagen – Dresden Festival of Contemporary Music: From 1–10 October in even years in the Festspielhaus Hellerau and other venues (www.hellerau.org).
Jewish Music and Theatre Week: Artists from home and abroad, professionals and amateurs, present Jewish culture at the end of Oct–early Nov (www.juedische-woche-dresden.de).
Unity.Dresden.Night: Germany's biggest inner-city party takes place between the main station and Neumarkt – in pubs, cinemas and department stores (www.unity-dresden-night.de).

NOVEMBER

Czech-German Culture Days in Dresden and the Elbe/Labe Euroregion: 14 days of art and culture (www.tschechische-kulturtage.de).
Jazztage Dresden: Saxony's biggest jazz festival with regional and international stars (www.jazztage-dresden.de).
Cynetart: International festival for computer-aided art and multi-disciplinary media projects (www.cynetart.de).

DECEMBER

Striezelmarkt: First held in 1434, this is one of Germany's oldest Christmas markets (www.dresden.de/striezelmarkt; ► 36).

Picture Credits

Credits

1st Edition 2016

Worldwide Distribution: Marco Polo Travel Publishing Ltd
Pinewood, Chineham Business Park
Crockford Lane, Chineham
Basingstoke, Hampshire RG24 8AL, United Kingdom.
© MAIRDUMONT GmbH & Co. KG, Ostfildern

Authors: Angela Stuhrberg
Editor: Frank Müller, Anja Schlatterer, Anette Vogt (red.sign, Stuttgart)
Translation: Robert Scott McInnes
Revised editing: Margaret Howie, www.fullproof.co.za
Program supervisor: Birgit Borowski
Chief editor: Rainer Eisenschmid

Cartography: © MAIRDUMONT GmbH & Co. KG, Ostfildern
3D-illustrations: jangled nerves, Stuttgart

Printed in China

Despite all of our authors' thorough research, errors can creep in. The publishers do not accept any liability for this. Whether you want to praise us, alert us to errors or give us a personal tip – please don't hesitate to email or post to:

MARCO POLO Travel Publishing Ltd
Pinewood, Chineham Business Park
Crockford Lane, Chineham
Basingstoke, Hampshire RG24 8AL
United Kingdom
Email: sales@marcopolouk.com

FSC
www.fsc.org
MIX
Paper from
responsible sources
FSC® C020056

10 REASONS
TO COME BACK AGAIN

1. It is only possible to visit fraction of the **more than 40 museums in Dresden** on one visit.

2. A **paddle-wheel steamer cruise** on the Elbe is too good not to be experienced a second time.

3. Enjoy the sunset from the **Brühlsche Terrasse** – a wonderful experience time and again.

4. The delicious **Dresdner _Eierschecke_** is not the only sweet pastry – there are others you need to try.

5. You had too little time for all the Baroque sights in **Innere Neustadt**.

6. You got to like the **forthright Dresdeners** (and their dialect).

7. Dresden does not just have one, but two **historic cable railways**.

8. Dresden is at its loveliest in **spring**. Or during an **Indian summer**. Or in **Advent**…

9. It is always worth visiting Dresden's **charming surroundings**.

10. **BRN, Elbhangfest, Stadtfest** – if you want to take part in more than one festival, you simply have to come more than once.